Issues in
Urban Society

**Edited by Ross Davies
and Peter Hall**

Penguin Books

Penguin Books Ltd, Harmondsworth,
Middlesex, England
Penguin Books, 625 Madison Avenue,
New York, New York 10022, U.S.A.
Penguin Books Australia Ltd, Ringwood,
Victoria, Australia
Penguin Books Canada Ltd, 2801 John Street,
Markham, Ontario, Canada L3R 1B4
Penguin Books (N.Z.) Ltd, 182–190 Wairau Road,
Auckland 10, New Zealand

First published 1978

Made and printed in Great Britain by
Hazell Watson & Viney Ltd
Aylesbury, Bucks
Set in Monotype Times Roman

Contents

List of Figures

List of Figures

List of Tables

Acknowledgements

Permission to reproduce statistical material is acknowledged to the following sources:

To the Director of publishing, H M S O, for Figure 3, 'Trends in New House and Housing Land Prices', Crown copyright.

To Macmillan, London and Basingstoke, for Table 11, 'Electoral support for the Scottish National Party and Plaid Cymru in General Elections, 1964–74', taken from *British Political Facts 1900–1975* by D. E. Butler and A. Sloman.

To the Chartered Institute of Public Finance and Accountancy for Tables 15, 16 and 17 from the *Return of Rates 1974–75*.

Introduction

Peter Hall

For producing a symposium such as this, there are two main contrasting methods, with any number of mixed or transitional modes. One is controlled and convergent: through a series of meetings, at which contributors present early drafts of their papers and hear them discussed by the others; all will tend to move towards some agreed central set of issues and even, perhaps, a common point of view. The other is anarchic and divergent: the contributors work in isolation with only a general note of guidance from the editors; so that in the end their basic approaches may prove to be very different. For this particular collection we perforce chose the anarchic method. The editors wanted the most expert contributors they could find, and there was neither time nor resources to ship them regularly to some central point for an extended set of conferences.

Hence the possibility that the papers, though individually rich, might fail to make any sort of coherent whole. But in the event that fear proved groundless; for the papers in fact focus quite sharply on a limited number of key issues. The explanation cannot be telepathy; rather it is that these are the issues dominating debate in Britain today among academics and professionals.

At the risk of slight over-simplification, these key issues may be summed up under two heads, themselves closely interrelated. One is the conflict between two main objectives of national policy: the promotion of economic growth, and the conservation of natural resources and environmental quality. The other is the need to trade off allocative efficiency against distributive justice in the public sector of the economy, a problem complicated by the lack

13

of clear criteria or methods for determining either quality with any precision. The first of these themes, it will be seen, has clear spatial implications; growth versus conservation is a battle fought particularly in certain areas of Britain, in the green belts around the major cities, on the sea coasts, in the National Parks. The second theme, efficiency versus equity, has important non-spatial aspects which many commentators, including the contributors to this volume, naturally tend to stress. But this theme also has its geographical implications, and they emerge clearly enough in some of the later essays in the book: subsidies for declining industries in declining cities or regions, encouraging small shops that will serve the relatively immobile poorer members of the community, finding ways of equalizing the rate burden on different groups in different local authorities, determining the right balance between spending on education and housing and roads in these same areas, are all aspects of the problem.

Growth versus conservation is a central concern of the early chapters by Champion, Warren, Sant, O'Sullivan, Davies and Hookway. Interestingly, these authors fall fairly clearly on to two different philosophical sides of the issue. Champion shows that though less rural land was taken for urban development in the 1960s than in the 1930s, nevertheless agricultural land was disappearing at the rate of 2·5 per cent over the decade; yet agricultural productivity was rising so fast that it more than compensated. We could do more to feed ourselves, for we import over one third of our needs of temperate foodstuffs; but that might demand an even more severe programme of containing urban growth, which has already had deleterious side effects such as higher land prices. By controlling land use but by failing consistently to control financial gains from land, the policies seem to have brought windfall profits for a few and more expensive houses for the many. Paradoxically, the answer at the end of Champion's analysis might well be that we either need a much more comprehensive system of control, or a much looser system of land-use planning; the half-way house, which we have had since the historic 1947 Planning Act, is simply inconsistent.

Kenneth Warren on resources is clearly if cautiously on the side of the conservationists. 'Short-term gain from resource exploitation', he concludes, 'may not only imply substantial loss to other sectors of society or other localities, but may also lead to long-term harmful effects and perhaps irreversible environmental damage.'[1] He points to a powerful body of opinion that rejects the 'profit ethic' in favour of a 'social ethic'. Unless this is done, he thinks, the struggle to maintain the standard of living may lead to a fall in the quality of life. He quotes examples such as oil-rig construction on Scottish highland lochs, or the invasion of National Parks by mineral workings.

Morgan Sant on regional development takes a more purist economic line. But he is at one with Kenneth Warren on the folly of short-term adaptive solutions that may do long-term harm. He thinks that because of an obsession with unemployment, politicians and planners may ignore the wider problems of national economic development. He points to the rapid 'tertiarization' of the British economy, which by the mid-1970s counted over 62 per cent of its labour force in service industries, and wonders how far this really represents a healthy economic development – a concern now shared by many economic commentators and apparently by the top advisers in the Treasury. Regional policy, he concludes from his own studies and those of workers like A. J. Brown or B. Moore and J. Rhodes, has brought extra jobs to the assisted areas but not nearly as many as would be needed to cut unemployment rates and raise activity rates to national averages, or to reduce outward net migration to zero. He calls for a broader-based longer-term regional development policy concerned with the structure and direction of change.

Patrick O'Sullivan joins Morgan Sant in taking a fairly strong economic line. British transport policy in the 1960s and 1970s, in his view, is marred by indiscriminate subsidy with little objective other than the preservation of jobs, particularly among railwaymen, at all costs. There is no evidence, he argues, that the railways could win back from the roads substantial volumes of freight traffic, so one argument for subsidy – that of cost reduction with increasing scale of operation – falls to the ground. And, anticipating the other major theme of the book, he seeks to show that

15

subsidies to rail commuter services are actually regressive in their income distribution effects since the main beneficiaries are London middle-class travellers. O'Sullivan's arguments here, and indeed most of his main line of approach, have been strongly endorsed since his essay was written by the government's consultative document on transport policy[2] – the conclusions of which were much criticized by the railwaymen, and were modified in the subsequent Transport White Paper.[3]

Ross Davies, writing on retail trade, also joins the ranks of the fairly hard line economists. No other country, he points out, has exerted such stringent planning controls over the location of new retailing – and that includes not only the relatively *laissez-faire* United States but also countries such as West Germany, France or Sweden, which might have been expected to be interventionist. The pressure for out-of-town and edge-of-town shopping has been resisted; instead, vast redevelopments have taken place in existing city centres. In some cases at least, it seems clear that the only reason has been the desire to protect existing retail interests; the loser, Davies makes clear, has been the customer, who suffers needlessly high prices and inconvenience. Even the argument, fashionable nowadays – that shopping policy should favour the less mobile car-less members of the community – cannot justify what has happened; for, as Davies clearly shows, the impact of the big city-centre schemes has been to reduce sharply the numbers of the small local shops that are of the greatest value to such customers. Just as with transport policy, we seem to have placated the existing producer interests without any thought to the needs of the customer; and among the latter, hardly anyone seems to have gained. Thus in both cases it can be argued that the policy was both economically inefficient and socially regressive.

Reginald Hookway on recreation takes a more cautious line, as befits the top official of the Countryside Commission. There is a real conflict, for Hookway, between the increasing pressures of demand on the coast and the countryside, and the fixed supply of scenic beauty. Yet the circle can be squared, he believes, through more intensive use of existing resources – particularly through greater spreading of the demand in time – coupled with multi-use of countryside for recreation and agriculture, recreation and forestry, recreation and resource development. Country Parks, developed near the cities as honeypots to catch short-distance recreationers, can also help relieve the pressure. Yet, as before, the paradox is that these measures may prove socially regressive: they may provide more resources to meet the insistent demands of higher-income mobile groups, while providing very little for the immobile poor in the inner cities.

Della Nevitt takes up this theme of public policy and its distributional impacts, and makes it the main theme of her essay on housing. Housing policy, she emphasizes, cannot be expected to work miracles for 100 per cent of the population. Over half a century in Britain, she concludes, housing policy has been highly successful in transferring real income to lower-income groups through public provision of housing and through rent controls, plus income subsidies to very low-income people. Yet some of the impacts have been perverse: tenants, and also their landlords, have had relatively little help, so that their market has tended constantly to contract, while owner-occupiers (who are in general the more affluent half of the population) have received generous subsidy through income tax relief. She emphasizes that this must be a mistaken policy since a rental sector will always be needed for new entrants to the housing market. But at the same time, as over much of the country the supply of and the demand for housing come into some kind of balance, she poses the uncomfortable question for policitians and social administrators: how big a role should housing play in the welfare state anyway?

The answer to this and related questions could lie in the principles put forward by Bleddyn Davies in his essay on welfare needs. The problem, Davies argues, is that we do not have any readily available set of social indicators that would indicate where we should put our scarce public resources. In fact we often do not have the raw material that would be needed – so obsessed have the Census authorities been with the needs of the housing managers and the transport planners. For instance, there are no census figures of the disabled, or of the numbers of people living without relatives or close friends nearby. Research should be encouraged, Davies thinks, to quantify what would be needed to provide services at a similar standard in different areas. It would be difficult, but by no means impossible.

Edward Craven on representation takes up a rather different side of the distributive issue, echoing Patrick O'Sullivan and Ross Davies when he argues that the growth of public participation has largely been through the agency of middle-class professionals who know how to manipulate the system and use their skills to get the result they want. In the process, he shows they become involved in 'zero-sum games' with the planners of motorways or airports, in that their gain is someone else's loss. Very often these losses are ignored; they take the form of traffic congestion, lack of opportunity, or continuing poor environmental conditions for someone else. The tendency, he argues, quoting Anthony Crosland, is for such middle-class groups to want to 'pull up the ladder' behind them, denying to wider groups of the population the advantages they have long enjoyed themselves. Doubtless this is human nature; the problem for decision-makers must be how to trade off the losses of a vocal few against the possible gains to the many.

Richard Jackman on financial allocation neatly ties together several of the themes of earlier authors. In the absence of rational decision criteria for public spending, he suggests, there is a tendency for people to argue that they have an absolute right to a particular social service – be it education, housing or transport. With some social services (as with medicine or most education) their right is admitted, but even then there are problems of resource allocation (kidney machines for a few against better diagnostic facilities for the many). But with others it may result in much bigger amounts of provision than the community would desire if it could ever reach a collective decision. (For instance, by building roads and subsidizing public transport we may be providing more transport than we would really want to have.) Cost–benefit analysis, Jackman thinks, would yield better results. Up to now it has generally been applied to choices within particular well-defined policy areas, such as transport, but hardly at all to questions of allocation between major public sectors. That would be possible, he thinks, only in relation to social indicators – which is where Jackman echoes Bleddyn Davies's plea.

At the end, the impression made by these essays is that we haven't planned very effectively in the past and that we should be doing better in the future. (Significantly, perhaps, two of the most critical commentators have underlined their strictures by emigrating.) We get the impression of an old, rather tired society, which has planned through a particularly disjointed kind of incremental-ism with the main aim of placating various vested interests, ranging from employees of dying industries, through middle-class defenders of rural acres, to big city housing departments and high-income owner-occupiers. Social policy has consisted of squeezing limited extra resources to pay new subsidies to groups that have campaigned the loudest, but in the process no other group must ever sacrifice any of its subsidies or privileges or doles. The result is a pattern that is both woefully inefficient – since efficiency is the last consideration in anyone's mind – and far less effective in redistributing real income than it could be or ought to be.

The reader must judge how far this is a caricature of the truth. I believe that it is very substantially correct, and that it explains in large measure both the abysmal record of economic growth in modern Britain and also the fairly widespread social discontent. The cynic might merely offer one corrective: that other nations are by no means free of the same vice. They, too, are apt to subsidize declining industries to keep their workers in employ-ment (both Germany and France maintain far larger railway networks, and far bigger rail employment, than Britain); they, too, are prone to distribute subsidies in a highly regressive way (consider the history of American housing policy since the Second World War); they, too, pay vast sums to maintain uneconomic producers in declining regions (as witness the whole history of EEC farm policy). The only difference perhaps is that despite these aberrations they have achieved economic growth – and thereby, the cynic might add, the means to even greater aberrations. A country with as poor an economic record as Britain, not number two but very nearly number *n* among major industrial nations, really ought to try harder.

References

1. See p. 81.
2. *Transport Policy: A Consultation Document*, vol. 1, London, H M S O, 1976.
3. Department of Transport, Scottish Development Office and the Welsh Office, *Transport Policy*, Cmnd 6836, London, H M S O, 1977.

Chapter 1

Issues over Land

A. G. Champion

The strong feelings which the subject of land stirs up in an advanced urban society like Britain arise from at least three sources. First, land is in virtually fixed supply, yet it is required to provide security in such forms as food and shelter for the individual and for a growing nation which is making ever increasing demands on space. Second, the nation's land area comprises a multitude of irregular units in the ownership and use of different individuals, whose decisions have repercussions on neighbouring units. The negative aspects of pollution and traffic generation caused by certain land uses are well publicized but, equally, positive effects can be bestowed on land units in certain circumstances, for instance the benefits derived by housing adjacent to a park or by rural land in proximity to the urban area. Third, land is the focus of much wealth, power and status. The traditional image is of the landlord controlling the activities of his tenants, but of greater current concern is the use of land as a vehicle for investment gain and tax avoidance and as a hedge against inflation in a climate of economic uncertainty.

These characteristics of land are not merely the subject of academic interest and informal debate, but are so fundamental to present-day society that they stimulate widespread government involvement. For the last sixty years the state has shown deep concern over the manner in which national land resources are used, leading for instance to the establishment of the Forestry Commission in 1919 and the progressive tightening-up of powers for restricting the expansion of the urban area at the expense of food-production potential. For even longer, local levels of government have recognized the problems arising from the concentration of interacting activities in compact built-up areas and have attempted to ensure that no new development falls below certain standards. The power and wealth of landowners have generated a long history of calls for land reform and land nationalization, calls receiving an increasingly sympathetic hearing by governments which feel that the actions of the landowners are largely responsible for frustrating the achievement of land-use planning objectives. Indeed the often unanticipated effects of government involvement in land matters are now at least as important in stirring up controversy over land as the original issues themselves. Land issues have become a battleground between political ideologies, particularly over how much public intervention there should be and the best approach towards reaching various goals.

The following account is structured around these three major sets of issues. Superficially at least, they can be considered to fit into a coherent framework of different spatial scales and time horizons, progressing from the more general to the more immediate and particular. The issues arising from the fixed supply of land are in the final analysis national in scale, and though they are sometimes put forward as an ever present threat to security, they constitute essentially a long-term consideration, stretching well into the next century. Matters relating to the organization of space and the interaction between land units are traditionally dealt with at local government level, though there has been increasing discussion about their treatment at the intermediate regional scale. Land-use planning policies tend to be formulated for a time-horizon of between five and twenty-five years, depending on the aspect involved and the degree of control over it. Finally, issues relating to the wealth element of land have to be considered at the micro scale of individual owners or occupiers, whether private or public, through whose decisions land-use change occurs. Collectively, these localized changes contribute to a land development process which normally takes place over a span of only a few years, though interest in land for development purposes may extend over a longer period.

The national land budget

The issues surrounding the allocation of the nation's land resources between different land uses focus very largely on the role of agriculture. Since food is essential to the population, its assured availability constitutes a fundamental element of social well-being and national security. The key issue therefore concerns the steps that are necessary to ensure that the United Kingdom can feed its population adequately in the future. The answer is by no means straightforward, since it involves looking a long way ahead into an uncertain future. Yet the issue is crucial, for on it depends the rate of agricultural land loss which can be tolerated and thus the density and location of future urban development. In this account we look briefly at the current situation and see how it has been changing recently, then go on to examine likely future trends in the factors affecting the competition for land, and finally assess their implications for national policy.

Current position and recent trends

Statistics show that, apart from some small island states, the United Kingdom is one of the most crowded nations in the world. At current dietary standards and at the present economic and technological levels, about 1 acre (0·40 ha) of average agricultural land is required per person for food production. The entire agricultural area in Britain, however, affords only 0·82 acres (0·33 ha)/person and the ratio drops to 0·54 acres (0·22 ha)/person if the much less productive hill lands are excluded from the calculations. This relationship between population and land resources is reflected in the degree of self-sufficiency in food. The nation produces roughly 50 per cent of its total food consumption and around 65 per cent of the temperate-climate food requirements.

While this situation is in itself a source of concern for many people, the problems are compounded by the nature of long-term trends. In the first place, the twentieth century has witnessed the growth of the UK population from 38 to over 55 million by 1971.

This rate of increase, approximately 0·5 per cent per year, is modest by comparison with the levels recorded in the previous century and with the experience of many other countries, but it has meant a substantial rise in the country's food requirements, particularly as it has been associated with a general improvement in dietary standards.

At the same time, the amount of space available for agriculture has been shrinking. Estimates of land-use change suggest that the area devoted to 'urban development and related uses such as motorways and airfields doubled over the first half of the century (Figure 1). Even during the 1960s, when the controls on urban

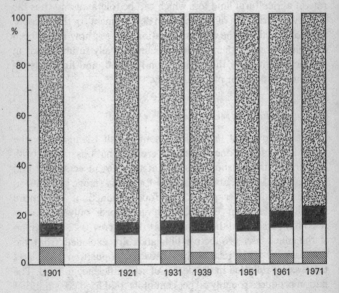

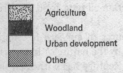

Agriculture
Woodland
Urban development
Other

1 Major land uses in England and Wales, 1901–71

expansion introduced after the Second World War were biting severely, the net transfer of agricultural land to urban use in the UK averaged 48,700 acres (19,700 ha) per year. Over the same period the government's energetic policy of afforestation was taking agricultural land at an average rate of 64,000 acres (26,000 ha) per year, though this generally involved very poor quality land. Altogether the other major uses consumed farmland at the rate of some 110,000–125,000 acres (45,000–50,000 ha) per year during the 1960s (Table 1), resulting in a net decline in the total recorded agricultural area of 2·5 per cent over the decade.

Table 1. **Annual average rate of land transfers between agriculture and other uses: United Kingdom, 1960–70** (thousand acres – hectares)

	Urban use	Forest and woodland	Government departments	Other changes	Total
England and Wales	39·8 (16·1)	15·0 (6·1)	+2·0 (+0·8)	4·2 (1·7)	57·1 (23·1)
Scotland	6·7 (2·7)	46·2 (18·7)	0·0 (0·0)	1·0 (0·4)	53·5 (21·7)
Great Britain	46·4 (18·8)	61·2 (24·8)	+2·0 (+0·8)	4·9 (2·0)	110·7 (44·8)
Northern Ireland	2·2 (0·9)	3·7 (1·5)	1·0 (0·4)		6·9 (2·8)
United Kingdom	48·6 (19·7)	64·5 (26·3)	4·0 (1·6)		117·5 (47·6)

Notes: + denotes a net gain to agriculture. Data for Northern Ireland relate to the years 1961–70.

Source: Champion, A. G., 'Competition for Agricultural Land', in Edwards, A. and Rogers, A., eds., *Agricultural Resources*, London, Faber, 1974, p. 218.

All the evidence presented so far suggests a worsening of the food supply situation in Britain, but the record of the agricultural industry over the last few decades points in a more optimistic direction and indicates a considerable capacity for expanding production when so required. The wartime years were rather exceptional, but even the long-term trends in peacetime show an increase in the contribution of domestic production to food requirements from not much more than 30 per cent in the 1930s to around 50 per cent today. During the 1950s and 1960s the net output of British agriculture increased by between 2 and 3 per cent per year in spite of the steady contraction of the farmland area. The reason for this growth in output lies in the achievement of higher levels of productivity per unit of land, which in turn have been made possible by technological and organizational changes in the industry itself and the stimulus of government financial support.

On the face of it, a national food crisis seemed no closer at the end of the 1960s than it was twenty years before; if anything, its prospect had been pushed back somewhat. Events since then, however, have put a new complexion on the situation. Rising prices on the world commodity markets and concern over Britain's continued economic difficulties have prompted a reassessment of the contribution of domestic agriculture, with the White Paper *Food from our own Resources*[1] recommending a substantial increase in the country's degree of self-sufficiency. Meanwhile, however, doubts have been cast on the long-term ability of the industry to sustain further increases in land productivity. These developments seem bound to intensify the pressure on land resources.

Future competition for land

In these circumstances the central question concerns the extent to which pressures on land are likely to intensify, since this will carry implications for the nature and scale of change in official attitudes towards land resources. Forecasting the future state of the national land budget is complicated by the variety of factors which bear on the situation and by the problem of uncertainty which attaches to each one. A useful approach to this task has been put forward by Edwards and Wibberley in *An Agricultural Land Budget for Britain 1965–2000* and has subsequently been adopted by the Centre for Agricultural Strategy in its report *Land for Agriculture*.[2] Though these studies pay little attention to developments in synthetic foods and to the future impact of EEC membership, the underlying methodological framework is simple and unchallengeable. It consists of estimating the likely future land requirements of each major activity and seeing whether altogether they can be accommodated by the total land resources available.

The two most significant non-agricultural land uses – forestry and urban development – were estimated by Edwards and Wibberley to require an additional 3·7 million acres (1·5 million ha) between them from 1965 to 2000, taking new land at an average rate of some 2·2 per cent of the country's total agricultural area per decade. Since this study was made, events suggest that the rate of land transfer may be somewhat lower. The government study *Forestry in Great Britain*[3] recommended a cut-back in the afforestation programme, although the worldwide escalation in timber prices immediately after may stimulate a further re-appraisal. As far as urban development is concerned the 1970s have seen a short-lived house-building boom and a longer period of recession, associated with slower economic growth and population increase than was expected. These checks, however, are likely to be only temporary and to have a fairly small effect on the rate of contraction in agricultural production potential.

Turning to the land requirements of agriculture itself, there are two fundamental considerations; first, the quantity of food which will need to be produced by the 'national farm' and, second, the progress in land productivity which farmers can achieve. The former depends in turn on several factors. Probably the one over which least uncertainty exists is the per capita level of food consumption, since this varies by only small amounts relative to rates of change in living standards. The overall demand for food in Britain is much more strongly influenced by total population numbers. Population projections, however, are notoriously un-reliable because of short-term fluctuations in the birth rate. The recent fall in the birth rate to below replacement level suggests the possibility of persistent natural decline setting in from the 1990s, but past experience indicates that a return to a long-term growth trend of around 5 per cent per decade may be at least as feasible.

Further difficulties are presented by the need to estimate the proportion of overall food consumption which domestic agri-culture will be required to provide. This depends on the country's degree of self-sufficiency and the possibility of further develop-ments in other food sources. At present, five sixths of Britain's food consumption consists of temperate-climate commodities broadly suited to the physical conditions of this country. Of this proportion, Britain imports 35 per cent. Therefore, to achieve self-sufficiency in respect of these products the agricultural industry would have to expand by some two thirds, while the attainment of overall self-sufficiency would mean a doubling in output, plus some changes in dietary patterns. The two main alternative sources of food supply are fisheries and synthetic products. Current signs suggest that natural fishing grounds have little potential for further exploitation, but qualified success has been achieved in essentially experimental fish farms. Synthetic food substitutes have so far been used mainly as additives, but recent research has confirmed the technical feasibility of generating protein from yeast and hydrocarbon bases. Extra contributions from both these developments may perhaps remain very small until the end of the century, though thereafter they may begin to take some of the pressure off agricultural land.

The most important consideration – but probably the least clearly known – is the progress that can be achieved in agriculture itself through raising yields. The experience of the 1950s and 1960s has stimulated many to forecast a doubling of land productivity over the last thirty years of the century. Others are not so optimistic, pointing to the evidence of soil deterioration observed by the Strutt Report[4] and to the ecological damage caused by increased applications of artificial fertilizers, pesticides, and herbicides. Some advocate a curb on these developments and a return to the sounder ecological principles of traditional husbandry, requiring a much higher input of labour and probably incurring the division of the 'national farm' into much smaller family-size units.[5] Judging by the examples of horticultural holdings in this country and of labour-intensive farming abroad, for instance in Japan, this pattern of agriculture could achieve much higher productivity per unit of land than is general in Britain today, but only of course at much greater cost.

Implications for national policy

The uncertainty inherent in these considerations poses very real problems for central government when making decisions affecting the allocation of land between activities. The nation has to resolve at least three issues of crucial significance: what is the desirable level of self-sufficiency in food supplies? To what extent should the transfer of agricultural land to other uses be restrained? How far should the state direct the activities of individual farmers? Each of these issues can in theory be reduced to a statement of costs and benefits, but the criteria are social as well as economic in nature and even the latter cannot be put on a firm financial basis.

As far as self-sufficiency in food supplies is concerned, the prospect of further price rises on international commodity markets supports the idea of aiming at an increase in the size of British agriculture. Currently the likelihood of being forced to rely on domestic farming alone is diminished by Britain's membership of the EEC, with its frequent food surpluses and sizeable regional policy, yet it is these two aspects which threaten the survival of the economic union. Wartime blockade and widespread harvest failure pose further dangers, but some would argue that in the short term they can best be countered by the use of a strategic reserve of stockpiled food and by rationing rather than by the large-scale expansion of agriculture as a purely precautionary measure. Behind this issue lies the fact that a substantial increase in the size of domestic agriculture would be costly, whether it is achieved through greater inputs of fertilizers or through the more intensive use of labour transferred from more productive activities. National policy has to strike a balance between greater security and higher food prices.

The issue concerning the rate of transfer of agricultural land to other uses revolves very largely around the rate of urban expansion, because this is responsible for the greater part of the loss of the country's more productive farmland. Here again the question involves relative costs, using the term 'costs' in its widest sense. There is little doubt that, given a sufficient period of adjustment, the average productivity of British farmland could be increased several times over if economic incentives stimulated a move towards more intensive enterprises and higher levels of input, thereby permitting a steady and perhaps increasing transfer of land to urban use. Alternatively, a total embargo on further urban expansion would keep food prices lower, but land scarcity and congestion would affect the cost and quality of life in the built-up areas. It is by no means easy to evaluate the relative costs of alternative levels of land transfer, but this must be attempted if the nation's elected representatives wish to make a definite decision about the most appropriate course of action.

The third issue is the extent to which the state should interfere with the activities of individual farmers. At present central government influences the level and nature of domestic agriculture through a wide range of indirect methods including grants, quotas, and advisory agencies, but the prospect of food shortages would bring calls for more direct action, as occurred in the Second World War. Even now the output of British agriculture could be increased substantially if all farms were to achieve the levels found in the best managed. An increasing number of holdings are run by so-called 'part-time' farmers, some highly productive but others operating at such a low level that they are ignored by the annual farm census. In this context decisions have to be made as to when, in an impending food crisis, direct state intervention becomes justified. The question arises whether it is perhaps more acceptable to opt for the less direct solution of preventing new urban expansion than to take over the running of a farm in the national interest (though, admittedly, international experience casts some doubts on the likely efficacy of the latter step).

It is also necessary to consider the time horizon used as the basis for these decisions. An economic approach to the land allocation question must take into account the length of time over which a particular investment is likely to yield a return. The conversion of land from agricultural to urban use represents a long-term investment; but how far into the future should policy decisions on the rate of urban expansion be based? What will be the relative significance of land in agricultural and urban uses at any particular time? Our previous experience has given the impression that the conversion process is irreversible except in isolated cases. Yet this may not be the correct viewpoint now. In the first place, a serious food shortage would attract less intensively developed parts of the urban area back into food production, as happened with sports fields in the Second World War. Secondly, the urban area is becoming increasingly dynamic, partly owing to rapid technological change but also due to the related shortening of the average life-expectancy of new development. A housing estate built at a relatively low density today does not necessarily commit the site to that level of use for ever. A decision has to be made on the most appropriate timespan over which to take precautions. Even so, whether it is fifty years or a hundred, the task of land budgeting is made extremely difficult, not only by the uncertainties of an unknown future but also by the need to take increasing account of the social values involved.

Land-use planning

The allocation of land between different activities within the nation is a long-established feature of government involvement in land matters, but in fact few of the issues raised in this connection are exclusively physical in nature. They have arisen because physical planning has been used to solve economic and social problems, based on the assumption that in a democratic country it is more acceptable to influence human activities through the less direct means of controlling land use rather than by overt economic planning and social manipulation. Initially, government concern focused on the problems which were posed mainly at a local scale by the concentration of different activities in congested urban locations. This led to restrictive legislation aimed at improving the layout of buildings and reducing the various forms of pollution. Subsequently, the extension of controls at this level has led to more comprehensive town plans and environmental management schemes, while at the same time the intensification of spatial interaction has prompted the widening of the scale perspective adopted in land-use planning to take in metropolitan and regional considerations. It is these essentially strategic considerations which appear to have dominated planning thought in recent years.

Postwar planning strategy

In Britain the broader economic and social issues which have drawn planning strategies into controversy have for several decades focused on two basic problems: regional variations in economic health and social well-being, resulting from the concentration of growth in a few more attractive regions, and the rapid expansion of conurbations and other major cities, involving the decentralization of homes and jobs at the local scale. The foundations of the official response to the problems were laid mainly during the 1940s through the Barlow Report on the distribution of industrial employment, the Scott Report on land use in rural areas, the Reith Report on new towns, and several other studies, most notably Abercrombie's influential plan for Greater London.[6] The general viewpoints which emerged were: first, an industrial strategy aimed at controlling employment growth in the attractive congested regions and diverting new growth to the slower-growing regions; secondly, a policy for the containment of major urban areas within strict boundaries and the accommodation of surplus development pressures in a surrounding ring of new towns, with the dual purpose of limiting the loss of agricultural land and providing a better standard of urban environment. Effective land-use planning powers were advocated to achieve these aims, resulting in the Distribution of Industry Act 1945, the New Towns Act 1946 and the Town and Country Planning Act 1947.

These ideas have been maintained in most of their original form over the last three decades and in some cases the legislative powers to enforce them have been strengthened and supplemented. The new towns programme, after an initial burst of activity in the late 1940s, saw a new lease of life in the 1960s. Publicly administered 'overspill' policies were extended in 1952 when the Town Development Act provided the framework for town expansion schemes. Powers for controlling rural land-use changes were reinforced for selected areas through the 1949 National Parks and Access to the Countryside Act, while from the mid-1950s the adoption of London's green belt concept by other major cities provided further scope for resisting the outward extension of urban development into the surrounding countryside. Moreover, urban containment policies in southern England, allied with direct floor-space controls, became an increasingly important tool in diverting new growth opportunities to the nation's more peripheral regions.

These policies have not gone unchallenged. Cherry has pointed to 1947 as the apogee of the 'consensus viewpoint' in land-use planning.[7] Though even at that time full agreement could not seriously be envisaged, it is certainly true that since then criticisms of the policies, their objectives and means of implementation has mounted steadily, culminating in a period of profound intro-spection in the planning profession in the 1960s. The challenge arose from at least three interrelated sources: the increasing public acceptance of more direct attention to social objectives in prefer-ence to the traditional preoccupation with physical aspects; changes in patterns of human organization leading to circum-stances very different from those anticipated in the 1940s; and – partly as a result of this – the discovery that planning policies were generating side-effects which were in some cases entirely opposite to their aims. Over the last fifteen years attempts have been made to solve these difficulties through the examination of alternative planning policies and through an overhaul of the machinery responsible for formulating them and carrying them out. These steps, including the introduction of structure planning and the reform of local government, seem, however, to have had the effect of fuelling the debate instead of cooling it down.

Controversy over policy and practice

Issues about the distribution of land-using activities within national space cover a range of themes, but it is helpful first to distinguish broadly between inter-regional and intra-regional considerations. The former encompass policies designed to secure some degree of balance in the distribution of population, jobs and resources between regions, while intra-regional planning relates to the internal structure of individual regions. It is often difficult to draw a line between the two, but in British planning the most commonly adopted definition of a region is the Standard Region recognized by the Census of Population.

The main issues involved in regional policy-making derive from the problem of what constitutes a satisfactory balance between regions. Here considerations of land supply and land planning take second place to the more fundamental question of whether the preservation of a nineteenth-century regional pattern constitutes a brake on the nation's overall prosperity and, if so, whether this is an acceptable price in terms of social and political goals. Even so, physical factors have been drawn into the debate on occasions, particularly in relation to the supply of land for urban development. It has been pointed out that regional policies have the effect of shifting growth towards the regions which are already the most congested. This is not merely a comment on their high-density urban environments inherited from the past, but also refers to the fact that some of these regions have the least land available for future development. As the interdepartmental study *Long Term Population Distribution in Great Britain*[8] has shown, the north-west and northern regions are at a serious disadvantage compared to the regions of southern England, even the south-east, once account is taken of the existing urban area, of land physically unsuitable for building and of land protected on amenity grounds (Figure 2). It would be equally possible, however, to argue in support of current regional policy, since major recreation areas such as the National Parks are more numerous in the north and west and agricultural land there is generally less productive than that further south.

At the intra-regional level controversy has focused largely on the concept of containment and raised a variety of issues concerned with green belts, new towns, and the problems of the major cities. In overall physical terms the containment approach has been highly effective, as witnessed by the reduction in the rate of rural–urban land transfers since the interwar period. Yet the achievement of this broad objective has not been accompanied by complete success in rationalizing land use at local level (see, for example the comments of Alice Coleman), nor has it been associated with the full range of benefits originally anticipated in social terms.

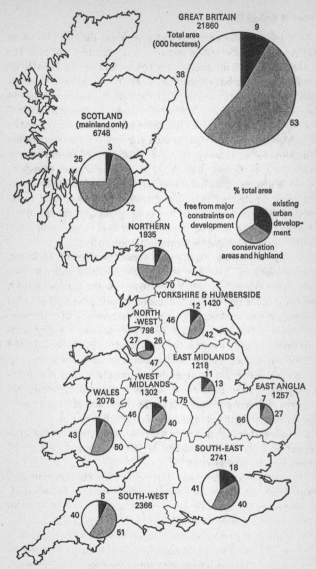

GREAT BRITAIN
21860
Total area
(000 hectares)

9
38
53

SCOTLAND
(mainland only)
6748
3
25
72

% total area

free from major
constraints on
development

existing
urban
develop-
ment

conservation
areas and highland

NORTHERN
1935
7
23
70

YORKSHIRE & HUMBERSIDE
12 1420
46
42

**NORTH
-WEST**
798
27 26
47

EAST MIDLANDS
1218
11
13
75

**WEST
MIDLANDS**
1302
14
46
40

WALES
2076
7
43
50

EAST ANGLIA
1257
7
66 27

SOUTH-EAST
2741
18
41
40

SOUTH-WEST
2366
8
40
51

2 Restraints on development, by regions, 1966–70

In most cases, criticism has been directed at the lack of positive action taken by the public sector in implementing policies. The clearest example is afforded by the role of green belts. It has been argued that these have been used to restrict development rather than to contribute to an improvement in the environment through the promotion of recreational space and amenities. Until recently, the only amenities available appeared to be wet gravel pits which increasingly became dumping grounds for waste rather than pleasurable picnic areas. The setting up of country parks under the 1968 Countryside Act and the preparation of experimental landscape plans for peri-urban areas have pointed the way to a more positive attitude. Yet despite exhortations that variations of the green-belt concept should be used to mould urban form and achieve a better integration of town and country, the '*cordon sanitaire*' principle seems firmly entrenched.

New towns, though one of the most positive elements of British physical planning, have also received considerable criticism. The main issues relate to whether new towns or the expanded town idea provide the best vehicle for accommodating overspill population and, more fundamentally, whether the principle of containing the major cities and 'decanting' their surplus development pressure to satellite towns is the right solution in practice. In the 1970s the first question has been rendered somewhat academic by the general reduction in development pressures, but it is noteworthy that by the 1960s the official new towns programme had begun to place greater emphasis on the expansion of large existing centres than on further designation of completely new sites. Though this meant rather higher land costs, great advantages were seen to be gained from the availability of labour, services and social facilities in the original core.

The broader concern over the validity of containment and decantation effectively challenges the whole basis of British land-use planning. Currently the main criticism comes from those who blame the new towns for robbing the inner parts of the conurbations of their demographic and economic vitality, through their selective accommodation of manufacturing industry and young skilled manual labour. The movement to the new towns, however, is only part of a more general process, as has been shown by a detailed study of the planning system carried out at Political and Economic Planning under the direction of Professor Peter Hall.[10] This study concluded that in many respects the containment approach has failed to achieve the objectives set out in the 1940s. It was found, for instance, that the average length of journeys to work had increased, instead of being reduced in the spirit of the garden city movement. The degree of social polarization was also shown to have risen. The majority of those who moved out of the congested cities comprised relatively well-off families, leaving behind in the inner parts of the cities the poorer elements, including the lowest paid, the elderly and cultural minority groups.

It could be argued that this pattern would have developed naturally without containment policies, but the PEP study produces two compelling reasons for thinking that they have produced greater economic inefficiency and social injustice than would have evolved in an essentially 'non-plan' situation. First, the characteristics of the 1947-type development plan, with its detailed zoning of land for up to twenty years ahead and an often considerable lapse of time between reviews, hampered the planner's ability to cope with unanticipated developments such as the upsurge in population growth rates and car-ownership levels during this period. This lack of flexibility was partly responsible for the increase in commuting distances, because the land allocations in the overspill schemes and development plans were insufficient to cope with the pressures placed on the major cities. The resulting scarcity and high price of housing there stimulated large numbers to seek accommodation beyond the green belt and commute back to their jobs.

Secondly, the inflexibility of the planning machinery was reinforced by the attitude of local government and political pressure groups, for they did not always want to go along with the natural trends. In particular, the major cities, which, as county boroughs, retained their independence in the 1947 Act, went to great lengths to keep within their boundaries as much employment as possible in order to ensure their source of taxable revenue. Space within their limited areas also had to be found for public housing, so little room was left for new private house building. The surrounding counties, for their part, were not keen to allow rapid new development, though generally they found private housing more acceptable than other forms of urban development. This polarization between public and private housing was intensified in the many cases where cities and counties were controlled by opposite political factions, since each had a vested interest in preventing a watering-down of its electoral support.

Reform and reconsideration

These two major obstacles to effective land-use planning and policy implementation have stimulated serious official concern over the last fifteen years. The search for a more flexible approach to planning led to the introduction of structure planning in the 1968 Town and Country Planning Act, while the difficulties arising from the division of authority between cities and counties reinforced calls for the overhaul of the anachronistic local government framework, leading to the Local Government Acts of 1972–3. At the same time, these issues raised even more fundamental questions, involving the reconsideration of the role of planning and the way in which goals are formulated.

The debate on the nature of policies and their underlying objectives is far from resolved. Structure planning itself soon came under criticism from those who advocated a closer integration of planning into a corporate framework of administration and budgeting. The main challenge, however, came from the breakdown of the 'consensus viewpoint' and the realization that society does not constitute a homogeneous whole. The move towards greater public participation, highlighted by the conflict of pressure groups on major issues such as the third London airport and London's motorway box, began to provide ample evidence that there exist many elements with often very different ideas and aspirations. As far as broad planning philosophy is concerned, one can detect the existence of a range of viewpoints within two extremes: at one end, those who would welcome the reduction of public powers to the simple restrictions operating at the end of the last century and, at the other, those who would prefer to see a positive move towards the original 'garden city' formula propounded by Ebenezer Howard at about the same time. The present climate of official opinion is coloured by the economic recession and demographic stabilization of the mid-1970s, but long-term strategy still seems to be sympathetic towards many elements of Howard's thinking. As such, it is rather different from the immediate postwar version, which emphasized physically separate, self-contained towns and an inviolable green belt of considerable dimensions; it relates much more to the 'social city' concept, involving the overspill of development pressures to a fairly dense network of smallish settlements with good links to the metropolitan nucleus. The regional strategies for the South-East and North-West, for instance, go some way towards this pattern, with their preference for clustered development in broad growth zones fairly close to the conurbations.

The inadequacy of the administrative machinery, though the object of more concrete action, also remains a leading issue since it is by no means clear that the reforms have really improved the situation. Indeed, judging by the intensity of the continuing debate the changes seem to have raised more problems than they have solved. The main set of difficulties centres on the reorganization of the plan-preparation process and the adoption of a two-tier pattern of local government. The 1968 Town and Country Planning Act introduced a two-stage approach to plan preparation. Under this arrangement, each county planning authority prepares the overall structure plan in diagrammatic form, indicating the general disposition of major features such as urban areas, industrial estates and roads, and within this framework local plans are produced when it is necessary to study a particular subject or to show the precise location of land uses. This step went a long way to meeting the criticisms made of the inflexibility of the detailed 'blue-print' approach of the earlier county development plans, but unfortunately the subsequent reform of local government in England and Wales led to the division of plan-preparation responsibilities between the two tiers of authorities. The task of producing local plans was taken away from the county councils and assigned to the lower tier of district authorities. Even in situations where amicable relations exist between a county and its districts, a certain amount of duplication of effort must be expected. Where the two levels are in conflict on various issues, plan preparation is likely to experience serious difficulties of co-ordination, as has already proved to be the case in the two-tier system created for Greater London in the mid-1960s.

As well as affecting plan preparation, local government reform appears to have done little to ease the observed problems facing the implementation of planning policies. In the first place, though county boroughs have been abolished, their areas have generally been retained as districts in the new two-tier system. Given the degree of autonomy accorded to the districts and the perpetuation of political cleavage between city and surrounding districts in many areas, these changes do not raise much hope for relaxation of those practices that led to severe containment and the associated problem of social polarization. Secondly, the reluctance of central government to accept the city-region as the basis for delineating the boundaries of the new counties has reduced the degree of control which each county can exercise over developments which may affect it and has therefore increased the need for cooperation between counties. On both these issues, it is the metropolitan counties which face particular difficulties, since their districts are relatively more powerful and their county boundaries are very tightly drawn round the existing built-up area, excluding a large part of their commuting hinterland. These problems are not likely to be resolved for some time to come, though the introduction of a more effective regional planning machinery may help to mitigate the most serious conflicts.

Land ownership and the development process

The third and most detailed scale at which issues over land can be identified is that of the individual property unit. The problem of individual rights is steeped in history and has crystallized around the power and wealth of the landowners. Repeated calls had been made for state intervention in the protection of individual rights even before Henry George, in the nineteenth century, advocated land nationalization. Traditionally this concern was stimulated largely by the plight of disadvantaged tenants and the landless, but more recently its chief significance has tended to derive from the issues outlined earlier in this chapter. In particular, the state itself has become increasingly aware that the effectiveness of its land-use policies may well be reduced unless it can achieve co-operation with, or control over, those who hold the rights in the individual parcels of land that comprise the mosaic of national territory.

The two key features in this debate are the mechanism for realizing the approved land-use patterns set out in local plans and the way in which financial gains generated by land-use change should be distributed. Both were considered during the formulation of the 1947 Town and Country Planning Act and have been given serious attention on several occasions subsequently. The efficiency of plan implementation was examined by the Dobry inquiry between 1973 and 1975, while the treatment of development gains has been scrutinized in a variety of ways over the last thirty years. The introduction of the Community Land Act and Development Land Tax in 1975/6 brought the most comprehensive moves yet seen in the attempts of the public sector to achieve its objectives, but the nature and intensity of the continuing arguments over this legislation suggest that it does not represent the last word in what is essentially a conflict of political ideologies.

Problems arising from the land development process

The background to the issues faced at this scale has been set out clearly in a number of official and professional reports including the Royal Town Planning Institute's paper *The Land Question*, the contribution by the Royal Institute of Chartered Surveyors on *The Land Problem* and the Government White Paper *Land*.[11] Underlying the situation is the general antipathy felt towards landowners by those without land, on account of the greater status, wealth, power and security which the former are considered to derive from land. More directly, however, three groups of reasons for confrontation can be identified. One concerns the alleged failings of the free-market system in providing an orderly and efficient pattern of development and emphasizes the negative effects of the property boom of the early 1970s. A second relates to the difficulties imposed on the public sector and its activities by the high price of development land, while thirdly, the increasing intervention of the state produces feelings of uncertainty and even resentment among those who have traditionally owned or occupied land for their own purposes.

The treatment of land as an investment medium has a long history related to the security element of a commodity in fixed supply and under steadily growing demand. Through much of the postwar period, the value of most rural land was enhanced by the special treatment which it received in the assessment of death duties and by its use to reduce the annual tax liability of firms, but a particularly strong boost was given to land prices in the early 1970s by the escalating rate of inflation and by the general collapse of the stock market of that time. All types of land were affected to some extent, but in absolute terms the price of development land rose most rapidly. Ever since planning policy had begun to limit the amount of land being taken for urban use, the 'artificial scarcity' so created had caused the price of land having the prospect of planning permission to rise far above that of purely agricultural land.

Besides the general rise in land prices, the market for building land was put under further pressure at about the same time by an upsurge in demand for private houses. A variety of problems emerged from this complicated situation. The attractiveness of land as an investment medium diverted capital away from the productive sectors where it was much needed to stimulate the country's economic growth. Excessive capital gains were to be made from trading in land designated for development, but they went only to the lucky few that held land in areas ordained by the government, while landowners in similar sites quite close by were denied these benefits. Meanwhile, for the agricultural industry in general, the land investment boom proved more of a problem than an asset, because land prices had risen to levels which were totally unrealistic in terms of rent from purely agricultural sources.

The gross overvaluation of agricultural land proved only a short-lived affair with the collapse of the property boom, but the longer established high price of 'artificially scarce' building land has continued to impose costs on all types of urban development and to exaggerate the financial burden of public sector programmes. Over the period 1963–75 the cost of building land increased in relative terms much more rapidly than the selling price of the overall housing package (Figure 3). The very high capital costs involved in developing urban fringe lands has affected the extension of public services by local authorities. In some cases a backlog of public work has resulted, as the cost of building up land for roads and schools has put back the schedule of improvement in other essential services, such as sewage disposal, while the provision of social services has been similarly – if anything worse – affected. The irritation of local authorities stems largely from the fact that for most of the postwar period the development value which they have helped to create by selective decisions on the extent and location of new building has not been returned to them, but instead has gone into private hands. This sense of injustice was aggravated by the 1959 ruling that the public sector should pay full market price for land under the 'alternative use' valuation, whereby compensation for land acquired for a school, for instance, would be put at residential land prices if housing represented the highest-value alternative use appropriate for the site. In this sense, they felt they were actually paying the landowner for the development value which they had in part generated.

Finally, there has been considerable resistance to the idea of state intervention among those elements of the general public who were most directly affected. The sharpest resentment tends to be expressed over the public powers of compulsory purchase, though the 1959 ruling clearly served to soften the blow for the landowner (if not for the tenant). The relations between local authority and developer, never very smooth under the 1947 legislation, appear in general to have worsened in recent years, although there are

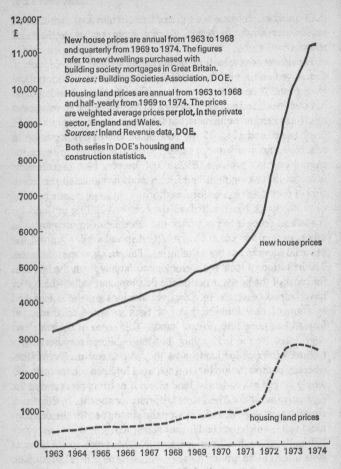

New house prices are annual from 1963 to 1968 and quarterly from 1969 to 1974. The figures refer to new dwellings purchased with building society mortgages in Great Britain. *Sources:* Building Societies Association, DOE.

Housing land prices are annual from 1963 to 1968 and half-yearly from 1969 to 1974. The prices are weighted average prices per plot, in the private sector, England and Wales. *Sources:* Inland Revenue data, DOE.

Both series in DOE's housing and construction statistics.

new house prices

housing land prices

3 Trends in new house and housing land prices

examples of fruitful cooperation. The conflict became particularly bitter in the early 1970s, when the building industry made strenuous efforts to meet the rapid growth in demand for private housing. The developers accused the local authorities of failing to make

44

available sufficient land for development, while the latter blamed landowners for holding back from the market in the hope of reaping even higher gains in the future. Land-hoarding arguments extended into the city centre, where the vacant office space of Centre Point brought discredit to the developers, though the latter in their turn were able to point to large areas of unused land held by local authorities, government departments and national corporations like British Rail. Though subsequent studies[12] suggested that the failings of local authorities and developers were of secondary importance compared to the availability of house-buying credit facilities, this controversy, plus the other related criticisms, highlighted the need for some fundamental rethinking over development procedures.

Policy solutions and practical experience

The provisions made for development plan implementation in the 1947 Town and Country Planning Act indicate that a general awareness of these problems existed at that time. Conformity of actual development with the plan was secured by the requirement that proposals for most types of land-use change should be submitted for the approval of the local planning authority. The treatment of financial gains arising from development largely followed the recommendations of the Uthwatt Report on Compensation and Betterment, in that a 100 per cent levy would be imposed on such gains and only the value of the land in its original use would be retained by the former owner.

The development control system, as opposed to the plan preparation machinery discussed earlier in the chapter, survived the thirty years after its inception virtually unchanged. The most fundamental criticisms have concerned the length of time which elapses between the submission of the initial (outline) application and the final decision from the planning authority. Particular frustration has been expressed in connection with major projects requiring lengthy negotiations with the local authority and perhaps appeal to the Minister responsible, but difficulties have also arisen on those occasions where the building industry in general has been placed under severe pressure from an upsurge in private house demand. It was such an instance which led to the setting up of the Dobry review of the control system in 1973. This inquiry's report[13] concluded that the system remained valid, but recommended that procedures should be made less cumbersome by giving more rapid treatment to the numerous applications which were simple, minor or uncontroversial in nature – a suggestion which has so far received less than full support from the government.

The treatment of development gains, by contrast, has had a much more stormy history. This can be attributed in part to the wide range of alternative approaches which have been suggested for dealing with the problem of excessive profits. Altogether, it is possible to identify at least five or six main lines of attack. The taxation of development gains, through a betterment levy or similar instrument, probably commands the widest support. Site-value rating, a type of tax more closely related to local authority rates, has been proposed, most notably by the Liberal party, as a general solution to the urban fringe problem and as a means of tackling the problem of vacant land and property inside the built-up area. Certain other taxes, such as capital transfer tax and the mooted wealth tax, have been offered as tools for helping to curb speculative interest in land, but their effects tend to be undermined by the special treatment claimed for agricultural land. A rather different approach is the provision of grants from the Exchequer to assist local authorities in acquiring land for essential services on the open market. Finally, there are the ideas of creating public 'land banks' and of nationalizing development land, or indeed all land, ideas which necessarily involve considerably higher degrees of public involvement in the land market.

In practice, the selection of the most appropriate alternative has formed the focus of a continuous confrontation between Conservative and Labour governments. The 100 per cent development charge introduced in 1947 by the Attlee administration was abolished by the Conservatives when they returned to power in 1951, while the ruling that local authorities could buy land at below market price was repealed in 1959. From that time, only new towns, under the 1946 legislation, were still able to acquire land at existing-use value. In 1967 the Labour government tried a new approach. The betterment levy was reintroduced, but was set at a lower level of 50–55 per cent in response to criticisms that the earlier 100 per cent level eliminated all incentive to bring forward land on to the market. In addition, the Land Commission was established with the task of buying up land well in advance of needs, thus providing a type of 'land bank' for future development, private and public alike, a scheme which at least superficially bore resemblance to the French practice of designating urban priority zones and freezing land prices at their original level. The Conservative party made no secret of its intention to repeal this legislation on its return to power, but later was itself forced to give the problem serious consideration. Its own proposals for a tax on development gains were ratified in 1974 by the incoming Labour government, which has subsequently produced its third major attack on this issue in the form of the Community Land Act and Development Land Tax.

This latest legislation gives wide-ranging responsibilities and powers to the local planning authorities. It requires that virtually all land needed for development and redevelopment should pass through public ownership. It makes land available to local authorities at existing-use value and permits its disposal through leasehold, freehold or other arrangements to take place at the going market price, thus allowing the 'community' to benefit from the value which it is said to have created. Needless to say, in view of the pressure that will be placed on local authorities and the 'hope value' expected by private landowners, this situation cannot be achieved overnight. Instead, the Act introduced the concept of a transition period during which the relevant public authorities start to implement a ten-year rolling programme of land acquisition and management and during which – until an appointed date, which is not the same for all areas and types of land – land transactions are still permitted on the open market. The latter, however, are subject to a development tax of not less than $66\frac{2}{3}$ per cent, rising to 100 per cent on the date set for the full implementation of the system. In this way, the Act is intended to reduce the cost of land to local authorities, maintain an orderly flow of land for development in general, and achieve an equitable move towards a new form of land market, where the 'community' as a whole benefits from the increase in land values through the acquisition scheme and the periodic renegotiation of leases.

The continuing debate

Judging by the variety of views expressed before the introduction of the Community Land Act, the debate over development land is by no means closed. The preferred solution of the Labour government falls short of the approach advocated by the self-styled Campaign for Nationalising Land,[14] while it awards a much more positive role to public authorities than is thought necessary or desirable by such bodies as the Royal Institution of Chartered Surveyors and the Institute of Economic Affairs.[15] The Conservative party has officially undertaken to repeal this latest attempt at public intervention in the private land market, though its poor record of urban land market management and embarrassment over being forced to consider the taxation of development gains have tended to curb its criticisms. Altogether the reforms come closest to the suggestions made by the two main pressure groups of professional planners, the Royal Town Planning Institute and the Town and Country Planning Association. The latter had consistently stood for the extension of New Towns Act principles to all types of urban development, while the former recognized the approach as the ultimate solution, at the same time recommending the less radical approach of public land banks as an interim measure.

Three questions lie at the forefront of the continuing debate: will party politics allow the Community Land Act experiment to run for a sufficient length of time to enable it to be given a fair judgement? Is the new system actually feasible, or will purely administrative and financial considerations prevent it from becoming fully operational? If it does get the chance to run, will it prove itself better than the alternative solutions outlined above? The answer to the first question is the most clear cut. Judging by

previous experience, the next Conservative government is likely
to repeal the legislation, or at least make such drastic changes that
the system will be incapable of operating as intended. Anticipation
of such changes may well encourage landowners to hold back
their land from the market in the immediate future, as tended to
happen during the life of the Land Commission. It was for this
reason that several professional and business organizations
recommended a less radical solution involving a development
gains tax and a limited 'land bank' system, which might have
had the support of both main political factions.

The feasibility of the preferred solution depends chiefly on
whether local government machinery is capable of carrying out
the extra work which it will be called upon to do. The delays noted
in the development control system, together with the pressures
placed on planning departments by local government reorganization and the introduction of structure planning, do not provide a
very encouraging outlook. The mid-1970s depression of the land
market and building industry perhaps reduces the scale of the
initial burden, but equally this is not a good time for local
authorities, already hard pressed in economic terms, to extend their
borrowing commitments in order to finance land acquisition.
The land acquisition programmes are likely to make only a slow
start since it is in the short-term financial interests of local authorities to hold back from the market until the development tax
rises to 100 per cent and until a quick turnover can be expected.
Even after the 'second appointed day', when the full range of
procedures is implemented, problems of staffing and operating
capital may remain powerful constraints for some time.

The most lively debate, however, focuses on whether the public
sector can hope to achieve better results than the normal workings
of the private land market. Views range from unqualified support
of government intervention to outright rejection of this approach.
At one end of the spectrum, it is argued that the public sector can
tackle the task of development on the urban fringe and in the city
both in a more efficient way, since it follows an orderly and
comprehensive programme, and in a more equitable way since
it takes a wider perspective than the pure economics of land

development. Opposing this view are those who express reservations about whether the public sector can respond to changing circumstances in such a sensitive way as the private developer can, and who therefore believe that it is likely to miss opportunities for reducing costs. This argument is taken to its furthest extreme in the observation that it is illogical to solve problems created by public intervention through the introduction of yet more public intervention and that, instead, all attempts at influencing urban development patterns through such mechanisms as zoning should be abandoned.

Such diverse arguments suggest that there is a long way to go before this issue will be resolved to the satisfaction of all concerned. The principle of state involvement in land-use planning is now, however, widely accepted in Britain and, with the Community Land Act, has run almost its full course. Even so, complete land nationalization has not taken place and still a great deal of importance is attached to the role of the private developer in the many stages beyond initial land assembly. Probably the most crucial issue on which the success of the Community Land Act hangs is whether good working relations can be built up between private and public sectors. This, in its turn, depends on the free flow of information between the two and an end to the secretive and sometimes underhand types of dealing which have generated much uncertainty and suspicion in recent years. If this is not achieved and the present system proves inadequate, then no doubt once again the solution will be sought in even more comprehensive government powers, eventually involving complete public control over the urban development process.

Conclusion

The issues over land which have been outlined in this account cover a wide range of scales in time and space and relate to many other aspects of British society. Even so the three-fold division followed here has been adopted largely for convenience of presentation. As has been intimated, the themes are often inter-related in complicated ways. Thus it has been shown that the allocation of land for development at local level depends to some extent on the value which is likely to be attached to agricultural land in the long-term national land budget. Similarly, experience has shown that local authorities stand a better chance of achieving their planning objectives if policies are formulated against the background of a clear understanding of the aims and aspirations of those who own or occupy individual land parcels.

Together, these three sets of issues show that land has been a foremost consideration in Britain during the last thirty years and has stimulated discussion for far longer. Moreover, from the above account it seems obvious that they will continue to generate a high level of discussion for many years to come. The safeguarding of our food supplies will remain a crucial concern in the land budget at least until technological developments allow land to become a considerably less important factor in food production. Issues over land-use planning, involving such questions as the relevance of containment policies, will remain for as long as physical plans are used as the principal method for directing patterns of human activity. The subject of land ownership and urban development involves a conflict of political ideologies which, as in several other areas, seems far from resolution. Even in the remote event of the Community Land Act receiving general acceptance, questions will still be raised about the validity of individual decisions, while as the inevitable side-effects are noticed, the competence of the public sector to manage the urban development process will be challenged. Conflicting ideologies and value-systems, differing levels of understanding about our problems, and uncertainties about future events will ensure that these issues over land will remain amongst the most fundamental of all those faced by our society.

References
1. Ministry of Agriculture, Fisheries and Food, *Food from our own Resources*, Cmnd 6020, London, HMSO, 1975.
2. Edwards, A. M., and Wibberley, G. P., *An Agricultural Land Budget for Britain 1965–2000*, Studies in Rural Land Use no. 10, Wye College, 1971; Centre for Agricultural Strategy, *Land for Agriculture*, CAS Report 1, University of Reading, 1976.

3. HM Treasury, *Forestry in Great Britain: An Interdepartmental Cost/Benefit Study*, London, HMSO, 1972.

4. Agricultural Advisory Council, *Modern Farming and the Soil* (Strutt Report), London, HMSO, 1970.

5. Waller, R., 'Prospects for British Agriculture', in Goldsmith, E., ed., *Can Britain Survive?*, Tom Stacey, 1971, pp. 113–20; Mellanby, K., *Can Britain Feed Itself?*, London, Merlin Press, 1975.

6. For concise outline, see Hall, P., *Urban and Regional Planning*, Penguin Books, 1974, chapter 5.

7. Cherry, G. E., 'The Development of Planning Thought', in Bruton, M. J., *The Spirit and Purpose of Planning*, London, Hutchinson Educational Books, 1974, pp. 66–84.

8. Department of the Environment, *Long Term Population Distribution in Great Britain – A Study*, Report by an Interdepartmental Study Group, London, HMSO, 1971.

9. Coleman, A., 'Is Planning Really Necessary?', *Geographical Journal*, vol. 142, no. 3, 1976, pp. 411–37.

10. Hall, P., Thomas, R., Gracey, H., and Drewett, R., *The Containment of Urban England*, 2 vols., London, Allen & Unwin, 1973.

11. Department of the Environment, Scottish Office and Welsh Office, *Land*, Cmnd 5730, London, HMSO, 1974; Royal Town Planning Institute, *The Land Question*, Planning Paper no. 4, 1974; Royal Institute of Chartered Surveyors, *The Land Problem – A Fresh Approach*, 1974.

12. For instance, Department of the Environment, *Housing Land Availability in the South East*, Report by the Economist Intelligence Unit, London, HMSO, 1975.

13. Department of the Environment, *Review of the Development Control System* (Dobry Report), London, HMSO, 1975.

14. Brocklebank, J., and others, *The Case for Nationalising Land*, Campaign for Nationalising Land, 1973.

15. Royal Institute of Chartered Surveyors, op cit.; Walters, A. A., and others, *Government and the Land*, London, Institute of Economic Affairs, 1974, p. 6.

Chapter 2
Issues over Resources — Cons'

Kenneth Warren

The nature of resources

Britain, plagued as it is with persistent economic problems, is frequently, and understandably, compared unfavourably with other advanced economies. Much of its industrial plant is obsolescent if not downright obsolete; there is a lack of dynamic industrial leadership and bad labour–management relationships. The national market is small as compared with that of the super-powers and as yet there is no evidence of significant advantages accruing from access to the wider market of the EEC. All these are common themes in the sad, continuous discussion of the British disease. Another, perhaps even more basic, limitation can be seen when comparisons are made between the resources of Britain and those of other countries. But is it in fact true to characterize Britain as a poorly endowed country? This of course raises the prior question of what is meant by the term 'resource'.

The word 'resource' is commonly used as more or less synony-mous with 'asset'. The Oxford Dictionary defines it concisely as 'means of supplying a want'. In the light of these definitions there is much to be said for the opinion that the greatest resource of an advanced economy is the skill of its people, the product of intelli-gence, of training and of imagination. W. Beckerman is a leading exponent of this view. Arguing for growth and against the stand-still arguments of those who hold what he regards as 'the fallacy of finite resources', Beckerman has summed up this philosophy of resources '. . . the world's chief resource is its population and the human capital thus represented. As long as there is no limit to human knowledge, there is no effective limit to any of the other resources that make up this universe.'[1] When one surveys the situation of many nations or regions, ranging from the overwhelming burdens of poor and over-populated Bangladesh or India to our own old, heavy industrial or highland problem regions, one has doubts about the practicability of Beckerman's approach. His view of a boundless human resource seems dangerously intangible, and is certainly not suitable for the same kind of analysis – including spatial analysis – that is necessary for dealing with physical needs. It ignores the very uneven areal incidence of economic difficulties, the conflicts over priorities for development, and variations in cultural and political attitudes towards problem solving. Above all it tempts the assumption that the scientist's laboratory can solve all problems. For these reasons a more restricted interpretation of 'resource' will be accepted here. A tentative definition of this more limited, earth-bound view might take the following form: resources are attributes of portions of the surface of the earth which give those parts especial value for particular purposes. Commonly this value is defined in economic terms but sometimes one is concerned with less tangible human values.

It must however be admitted that Beckerman has stressed a factor in resource development which is all too easily overlooked or underplayed. Though it may be convenient to concentrate on material resources, the active agent giving them value is his 'human ingenuity and technical knowledge'. Moreover as these human resources develop so must the interpretation of other resources change. Only changing human wants and capabilities can transform 'earth stuff' into resources. As E. Zimmermann summed it up many years, ago 'Resources are not; they become.'[2] Rising standards of living and increasing population provide the motives for extending the exploitation of resources; better knowledge, organization and investment bring it to fruition. Consequently a material or quality of the earth not regarded as a resource at one stage of development may become one later. For the same reasons the vital resources of one period may be superseded in the next one. Shallow coal seams near the outcrop were an important resource in the age of bell pits in the eighteenth century but ceased to be so with the economics of large-scale deep-shaft mining in the Victorian age. They became so again with new national needs and the innovations in mass excavating and moving machinery involved in open-cast working over the last thirty years. Clay-band and black-band iron ore from the coal measures, once a major national resource, provider of employment for thousands and incidentally a prime factor in much of the present location pattern for steelmaking, is effectively not a resource at all now. North Sea gas and oil represent the quite exceptional case of recent prime national resources – resources which indeed in the mouths of politicians are pointed to as the very base for our future economic salvation, a veritable *deus ex machina* – whose existence was not even suspected until a few years ago. On a different plane, the beauties of Snowdonia or of the Lake District were not a national resource when there prevailed a pre-Romantic aversion to wild landscapes. Beaches, sea and the ozone beloved of seaside propagandists required a wider-spreading wealth in the new Victorian urban/industrial regions, the development of rail transport and the gradual acceptance of the idea of a seaside holiday as part of the structure of the year, to convert them into the foundations for the mushrooming growth of the resort towns.

Increasing population, the appetite of individual wants and the progress made in satisfying more of them cause both a demand for new resources and for more of the existing ones. Given that there is a finite national space, this necessarily increases both the pressure on resource availability and the probability of conflict over the use of a particular area. Assessments of resource abundance and allocation of land to various uses are essential parts of the question of resource exploitation. They make up the planning counterpart of the economics of resource development. Increasingly, modern societies are recognizing that there are two other, even more fundamental aspects of resource development.

One is the effective exhaustion of a particular resource. The other, obviously interrelated, is the question of the long-term impact on the physical environment, the role of resource exploitation in the eco-system. What seems a perfectly logical, commercially viable resource prospect may look less so if the longer-term interest of society at large is taken into account, and positively undesirable if the long-term ecological effects are considered.[3] In all aspects of the consideration of resources the scale factor must be kept in mind. A development considered catastrophic to the local environment or by a local community may perhaps be justified in some wider national good, proved or assumed. Whether the proved high lead levels in the air near to the Gravelly Hill interchange at the heart of the Midland motorway network can be justified on these grounds is a nice debating point, but this case exemplifies the local/general conflict that can arise from a particular development, the wider resources being gained here being nodality. On the other hand projects in a national programme may not harmonize with the broadest interests of multi-national groups, such as a trading block, and may be to the disadvantage of poorer countries already severely handicapped. Britain has, for instance, proved uncooperative in some EEC pollution control schemes.

Such conflicts over the use of resources are conspicuous in Britain because of the country's small size, high density of population, early economic growth and high level of development. In this essay, two sets of problems are considered: those associated with generally interior, landward resources – farming, the needs of the uplands, water provision and mineral working – and those which are associated with outward-facing Britain, such as the space demands of extensive modern industries and the impact of oil and gas supply and processing, a group of resource problems which, though not confined to it, are focused on the coast. After examining the nature of these different resources, discussion next passes to the difficult question of decision-taking in resource exploitation and the possible need for a new framework of thinking about resources in the last part of the twentieth century.

Britain's resources

In spite of the limitations suggested above it would be pedantic to discount the tremendous importance of human capital, the inheritance in the way of settlements, industrial plants, farming systems and buildings and means of communication, and the present population with all its physical and mental qualities. As suggested above, any resource inventory is possible only within the context of a given society's interpretation of wants and possibilities, and the actions and the interpretations of one age become the constraints and conditioning for the next. An objective assessment of material resources is therefore difficult. Classification into neat and distinct groups will prove impossible but the attempt to disentangle them will itself reveal some of the resource development issues.[4]

Land

Land is one of the most basic of all resources when it is taken in its simplest sense to mean human occupancy or extension: providing space for living and moving, for association, for interaction and for isolation, for the areal specialization of economy and society which is of the very essence in a modern advanced affluent nation. In Britain a population of 55 millions now lives where only 37 millions lived in 1901 and 10·5 millions in 1801. The vast increase in personal mobility for work and pleasure, taken with this rise in numbers, means that British planners can ill afford to ignore the importance of space or to underestimate the increasing pressures on it. This pressure is greatly increased by the extremely low population densities of highland Britain, particularly in those tracts north of the Highland boundary fault. The need to accommodate the demands of the urbanized mass for more recreation space has become one of the predominating influences in Britain's resources policy. It is well to recognize that it is a relatively new influence. At an earlier stage not only were numbers and per capita wealth smaller, but easy movement was available to only a small section of the population and was less pervasive anyway. Outside the industrialized areas, which were admittedly treated with quite unbridled savagery by nineteenth-century man, the environment was not widely at risk.

Rural land

Between the great urban/industrial agglomerations, the free-standing industrial centres and the market town and other settlements of the country-wide services hierarchy, and away from the transport lines which link them and articulate the national economy, lies the surviving rural land of Britain. Those factors which determine its use in any area are essentially: its physical endowment – the intrinsic qualities of the site and local climate, proximity to urban workplaces and urban markets, the heritage of localized human skills, and, increasingly, various national government policies. Because of a widening range of uses, rural land is not only more intensively but also more extensively employed than ever before. The parts within the widening commuting range of urban centres are becoming rururbanized. Beyond, in the so-called deep countryside, there is a general decay of traditional rural communities and conflicts in new forms of occupancy: on the one hand agriculture, grazing, urban recreation, water storage and water sports compete for the land; on the other there is too often '. . . a gloomy picture of villages without transport, social services, jobs for local people, schools for their children, and shops for their housewives'.[5] Still more remote, poorer, usually upland areas suffer from outright social decline and experience land-use conflicts between extensive grazing and forestry. Further again, in the lands which were once barren, or merely the seasonal grouse shooting or fishing lands of an élite, are the immensely valued wilderness lands which have a rapidly increasing importance in terms of their 'psychic yield', their contribution above all to the mental wellbeing of ordinary urban dwellers. New uses here can become so intensive that the general resource is depreciated; thus, for example, '. . . the grey emptiness of the Cairngorms is being invaded by new roads and chair lifts, rare wildlife is endangered by pesticides, and places of scientific importance are being slowly put to waste'.[6]

Here and there within rural Britain are localized areas of special resource endowment: for example minerals, outsanding amenities, or sites of particular scientific interest. The fewer the occurrences of any, the stronger the claim for special treatment. The scope for conflict over development, resulting from incompatibility of land uses, is great and is increasing. No use illustrates this better, more widely, or with rational argument more easily becoming tinged with emotion, than the case of agriculture.

Agriculture

The farmer struggles against a legion of other users competing for the land. At present about 47 million acres (19 million ha) of the United Kingdom are in farmland and the annual loss to all other uses is about 144,000 acres (58,000 ha). This yearly subtraction from the farm acreage does not, however, constitute the full range of pressures on farm land.

Even though in Britain it has so far proved possible generally to avoid the 'urban fallow' of wasteland which surrounds the advancing front of suburban development in North America, trespass, vandalism, litter, prowling dogs, and fire make up a formidable array of troubles for the farmer close to an urban area and even for those further away. He may be tempted by the offers of land developers or bludgeoned by the impact of compulsory purchase. Towards the upland edge of farming the value of the land as a resource for such various uses as military training, water gathering and storage, afforestation and amenity has increased greatly in the twentieth century. How should government help in the allocation of the resources of rural land between conflicting claimants?[7]

Some years ago G. P. Wibberley[8] suggested that it might be desirable to zone the use of agricultural land, giving the town dweller freer access near to centres of population or major transport arteries while giving farming undoubted pre-eminence in remoter areas or on land of higher quality. The priority given to agriculture will vary according to how highly a large domestic food production is valued. It is interesting to see how quickly evaluation of such a national resource can change. In the early and mid sixties there was a widespread feeling that an increase in agricultural imports from other temperate areas might be better than major increases in home agriculture. In 1964 C. Buchanan wrote that industrial Britain might need to keep its agriculture active . . . 'for perhaps no other reason than to have a smiling countryside for its own delight and mental and physical recreation'.[9]

Within a few years, increasing balance of payments difficulties and, later, the prospect of long-term world food shortages caused a reassessment and new expansionist thinking. By 1975 Mellanby was insisting that Britain could feed itself and be healthier in the process.[10] The National Farmers' Union was pressing for increased output to cut down on the 1974 bill of £1600 million paid for imported temperate foodstuffs and the government responded with a White Paper which aimed for a £530 million reduction in the annual food import bill by 1980. It stressed that land taken for development should wherever possible be of low quality. These policies towards 'home grown' food production also have considerable international significance: it is said that our continuing importation of four million tons of grain to be used as animal feed means a loss to the Third World of food for twenty million people.[11]

Upland resources: sheep and trees

In the British uplands there is land-use conflict between the farmer, the forester, water boards and the recreationist. Though generally of less significance, in some areas military training grounds are locally important and raise high emotions.* Sometimes the conflicts are internal to the farming community – as in the case of tourism, where some farmers can obtain supplementary sources of income while others find it an obstacle to efficient operations. In other instances clashes of interest are between different communities, or even different national groups (such as over the issue of providing water resources in Wales for Merseyside and the Midlands).

The conflict between forestry and upland grazing has been protracted, keen and fought on a variety of fronts – commercial

* In 1973 629,000 acres (246,000 ha) of land was held by the services in Britain, and considerable parts of this, and, with the exception of Salisbury Plain, the biggest sites, were in the uplands.[12]

and aesthetic, sectional versus general regional interests, local and national. The position of the various parties has shifted and continues to do so. Classifications of upland farming alone differ considerably. The Economic Development Council for Agriculture reckons that hill farms cover 14 million acres (5·6 million ha) in the United Kingdom and are made up of 26,000 farms and 35,000 part-time units. On the other hand agricultural land classified as 'hill and upland' covers 15·5 million acres (6·3 million ha) in Britain. From this a little less than 10 per cent of the viable holdings in Britain produce about 5 per cent of the national value of farming or almost £200 million gross output in 1974.[13] Nationally the most valuable function of hill farming is the breeding and rearing of cattle and sheep to be sold before winter to lowland farms for fattening. In this way hill farms play a vital role in the whole farm economy: change in the uplands will have wide repercussions.

Technical change has meant that the grazing potential of the uplands has been increasing rapidly. In recent years, the spraying of bracken, fertilizing of the soil and surface seeding carried out intensively over small areas has resulted in productivity increases far in excess of those predicted by Sir George Stapledon in his celebrated experiments forty years ago. On one Lakeland hill numbers of livestock doubled by these means in a year. Even more impressive, at over 1650 feet at Pwllpeiran in Wales, various treatment measures quadrupled the number of sheep that could be grazed and increased the productivity per animal as well.

The situation of forestry and its case for an increasing share of the uplands has also altered. The Forestry Commission began work in the aftermath of the timber shortages of the First World War. By the 1960s, when its first plantings were still far from mature, and any trees which it had planted since the Second World War were only just beginning to yield thinnings, it had begun to look as if afforestation on this scale was strictly speaking uneconomic. As part of EFTA the United Kingdom at that time had free access to Scandinavian timber. Yet, in spite of this, the Forestry Commission continued and even increased its planting programme partly perhaps because of the natural momentum that had been gained from a major going concern, but also because of the wider returns that were envisaged – additional employment in the uplands, a general beneficial impression of activity and progress, a regional economic 'warming' effect which was especially noteworthy in the Scottish Highlands. In the 1970s Britain's departure from EFTA when it joined the EEC, a sharply rising bill for imported wood products (Britain now supplies only about 8 per cent of its timber needs, and the 1974 bill for imported timber and timber products was £1800 million or almost 42 per cent of that for oil, though some of this was for woods which could not be grown in a British climate) and the trend to a new 'siege' economy framework of thinking in which savings in foreign exchange are vital, point to a strengthening of the case for forestry in the uplands of Britain. In short, changes in forestry, in grazing and in the national economic situation mean that the conflict for the use of the resources of the uplands has become keener. There are additional complications.

A wide difference between the initial and recurrent investments of the two forms of activity and between the timings of the returns from these expenditures makes comparison of the two difficult even allowing for discounting to a common base year. Then there are changes in techniques, trading conditions and consumer tastes and value judgements to complicate the issue. Some of these changes are rapid – land purchase prices in the 1974/5 Forestry Commission year averaged more than double those of the previous year – others, though slower, can still change the whole context of consideration. One example of the latter is the change in the organization of forestry work which makes the social argument for forestry different and probably weaker than it was. Now more and more forestry work involves contractors who shift men from site to site rendering the idea of forest villages and new localized growth centres for people in upland society much less tenable than a decade or so ago. Other considerations difficult to quantify include the contribution of forestry to run-off control, and the increasingly active policy of the Forestry Commission in providing facilities for tourism. When aesthetics and value judgements are openly brought into the argument, dispassionate evaluation is all but dispensed with. Some critics write with passionate conviction of the unacceptability of masses of dark conifers on what was previously a bare moorland; others support the hill farmer on the grounds that he '. . . provides much of the social character of the countryside and contributes to its appearance'.[14]

The proponents of the National Parks, which cover 9 per cent of the area of England and Wales, have sometimes dealt harshly with both farming and forestry interests. A 1974 review of the Parks concluded that there should be a strong presumption against development which would be out of accord with park purposes. 'In the most beautiful parts which remain unspoiled it should amount to a prohibition to be breached only in the case of a most compelling national necessity.'[15] Apart from war, it is difficult to obtain unanimity about what constitutes 'a most compelling national necessity'.

Water

At the beginning of the century, in his celebrated yet contentious work *On the Location of Industry*, Alfred Weber wrote of water as a ubiquity in terms of its availability for manufacturing industry. Growth of large-scale manufacturing and more widely increased population and its extending personal necessities have rendered this description most inappropriate. Indeed, water is now regarded as a relatively scarce resource and several major issues surround its exploitation or supply – the reconciliation of local values with national needs, the desirability for working out an overall strategy rather than a series of short-term policies, and the organizational and psychological constraints involved in securing adequate future amounts. The long-term organizational barrier to a national approach to the exploitation of Britain's water resources was the existence of some 200 separate water supply undertakings. These have now been merged into ten regional authorities. The psychological barrier is to be found in the public's unwillingness to bear the real cost of a level of water consumption which by the mid-seventies has reached 36,000 gallons (163,000 litres) per head per year – excluding agricultural and industrial use – and is expected to reach 77,000 gallons (350,000 litres) by 2000 A D. There remains a deep seated assumption that water should be a cheap good, presumably based both on its essential contribution to human life and the naïve belief that 'Nature provides it'.

In Britain the local versus national clash of interest derives from the spatial dichotomy between the supply and demand for water. Excluding river water and a few major aquifers in the chalk and limestone of south-east England, the main sources of supply are the upland areas of the north and west. A few years ago, there was some popularity for the idea that future increases in demand should be met by building estuarine barrages, some of which could be multi-purpose. The chief of these involved the Dee, Wash, Morecambe Bay and Solway Firth. They were, however, very costly and also likely to provide a major disruption for wild life. Apart from the Dee project they have now faded from the planning scene. Desalination of sea water is not likely to be a commercially viable alternative. In 1972 the Water Resources Board reckoned that even in the high-cost water area of south-east England desalinated water would cost anything from 2·5 to fifteen times as much as water from conventional supplies at source. Throughout the country as a whole, the main source of supply will inevitably be the uplands though provision will still be expensive. In a major report in 1974 the Water Resources Board suggested a development scheme for England and Wales which, even at 1972 prices, may well cost as much as £1,500 million in capital and operating costs to the end of the century. Existing reservoirs will be enlarged, some of them will be reoriented to deliver to new consuming areas and major new upland reservoirs will be built. Much water transfer between and within regions will be by river as well as by aqueduct.[16]

The conflict between local and wider interests and between short- and long-term solutions may be highlighted from north-east England. As late as spring 1967 the way was cleared for the construction of a major reservoir at Cow Green above Cauldron Snout in Upper Teesdale. The struggle for the approval of this scheme had been long and hard but in spite of opposition on the grounds of the unique botanical and geological quality of the area, the extension of ICI on Teesside and the threat of potential redundancies there if the reservoir was not built proved decisive.[17] Before the Cow Green scheme was completed attention had shifted to a new, much bigger project again designed in large part to supply industrial Teesside. Cutting between the huge expanses of Wark and Kielder forests, the North Tyne Valley above Bellingham is one of the most attractive rural areas of the north-east. Since, in a typical case of narrowly conceived planning, British Railways abandoned the North Tyne railway from Hexham to Riccarton Junction, this valley has been accessible only by unclassified roads and therefore has a wilderness quality even though its bottom lands are cultivated and it lies only some thirty miles by road from the western edge of industrial Tyneside. In 1975, however, after extensive public hearings, approval was given for a large reservoir in the upper section of the valley. A major national water source and some 200 jobs will thus be created at the cost of the transformation of a landscape, a great deal of local physical and social disturbance and the bringing in of an alien way of life associated with a range of water sports. If a wider, longer view had been taken in the mid 1960s it is at least probable that the loss of the Kielder section of the north Tyne might have saved the Pleistocene flora of Cow Green.

Mineral resources and manufacturing

Like other major European industrial nations, Britain has increasingly become an importer of mineral supplies. Some 120 years ago it was not only the world's leading coal producer but the leader also in iron ore and non-ferrous metals. The flood of oil imports in the last quarter-century, the shrinking of home coal production, the rapid dwindling of home iron ore production since the mid-sixties (Northampton Sand ore output was 6·9 million tons (7 million tonnes) 1967, 1·3 million tons (1·3 million tonnes) 1974), and the almost complete annihilation of British base metal production seem to suggest that mining is of negligible importance as a British resource (Table 2). However, this is to

Table 2. **United Kingdom iron ore supply 1950–74**
(thousand tons – thousand tonnes – ore as charged)

	Home	Imported
1950	12·3 (12·5)	8·7 (8·8)
1955	15·8 (16·0)	12·2 (12·4)
1960	16·9 (17·1)	16·1 (16·4)
1965	15·4 (15·6)	17·9 (18·2)
1970	11·7 (11·9)	19·6 (19·9)
1974	3·9 (4·0)	18·3 (18·6)

Source: British Iron and Steel Federation
and British Steel Corporation, *Annual Statistics*.

ignore the extraordinarily wide range of British mineral products and the very impressive increase in recent years in the output of some of the non-metallic minerals, particularly sand and gravel, limestone and other constructional materials (Table 3).[18] If balance of payments difficulties continue to increase and if the attempted world associations of mineral exporters even nearly approach the effectiveness of OPEC it may be that there will be a revival in other lines of home mineral production. By the seventies there was a strong commercial and political lobby in favour of easier conditions for home metalliferous mining. Its supporters pointed on the one hand to the outdated, restrictive tax treatment of mining in the United Kingdom, and on the other to the impressive growth in non-ferrous-metal mining which had followed new mining legislation in Eire. Some government assistance to Cornish tin mining was given in 1975.

The problems associated with mineral working in a densely peopled, affluent and mobile nation, such as Britain, are considerable. Sand and gravel and even major unworked coal deposits are commonly found under agricultural land in lowland parts of the country. The landscape transformation associated with large-scale sand and gravel working is all too familiar in the riverine lowlands of southern England. Even where physical conditions are suitable for the creation of wet pits, a continuing supply of

Table 3. **United Kingdom production of selected minerals 1950, 1960, 1974** (thousand tons – thousand tonnes)

	1950		1960		1974	
coal	219,500	(223,000)	197,800	(200,965)	110,200	(111,963)
natural gas (coal equivalent)	—		110	(112)	51,957	(52,423)
crude oil	46	(47)	87	(88)	88	(89·41)
shale oil	113	(114)	61	(621)	Nil	(Nil)
iron ore	13,171	(13,381)	17,361	(17,639)	3,602	(3,660)
tin	1·4	(1·4)	1·9	(1·9)	9·9	(10·0)
lead and zinc	4·4	(4·5)	2·5	(2·5)	5·5	(5·6)
china clay and stone	816	(829)	1,713	(1,740)	4,298	(4,367)
slate	150	(152)	95	(96)	64	(65)
imestone	25,365	(25,771)	40,772	(41,374)	100,915	(102,530)
chalk	13,138	(13,348)	15,754	(16,006)	20,415	(20,742)
sand and gravel	38,000	(38,610)	77,200	(78,281)	105,000	(106,680)
(of which marine)	(—)	(—)	(4,200)	(4,267)	(15,300)	(15,545)
igneous rock	11,423	(11,606)	16,523	(16,787)	41,717	(42,384)
rock salt and brine	4,313	(4,382)	5,860	(5,954)	8,421	(8,556)

Note: The changing spatial impact associated with alterations in the pattern of production will be noted, for instance of the differential growth rates of limestone and chalk or the declines for iron ore, slate or shale.

Source: Institute of Geological Sciences, *United Kingdom Mineral Statistics*, 1975.

boating marinas or wildlife reserves cannot fully compensate for the loss of land or the creation of extensive, permanent sandy tracts in the most populous parts of Britain. In the recently formulated NCB expansion plans (costing a total of £1400 million) the development of the Selby coalfield raises a host of questions.

In 1975 the NCB was looking ahead to a production of ten million tons of coal from the Barnsley seam of the Selby coalfield by the mid 1980s or about 6·5 per cent of their target national output. The capital cost was estimated to be £60 to £80 million at 1974 prices but by 1976 had already increased to a multiple of this sum. The coal will be worked over 100 square miles (282 km^2) of the seam centred on the village of Riccall on the A19 road from Selby to York, access being through five shafts dotted over an area classed by the Land Utilisation Survey as being good general-purpose agricultural land. The coal will be drawn from the workings by slopes near Monk Fryston and delivered by 'merry-go-round' train to the established nearby major power stations at

Eggborough and Drax. Amenity objections to industrial instal-
lations, fear of extensive subsidence and its effects not only on
buildings but also on land already subject to occasional severe
flooding, doubts about the influx of 4000 men and their families
into what is now an almost wholly farming area, and the impact
in terms of possible more rapid run-down in the existing major
coal areas of west Yorkshire, make up a complex of unknowns or
fears about the development. Yet, accepting these 'local concerns',
the Selby field is clearly a major national resource. However, even
if it is reckoned essential to develop it the costs to society are
clearly going to be much greater (though perhaps less tangible)
than the estimate for the direct cost of development.

A more modest example of the effects on coal production of the
energy crisis has been the new impetus given to the activities of the
NCB's Open Cast Mining Executive. Ten or fifteen years ago,
the economic case for open-cast mining was relatively weak and
production was actually reduced to save jobs in deep mining at a
time of rapid contraction in coal consumption. In recent years,
however, technical improvements, allowing for larger-scale surface
digging, led to renewed activities. The rising prices of the mid-
seventies have now made some of these projects into highly
commercial propositions. In 1970 an application by the NCB to
open a big site at Butterwell near Morpeth on the edge of the
Northumberland coalfield was heard before a public inquiry: it
was subsequently rejected by the Minister. Another public inquiry
in March 1975 was followed by approval for the scheme in August.
2000 acres will be worked to produce 12 million tons (12·2 million
tonnes) of coal over ten years. Time and economic crises clearly
make ancient goods uncouth: 'resources are not – they become'.

Non-ferrous metal exploration and mining and also the development of non-metallic minerals in National Parks or areas of high
recreational value, have become highly contentious issues in the
last decade. Among very many other, less widely publicized
schemes, there has been controversy over tin in Cornwall, potash
working at three sites in the North York Moors National Park,
limestone working in the Peak District and controversial proposals
from Rio Tinto Zinc for dredging gold from the Mawddach

estuary and open-pit copper working near Capel Hermon in the southern part of the Snowdonia National Park[19] (Figure 4).

In these instances partisanship has sometimes overwhelmed calm analysis, on both sides. An alleged middle-class preoccupation with landscape before jobs was met on the other hand not only by a good deal of genuine concern to minimize the impact on the landscape, but also with some deviousness, as when RTZ apparently carried on its exploratory work in the Mawddach largely with the intention of a later strategic withdrawal in order to secure a wider public sympathy for its Snowdonia copper project.[20] Having suggested in a very small part of a general survey of mineral resources that renewed tin mining in Cornwall might not only deprive the Third World of invaluable jobs and income but would make a new, unsightly impact on the Cornish landscape, the present writer was denounced in Cornwall by a mining spokesman as 'an academic with his head in the clouds'. (It was interesting to hear incidentally that far from soaking up a great deal of Cornish unemployment, the number of jobs created was few and some of these had been taken up by migrants from Derbyshire.)

Industrial sites and the British estuaries

In a small country with an advanced economy the large scale of modern industry puts a premium on good sites – areas of flat land with good foundations and occasionally amounting to as much as several thousands of acres. Such sites need good service facilities, notably road and rail access, and bulk water supply. Because of the growing dependence on imported bulk raw materials and the growth in the size of the vessels involved in movements which are increasingly world wide, deep and open water approaches to the large sites have become increasingly important. A final factor which increases – or which in really well-rounded development schemes *should* increase – the area needed is the natural or planned associations of activities into interlinked complexes – oil and petrochemicals, steel and metal-working – and the wider associations of these into multiple-activity complexes along with

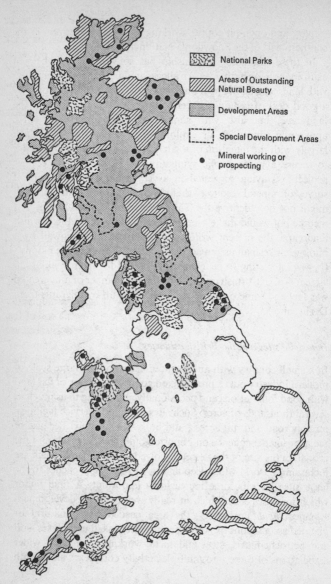

	National Parks
	Areas of Outstanding Natural Beauty
	Development Areas
	Special Development Areas
●	Mineral working or prospecting

4 Mineral development, problem regions and environment

other space-extensive activities such as power stations or dock developments. Even in a country so well endowed with estuaries as Great Britain, sites which meet all these requirements are becoming rare. Almost twenty years ago the managing director of Richard Thomas and Baldwins, then planning the major steel and strip mill project which later became the Llanwern works at Newport, remarked that sites suitable for such a project in Britain could be numbered on the fingers of one hand. In the late sixties the full potential of the estuarine lowlands began to be realized and study of the prospects of what were now frequently called Maritime Industrial Development Areas (MIDAS) was begun. A series of projects resulted – for Severnside, for Humberside and the proposed Ocean Span project involving above all the tremendous growth possibilities of the Firth of Clyde, an area quite uniquely favoured not only in terms of flat land and deep water, but also, above all, by the width and sheltered nature of the approaches. Unfortunately, this systematic survey followed many years of uncoordinated development, so that the scope for maximizing economy by concentration of very large developments on one or two estuaries had already been lost – by the end of the sixties, for instance, seven out of the ten major British estuaries already had oil refineries and petrochemical plants. Only two, Teesside and Severnside, had tide-water steelworks, but in that industry the established pattern of inland production centres and strong, established social interests lessened the possibility of change. In the early seventies slower economic growth seemed to the government to necessitate parsimony and the systematic evaluation of estuarine growth prospects was abandoned. From the point of view of rational development of a major national resource this is to be deplored as sheer shortsightedness. The fear remains that the existence of too many estuaries and of too many regional pressure groups may confound wise development of this resource; one indeed in which Britain is more favoured than any other country in north-western Europe.

Oil and natural gas

The development of gas fields in the southern part of the North
Sea, and the later development of oil fields much further north,
has played a central role in changing the British energy situation
and prospects since the mid-sixties. Full-scale exploitation of
North Sea hydrocarbons, however, began only in 1964. By 1975
there were five major gas-producing fields south of the latitude
of Flamborough Head. Some 380 miles to the north, the Frigg
field, straddling the boundary of the British and the Norwegian
concessions, was in production to supply gas to Britain by 1977.
In 1973 9·2 thousand million out of a total gas supply of 11·6
thousand million therms was natural gas. One result of this supply
has been a rapid advance in gas consumption. Between 1963 and
1973 British electricity production went up 68·5 per cent, but for
gas the increase was 257·2 per cent.

The first North Sea oil was brought ashore only in autumn 1975
but the importance of this new resource is likely to be much
greater still, Britain's foreign exchange losses from oil production
being replaced, by the 1980s, by net sales to overseas buyers; the
total government annual revenue from royalties and taxes on
North Sea oil may be as much as £3000 million.

The first major discovery in the British sector of the North Sea,
the proving of the Forties field, was announced in 1970; by mid
summer 1975 there were fourteen proved oil fields rated as
commercially important in this sector. Britain's energy-supply
pattern will obviously be radically altered by this development
(Table 4). Development costs in the North Sea, particularly in the
northern oil-yielding districts, however, are exceptionally high
and there remains doubt as to the degree to which the oil production
will be strictly speaking economic. The vital relationship is that
between escalating North Sea oil development costs and the very
uncertain course of world oil prices. When an OECD energy
report was prepared in 1974, production costs for North Sea oil
were put at $2 per barrel; by early 1975 they were at least double
that.[21] The cost of BP's Forties field development went up £50
million between early 1975 and September 1975, but clearly, with

outlay on a scale unprecedented even in the oil industry, once North Sea oil resources are opened they must be used, in order to give a revenue flow to match the extraordinarily heavy capital charges. The wider impacts of this major extension of Britain's energy base are also of great significance.

Table 4. **British energy supply 1960, 1973 and projected 1980**
(million tons – million tonnes – coal equivalent)

	Coal	Oil	Natural gas	Hydro and nuclear power	Total
1960	197 (200)	66[a] (67)	0 (0)	3 (3)	265 (269)
1973	131 (133)	159[a] (162)	40 (41)	12 (12)	342 (347)
1980	140 (142)	118[b] (120)	90 (91)	22 (22)	370 (376)

[a] All imported.   [b] Perhaps 100 million tons (102 m. tonnes) from the North Sea.

Based on: Cambridge Economic Policy Review, February 1975, and National Institute of Economic and Social Research, February 1975.

The regional effect has already been impressive. Some years ago wages in the Aberdeen area ranged about 10 per cent below the British average but by summer 1974 they were already 10 per cent above it; house prices were approaching those of south-east England and housing was in short supply. Direct employment of about 5000 in oil and substantial further multiplier effects by no means represented a clear gain, for many firms had lost workers to the higher paid oil-related trades and for some of these activities wage inflation had narrowed their competitive edge. Yet the boom in Aberdeen, the localized expansion at other points on the Scottish coast as at Leith or in old, decaying, former coal-export ports, such as Methil, Fife or at Burntisland, or above all on the Clyde, where about half the jobs in oil-related manufacturing are located, still fails to fully compensate for shortfalls in other sectors of the Scottish economy. By the late seventies it has been estimated that there may be 35,000 jobs in oil. Taking into account the multiplier effects of these, perhaps as many as 60,000 jobs will have been created. Much of this development will be in north-east Scotland: in the same period it is reckoned likely that up to 70,000 to 80,000 jobs will be lost in the older, declining industries of west central Scotland alone.

In short, though a boom to the national economy and particularly to the Scottish economy, oil will not provide the growth impetus in the sub-regions where it is most required. Major contrasts in regional prosperity will remain and even be accentuated by the impact of oil. More specifically, more locally and in many ways much more disturbingly, there will be the impression on the landscape of oil-related developments.

North Sea oil is to come ashore at four points – Teesside for the Ekofisk field, at Peterhead and in South Orkney for the southern group of British fields, and at Sullom Voe in the north part of the Shetland island of Zetland from the much larger northern group of fields. There will be benefits for the landing points. It has been reckoned that Shetland will receive £25 million by the year 2000 from the compensation fund based on the pipeline flow to the Sullom Voe tanker terminal. The price has already been paid in a shattering of the traditional island social life and in a very considerable disturbance to the local landscape.

Elsewhere round the coast of Scotland and to a limited extent also in north-east England, oil-rig construction or servicing activities have transformed local conditions, economically, socially and environmentally. In some instances, as with the Marathon yard at Clydebank, another yard at Methil and the Graythorpe yard on the Tees, oil-rig construction has replaced shipbuilding and has thereby fitted in easily with landscape, employment and social conditions. In other areas, the situation has been far less happy. In 1974, after a long public inquiry, an application for permission to build production platforms at Drumbuie in Wester Ross was refused but construction for the Ninian field at Kishorn near the foot of the beautiful 'cattle trail' road to Applecross was allowed. In the course of 1975 it became clear that the Kishorn site, originally expected to be fairly small, had been greatly extended. Other yards are at Ardyne Point, on the Argyll side of the Firth of Clyde, at Portavadie on Loch Fyne, and at Ardersier and Nigg Bay on the Moray Firth. In addition, at deep-water sites offshore in the Inner Sound of Raasay, steel decks and other equipment will be built onto concrete platforms floated in from the other Scottish production points.

Deep water is the dominating influence in the choice of sites for building and for assembling the new concrete-built platforms, though not for the earlier steel ones. Unfortunately, the deep-water lochs ideal for this are also one of the chief scenic glories of western Scotland. Even so, many have argued that economic necessity must come first. As one propagandist put it 'We have a right to require the crofters, the National Trust, the tourists, and any vested interest [*sic*] whatsoever, to cooperate and make sacrifices if necessary, to ensure the speedy construction of the rigs without further delay.'[22] In fact, both the 1970–74 Conservative administration and the Labour government which succeeded it acted to short circuit or speed planning approval for sites connected with North Sea development.

The coastline of Britain: a focus for resource conflicts

In the past resource development and associated conflicts were largely land based, as with coal and other minerals, power station sites, the extension of urban areas, disputes between farming and forestry. It is now increasingly clear that the coastline is the new major focus. Great new industrial projects in steel, oil refining and chemicals are seeking out ample deep-water sites. These include not only British concerns but also certain Common Market and other overseas firms; for example, Krupp and an Italian group have been interested in various prospects along the Firth of Clyde and another German steel group was said to be involved at one stage in the proposed Maplin port development. The landing of North Sea oil and gas, together with the future possibilities of these resources from the Celtic Seas, constitutes another group of pressures. Disposal of wastes of all kinds is another one. In a 1972 report the Royal Commission on Environmental Pollution observed that the estuaries of Britain provided a '... convenient and cheap sink for domestic and industrial wastes'.[23] The wider costs to society are not only the losses of general amenities but also, more directly, the deleterious effects on such activities as inshore fishing. The long-term environmental impact is less easily costed, but nonetheless it will probably be great. The expense of adequate cleansing facilities is high – it was estimated in the early 1970s as likely to amount to an extra 10 per cent on the capital cost of a new oil refinery.[24]

Nuclear power stations needing large amounts of cooling water, very firm foundations and safety-motivated remoteness from big centres of population are yet another coastal pressure. By 1974 the Council for the Protection of Rural England was predicting that within the next twenty years as many as twenty-five nuclear stations would be set up on remote sections of the British coastline. Several War Department training grounds have recently been relinquished to provide more space for public use – as, for instance, near Lulworth Cove – but there remain considerable areas given over to military purposes. Even housing or planned recreation may represent a most unwelcome intrusion to those who value the coastline from the point of view of wilderness. Peacehaven had become an interwar symbol of what not to do to the coast and thirty years ago Joad could already write, though with obvious hyperbole, 'The South Coast, along the greater part of its length is already "done for".'[25] Recently, at Druridge Bay in Northumberland, the NCB and the County Council were 'developing' as a major recreation area what, in spite of open-cast coal working a little way on the landward side, has until now been a magnificent long stretch of wilderness beach (Figure 5).

Decision-taking on resource development and land use

The processes through which decisions are reached over land-use conflicts are complex and not altogether satisfactory. It must be stressed from the outset that there is no likelihood that any wholly satisfactory formula will be found; interests will always vary and the invocation of some overruling national interest not only smacks of a totalitarian state but is usually extremely difficult to prove.

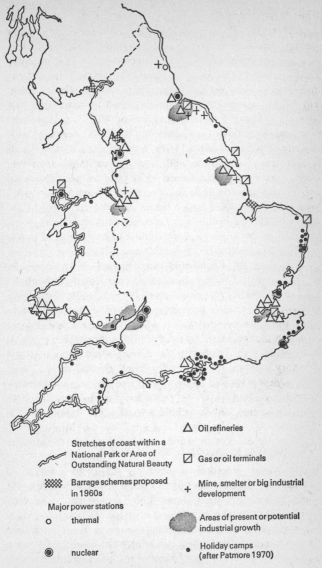

Oil refineries △

Stretches of coast within a
National Park or Area of
Outstanding Natural Beauty

Gas or oil terminals ⊡

Barrage schemes proposed
in 1960s

Mine, smelter or big industrial
development +

Major power stations

○ thermal

Areas of present or potential
industrial growth

◉ nuclear

Holiday camps
(after Patmore 1970)

**5 The coastline of England and Wales – resources and development
pressures**

Until the mid nineteenth century a landowner could develop the resources of his own land with little or no outside control. It is true that if his development of the land created nuisance for others the courts could restrain or fine him. One example of the latter is the almost constant recourse to litigation by landowners or farmers seeking recompense for the damage caused by fumes from the chemical works of Tyneside, St Helens or Widnes. (A later outcome was the setting of environmental standards, beginning with the Alkali Act of 1863 and the establishment of the Alkali Inspectorate.) Even in the wild heyday of capitalism there was some provision for the assumed wider good to take precedence over private interests. If he could secure a private Act of Parliament a developer could exploit the resources of land which he did not own. This procedure was especially important in the construction of the railway system. From the beginnings of public health legislation (the first general Public Health Act dated from 1848) another set of constraints was imposed on developers. In the course of the twentieth century, and particularly through the Town and Country Planning Acts of 1947 and 1971, increasingly complex controls have been established. Today broad structure plans form the context within which individual development proposals are considered by the planning authority. If a proposal is rejected by this authority the developer may appeal to the Secretary of State for the Environment. Even if the proposed development is allowed by the appropriate planning authority the Secretary of State may be petitioned by objectors. In both instances he may decide to hold a local public inquiry. This is conducted by an inspector appointed by the Minister. The inspector passes his findings and recommendations to the Minister who may accept or reject them.

The inquiry procedure is inevitably subject to a variety of political pressures at every stage – when decisions are made by the planning authority itself, when lobby groups can voice their opinions at the public inquiry, and when the Minister has to show some regard for the attitudes of his own party. Even in the open forums of public debate there can be little unruffled consideration and no calm objectivity in dealing with conflicting interests over resource development.[26] Even if the preconceptions of the various immediately interested parties could be set aside, it is difficult, perhaps practically impossible, to decide conclusively what is in the public interest. Does 'public interest' imply the whole rather than the part? How then can one balance national gain against local loss? Are we concerned with the immediate or the long-term public interest, and, if the latter, over what length of time?

It is clear that in the past many planning decisions have been partial ones. Sometimes there has been good physical planning but a neglect of social and economic issues; sometimes piecemeal planning has led to a duplication of resources and a consequent waste both of investment funds and of land. The Council for the Protection of Rural England, in commenting on the Water Resources Board's estimates for water demand to the end of the century and their consequent reservoir-building programme, has suggested that they are based on a crude aggregation of the projections made by the officials of the former local water undertakings and, as a result, involve over-provision at very high cost in both land and outlay. Even more explosively, a Commons Committee report of mid-1974 and a detailed study in 1975 suggested there has been gross over-provision of oil-platform construction capacity. By the end of 1975 some Scottish yards had still received no orders. By implication a number of the sites need not have been developed, a conclusion which is highly inflamatory to the conservationist.[27]

Apart from the division of decision-taking which often leads to duplication of development by private industry, there are sometimes strong social pressures for development even if this leads to a serious conflict with local amenity. In the late 1950s North Uist pressed for jobs in a rocket base whatever the environmental impact; more recently, the prospect of 500 jobs in construction (though many fewer permanent jobs) encouraged Anglesey interests to support Shell's application for permission to build a deep-water terminal there, even though it was widely maintained that the changing national oil supply situation made this no longer necessary. Much has been claimed for the use of cost–benefit analysis in such exercises. Whereas appraisal of possible investment by firms emphasizes private costs and benefits and the decision to go ahead is taken if the revenue from the latter exceeds the investment of the former by what is considered a satisfactory amount, modern cost–benefit analysis emphasizes social costs and social benefits as well. In a big mineral resource project, for instance, the real costs to society involve not only the direct outlay for the mine and smelter, wages or freight charges on ore transport, but also such considerations as disturbance to old traffic flows, noise and other environmental nuisance and interference with other possible land uses. The benefits include not only the profits which may accrue to the firm, but also the potential created for new employment, the regional multiplier effect and the wider possibilities of economic growth, perhaps bringing about a retardation of population decline but sometimes leading to the breakdown of a local society. Costs are incurred and benefits accrue at different times and so both must be discounted in order to permit a comparison of their present worth.

There are some grave weaknesses in cost–benefit analysis, however. A limited area must be assumed for the assessment, for otherwise the calculations become unwieldy, but in fact the true costs of developing North Sea oil include a slower development of national coal resources or possibly a reduced expansion of Merseyside or Severn estuary employment in oil refineries. It is assumed that all costs and benefits can be quantified and expressed in money terms for purposes of comparison. This exposes the method to ridicule. Even a human life has been valued – in the early 1970s at from £5000 to £7000, but varying with age and sex on the assumption that a young man will contribute more to society than an older one or a woman. In crude terms '. . . it follows that his net benefit is his expected future earnings less his cost in terms of consumption of goods and services.'[28] This *reductio ad absurdum* is paralleled by that which assumes a price can be put on amenity. Conversely, the yachtsmen or wealthier Glasgow commuters who fought strongly against big industrial developments on the shores of the Firth of Clyde on the grounds of its tremendous amenity value or those who opposed R T Z's Snowdonia copper-mining inclinations have maintained that certain values cannot be costed in monetary terms; their returns are in personal physical or psychic satisfaction. To these protagonists and indeed to most people the suggestion that scenery can be valued in terms of what people are prepared to pay to visit it are not at all convincing.

Cost–benefit analysis does not then provide a clear-cut answer to the question – should a particular resource project be allowed or not? It merely itemizes – within limitations of space and time – all those costs and benefits which can be quantified, and attempts to point up the significance of many which cannot. Subjective decisions still have to be taken by central government or some other public body. Even so, with all its many weaknesses, it represents an advance on former methods of decision-taking based on intuition and influence expected by particular pressure groups. The technique provides a systematic assessment of a new wealth of information about possible alternatives.

A wider framework for resource development

Short-term gain from resource exploitation may not only imply substantial loss to other sectors of society or other localities, but may also lead to long-term harmful effects and perhaps irreversible environmental damage. As Smith and his collaborators pointed out[29] pressure on the British standard of living, and questions about Britain's future as an industrial nation, are now causing a reassessment of its own resource potential. Is it wise to destroy even a portion of a National Park for a few million pounds reduction in foreign-exchange spending? Are not other economies in our manner of living possible and desirable as alternatives? Recently, one spokesman for an alternative society has pleaded for a replacement of the old 'profit ethic', a replacement which would have major implications for resource development.[30] 'In my view, Britain will return to the ethic that existed in societies long before that of profit. This is the ethic of social obligation.' Unfortunately, even if social ethics replace economic ethics it will still be necessary to find some way to 'economize' in resource exploitation, to decide on difficult choices between alternatives.

Where pressures of population and space are particularly great conflicts cannot be eliminated and indeed they seem likely to become ever keener. Clearly solutions to many resource issues will never be satisfactory to everyone. Yet even so, it is well to heed the alarmist warnings. A more immediate danger must not hide the long-term issues, but calls for urgent attention. In the siege economy that has followed from the energy crisis of 1973, a sense of urgency has grown up about the need to develop more fully our own home resources. This suggests a renewed danger of short-term expediency taking precedence over long-term planning. If resource exploitation policy continues to be short-sighted and narrow – if, for instance, the relationship between our resource policy and the situation of the Third World is ignored – a high price will eventually have to be paid. At home, an early casualty of the struggle to maintain the standard of living may be that more elusive but in the end more vital consideration of the quality of life. To an urbanized, affluent society resource issues are vital. Recognizing this, in tackling our economic problems in the late twentieth century, we must also see that it is more necessary to get the economic machinery and social structure right than to pull to pieces the national building in which they are housed in order to provide emergency fuel to keep the machinery creaking along in its old form a little longer. Perhaps, after all, Britain is not a resource-poor country but the challenge to planners in ordering priorities in development is a formidable one. It is becoming a progressively more daunting but more important task.

References

1. Beckerman, W., 'The fallacy of finite resources', *Bank of New South Wales Review*, 14 April 1975, pp. 10–15.
2. Zimmermann, E., *World Resources and Industries*, New York, Harper & Row, 1951, chapter 1, 'Meaning and nature of resources'.
3. Ward, B., and Dubos, R., *Only One Earth. The Care and Maintenance of a Small Planet*, Penguin Books, 1972.
4. Chisholm, Michael, ed., *Resources for Britain's Future*, Penguin Books, 1972.

5. Perry, G., 'Halting the neglect of rural Britain', report of the meeting of the CPRE, *Guardian*, 22 September 1975.

6. Faux, R., *The Times*, 9 September 1974.

7. Coppock, J. T., 'Farming for an urban nation', in Chisholm, op. cit.; also other articles in this book.

8. Wibberley, G., 'The preservation of Britain's rural land', in Ashton, T., and Rogers, S. J., *Economic Change and Agriculture*, Oliver & Boyd, 1976, p. 166.

9. Buchanan, C., *Guardian*, 2 November 1964.

10. Mellanby, K., *Can Britain Feed Itself?*, London, Merlin Press, 1975.

11. Laidlaw, K., 'Why Britain keeps 20,000,000 people hungry', *The Times*, 4 April 1975.

12. Defence Lands Committee, *Report*, HMSO, 1973.

13. Jones, Sir E., article on hill farming in special report on 'Grassland Management', *The Times*, 13 May 1974.

14. *The Times*, 'Brecon Beacons farming', 26 February 1973.

15. National Park Policies Review Committee, *Report*, HMSO, 1974.

16. Rees, J., in Chisholm, op. cit.; Water Resources Board, *Water Resources in England and Wales*, HMSO, 1974; Lingard, J., 'Pricing water to domestic consumers', *National Westminster Bank Review*, February 1974, pp. 34–43.

17. Gregory, R., 'The Cow Green Reservoir', in Smith, J. R., ed., *The Politics of Physical Resources*, Penguin Education, 1975.

18. Blunden, J. R., *The Mineral Resources of Britain*, London, Hutchinson, 1975.

19. Smith, op. cit. See also Blunden, op. cit.

20. Searle, G., in Smith, op. cit.

21. OECD, *Energy Prospects to 1985*, OECD, 1974.

22. Urquhart, Sir R., letter to *The Times*, 9 September 1974.

23. Royal Commission on Environmental Pollution, *Pollution in Some English Estuaries and Coastal Waters*, HMSO, 1972.

24. ibid.

25. Joad, E. M., *The Untutored Townsman's Invasion of the Country*, London, Faber, 1946, p. 153.

26. Smith, op cit.

27. House of Commons Science and Technology Committee on North Sea Development Problems, *Report*, HMSO, 1974.

28. Dewhurst, J., 'Putting a price on people', *The Times*, 31 January 1973.

29. Smith, op. cit.

30. Newbould, G. D., in a lecture to the sociology section of the British Association, 1975.

Chapter 3

Issues in Employment

Morgan Sant

Introduction

There is in Britain a pathological concern for employment and unemployment. Much of this is justifiable; there are broad inter-regional and inter-urban disparities in the demand for labour and significant variations in unemployment as a result. Yet attitudes can be ambivalent; slow growth in total employment (which inevitably has meant decline for some regions) has exacerbated the problems of regional development, but rapid growth in some places has created embarrassing difficulties of absorption. Like the proverbial farmer for whom no weather conditions are ideal, there is a tendency among regional planners (academic and practising) to find a cloud in every silver lining. Within such a highly integrated regional economic system as that found in Britain, and in a situation of slow growth – in incomes and population as well as employment – it may not be feasible to solve every problem; indeed it may not be possible to solve *any* problems to the satisfaction of all concerned. Solutions in one place or economic sector create difficulties elsewhere. For example: the growth of new towns diverts jobs away from the assisted areas; industrial movement to the assisted areas has contributed to the present problems of London; but if there were an easing of locational controls on London and the South-East the assisted areas would suffer. Faced with such intricate webs of cause and effect, an economic geography as complex as Britain's, and vociferous electorates, it is creditable that regional planning has achieved as much as it has.

At a time when the number out of work has climbed well above one million it may appear complacent – if not actually heretical –

84

to assert that less attention should be paid to a short-term indicator like unemployment. But it is an underlying theme of this chapter that excessive emphasis on this aspect of the economy diverts attention away from longer-term issues. Many examples have occurred of decisions which have been postponed or avoided because of the need to 'safeguard' established interests under the banner of preserving employment: the failure to scrap Concorde, the bailing out of Chrysler, the delay in implementing sex-equality in employment are but three of more recent cases. Yet there are times when one wonders just what is being safeguarded. Certainly it is unwise, as well as impossible, to neglect the short term: and it is equally false to assert that British planning has no long-term focus. But the question is one of integration and balance – making the short term serve the long term, and vice versa. In this the British experience and aspirations fall far short of adequacy (although it must be emphasized that this is not a peculiarly British failing, but one that is found in many countries regardless of political system or level of development).

The principal concern of this chapter is regional economic policy, the basis of which is the level of employment and un-employment in different parts of the country. Most of what follows is descriptive: there are sections on trends in employment and related indicators and on the effects of regional policy. Running through this is an attempt to be argumentative. Policies are not bureaucratic conveniences, but are the outcome of a mixture of values and philosophies together with logic and empiricism. All of these need to be under constant scrutiny.

Trends and distributions

For decades the level of aggregate employment has grown slowly. Since 1955 (the base year for Table 5) the main portion of the increase has come from rising female participation rates while the number of males in the total workforce appears to have fallen from a peak reached in the mid-sixties. But there have been limits to the growth of the female workforce; there were fairly high participation rates before 1955 in many cities and the untapped reserve was not very large. In addition, the number of students in higher education has increased and international migration, except in occasional years, has been fairly balanced.

Table 5. **Total working population,**
United Kingdom, 1955–74
(millions – figures rounded)

Year	Males	Females	Total
1955	16·47	8·01	24·49
1960	16·66	8·44	25·10
1965	17·07	9·02	26·10
1970	16·36	8·94	25·29
1974	16·05	9·60	25·65

Source: *Annual Abstract of Statistics.*

Although the total has been stable in the long term there have, however, been several important sources of variation among industries, cities and regions. These need to be considered against the background of the *cyclical* progression of the British economy. Far from being a smooth sequence of even-paced development, the national economy has been characterized by a series of accelerating and decelerating upward and downward movements (Figure 6), generally accompanied by a 'stop-go' two-step by different Chancellors with varying degrees of elegance and usually poor timing. These fluctuations have differed in their amplitudes and effects, and sometimes in their causes as well, but they have one thing in common – namely the small degree to which they are understood. Notwithstanding the occurrence of localized secular trends leading to the rapid rise or stagnation of particular places, the alternation of faster and slower rates of change is probably one of the most potent forces for shaping the structure of the national workforce and its regional distribution. For example, we know much about the casualties of recessions: older industries receiving death-blows, and some newer ones tottering under falling demand;[1] the regional and localized disparities that

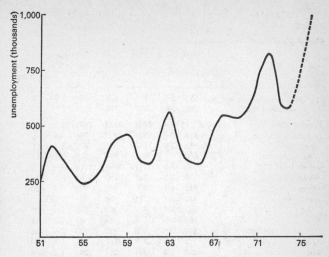

6 Numbers unemployed 1951–75 (June totals): United Kingdom

result from the incidence of these effects.[2] But we have far less information about the contribution of geographical imbalances in supply and demand to the causes of recessions, or about the transmission process of changes in demand upon regional economies, or about the transfer of resources between industries and regions during cyclical recoveries.

Structural changes in employment

Among the *structural* changes in national employment particular importance must be attached to the fortunes of different industries (Table 6). As in most post-industrial societies the shift here has been marked by the relatively rapid growth of the tertiary sector; between 1960 and 1974 it expanded its share of total employment from 54 per cent to 62 per cent. More precisely it was the 'white-collar' services – finance, insurance, administration, education, health and the like – which accounted for this growth. At the same time the manufacturing sector lost ground both absolutely

Table 6. **Total employment by major industrial category, United Kingdom, 1960–74** (thousands)

Industry	1960 no.	%	1965 no.	1970 no.	1974 no.	%	1960–75 percentage change
agriculture, forestry, fishing	635	2·8	497	468	417	1·8	−34
mining and quarrying	769	3·4	629	410	349	1·5	−55
Manufacturing	8851	39·4	9028	8339	7871	34·5	−11
food, drink, tobacco	815	3·6	839	792	766	3·4	−6
chemicals	531	2·4	518	491	475	2·1	−11
metal manufacture	618	2·8	632	594	507	2·2	−18
engineering	2049	9·1	2287	2095	1980	8·7	−3
shipbuilding	278	1·2	219	190	185	0·8	−33
vehicles	920	4·1	870	840	792	3·5	−14
metal goods	546	2·4	591	596	582	2·6	+7
textiles	902	4·0	819	678	585	2·6	−35
leather	64	0·3	61	49	43	0·2	−33
clothing and footwear	591	2·6	558	455	427	1·9	−28
bricks, pottery, glass, cement	339	1·5	358	318	301	1·3	−11
timber, furniture	293	1·3	301	271	283	1·2	−4
paper, printing, publishing	603	2·7	639	626	589	2·6	−2
other manufacturing	302	1·3	335	345	358	1·6	+19
Services	12,214	54·3	13,467	13,254	14,153	62·1	+16
construction	1459	6·5	1700	1335	1328	5·8	−9
gas, electricity, water	378	1·7	419	391	347	1·5	−8
transport and communication	1707	7·6	1655	1573	1506	6·6	−12
distributive trades	2833	12·6	3023	2676	2761	12·1	−3
finance, professional, scientific	2562	11·4	3108	3853	4490	19·7	+75
miscellaneous services	1998	8·9	2226	1947	2125	9·3	+6
national government	526	2·3	566	589	610	2·7	+16
local government	751	3·3	772	890	986	4·3	+31
Total	22,489	100	23,621	22,471	22,790	100	+1

Source: *Annual Abstract of Statistics.*

and relatively; after 1960 it lost over 10 per cent of its total employment and its share fell from 39 per cent to 35 per cent. In several industries the downward trend was well in evidence before 1960 (for example, textiles and shipbuilding) but although most other industries continued to expand slowly into the mid-sixties their trends have since been downward, with few exceptions. If one could be sure that the shift from manufacturing to services was justified by rapidly increasing production in the former and a massive growth of the latter's export potential there would be little cause for concern. However, between 1968 and 1974 the biggest gains in manufacturing production came in the consumer-goods industries (excluding cars), while the investment-goods and intermediate-goods industries registered a very slow growth. In the light of what was happening in other parts of the world – and particularly in Britain's competitors – where capital intensity was increasing rapidly, this could hardly be a satisfactory balance.

For many years a criticism levelled generally against manufacturing industries (and mining) was that they were guilty of overmanning. Often added to this was a charge that trade union power lay behind this inefficiency. The latter claim was always dubious: restrictive practices are, after all, no more than a bargaining tool and less a cause of inefficiency than a response to uncertainty about the gains from innovation. In turn industrial managements have themselves been affected by a series of uncertainties (for example, indecision over membership of the EEC, recessions in the late 1960s and early 1970s, vacillation by government over its intervention in, and assistance to, the private sector) accompanied by a rising trend in interest rates. So the conditions for substantial increases in labour productivity have generally been lacking. Indeed, by making certain kinds of labour cheaper (for example, through the differentials in the Selective Employment Tax, and by the use of the Regional Employment Premium) there have been marginal incentives against increased productivity.

It is, of course, impossible to predict precisely in what shape the manufacturing sector will emerge from the present recession. Although it is clear that a significant amount of labour-shedding has occurred it cannot be stated with any certainty that this will be met with substantially increased investment per employee and correspondingly higher international competitiveness. The National Enterprise Board may succeed in injecting capital into the larger firms (which account for the greater share of employment and output) but the reabsorption of over a million unemployed means that Britain will be a cheap labour economy for some years to come.

The growth of the service sector is, in one sense, understated by the statistics in Table 6. Within the manufacturing sector there has been a significant shift into 'non-operative' jobs – a broad category which includes professional and technical workers, warehousing, storekeeping, packaging, sales staff, clerical and administration staff and management. The proportion of employment in manufacturing industries accounted for by these occupations has risen steadily for many years; taking administrative, technical and clerical workers alone the proportion in 1924 was about 10 per cent, in 1954 about 18 per cent, and in 1974 it had reached 27 per cent. The trend is one that pervades almost all manufacturing industries. Moreover, the main components of the shift were found in the increase of women in clerical jobs and both men and women in administrative jobs. Explaining these changes is not straightforward, but it is not unreasonable to suggest that they are in some measure associated with changes in the corporate structure of industry and the growth of multi-plant firms which require a more 'top-heavy' organization. Of course, there is no reason to find fault in this trend if it enables industry to operate more productively. However, in view of the record of much of British industry, the unavoidable conclusion is that a significant number of firms have been more concerned about their offices than about their shop floors.

The trend in the manufacturing sector poses a major dilemma for the future of regional policy. In the past this has relied on the relocation of manufacturing industry, but if the supply of potentially mobile firms begins to dry up where will be the resources for job creation in the assisted areas in coming years? The answer is not totally pessimistic for there remain some areas of growth within the manufacturing sector and there have been actions to stimulate other instruments of policy (for example, office movement and 'indigenous' growth). But it now looks as if the scale of industrial movement achieved in the 1960s will be very difficult to repeat.

Geographical dimensions of change   rural & pop

The spatial variations in employment need to be examined at several different scales and in terms of several different processes. The broad pattern of disparities in the last few decades is now well known: the southern half of England expanded faster than average, while the remainder of the country grew slowly. But this is an over-generalization: there were wide variations within both sets of regions. In southern England many rural areas continually lost jobs, principally through the contraction of agricultural employment, and in Greater London the growth of service employment since 1960 has been more than offset by the contraction of its manufacturing sector, due mainly to its role as the chief supplier of mobile industry to the assisted areas and the rest of the South-East. Other conurbations in Britain have experienced similar trends and the growth areas have tended to be not the largest cities but those in the lower tiers (including the new towns and expanding towns).

At a broad regional level this distribution is related to the pattern of migration described by A. J. Brown.[3] This identifies the major flows of economically active migrants as being directed from northern Britain towards the South-East and London, with subsidiary flows to the Midlands. At the same time there are regions – East Anglia, the South-West and the East Midlands – which have received migrants in large numbers from the South-East and London. One is tempted to draw an analogy with a water tap being turned on and the water left to flood out over the container, although this is perhaps somewhat far-fetched. If we allowed our imagination to run full rein, however, we might ask to what extent the volume and direction of the flow could be regulated and what would be the secondary effects (beyond the impact on Wales and northern Britain and London and the south-east, that is) if it was in fact more closely controlled.

Despite the existence of a large body of research on the characteristics and direct impact of migration[4] there remain many unanswered questions about its effects on national and regional economies. As an equilibrating mechanism able to reduce regional disparities there must be grave doubts, but there are also grounds for arguing that migration on the scale experienced in Britain does not significantly harm the prospects of the regions. After all, migration is chiefly a response to conditions already existing and expected to continue, and is not therefore a principal cause of disparities. If regional policy has not succeeded in reducing the gap in income and unemployment rates between regions it is not due to migration from the assisted areas. This assertion partly contradicts the consensus view held in the 1960s which pointed to the negative multiplier effects in the depleted regions and the positive effects amongst the recipients; for example, for every five migrants to the South-East sufficient demand for goods and services was created to support one more.[5] But the argument can be extended. Industrial movement to the assisted areas has depended upon the growth of firms in the south-east and Midlands which in turn has partly depended on their labour supply. So to some extent migration may have aided regional policy.

The direction of industrial movement has generally been the opposite of migration.[6] With one exception, in the 1950s when the new towns programme absorbed a large share, regional policy has deliberately concentrated on moving the demand for labour to the north and west of Britain (Figure 7). Time-series analyses of industrial movement for the country as a whole and for individual regions show how this policy has been influential (Figure 8). In each series there are two groups of factors at work. One is *cyclical* and controls the year-by-year fluctuations in the volume of movement. Inevitably it contains the same factors which affect the level of industrial investment. The other group is *structural* and influences the overall level around which the annual fluctuations occur. Here the influence of regional policy is seen to have been highly effective. Changes in the controls on, and incentives for, industrial movement in the 1960s were matched by corresponding increases in the number of firms moving to, or setting up branches in, the assisted regions. To some extent this involved the 'creation' of extra mobility; the national profile as a whole underwent an upward shift. However, the greater part of the effect of the

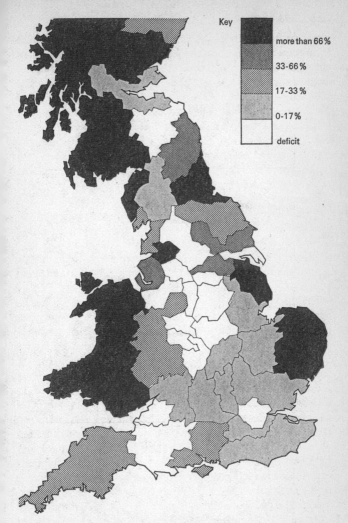

Key

more than 66 %

33–66 %

17–33 %

0–17 %

deficit

7 The contributions of industrial movement to employment change

$$\left(\frac{\text{Net employment in moves, 1945–65}}{\text{Change in employment, 1951–66}} \times 100 \right)$$

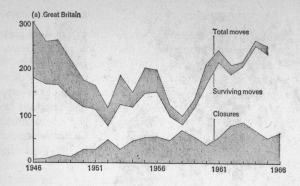

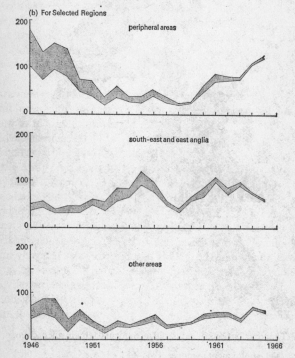

8 Time-series analyses of industrial movement: (a) in Great Britain, (b) for selected regions

strengthening of regional policy was to 'divert' industrial growth greatly raising the proportion going to the assisted regions.

Herein lie two major practical problems of regional policy. The first is that the estimated needs of the assisted areas (outlined later) outweigh the capacity of the non-assisted areas to supply them. The problem is exacerbated when the demands (and attractions) of new towns are also taken into account. But running faster to meet these needs puts extra pressure on the metropolitan regions. Both Greater London and the West Midlands have witnessed a depletion of their growth potential and have laid predictable claims for a relaxation of controls on their industrial expansion. In the case of the West Midlands this can be backed by showing that its industrial structure is not substantially stronger than that of some assisted areas and, like a house of cards, if the major underpinning (the modern engineering sector) has its expansion restrained or siphoned off, then the rest will suffer.

The second problem relates to the employment which is diverted. Here the greatest success has been in moving medium-sized firms and branch plants, together with a substantial amount of ware-housing. The majority of jobs involved are semi-skilled and a high proportion are for women. Meanwhile, other occupations – particularly the higher paid, more prestigious head-office jobs – have become increasingly concentrated in London and the South-East.[7] Whether this matters much from the viewpoint of efficient resource allocation is debatable. As part of a broader economic system (the EEC) it may be advantageous to have a greater concentration of control and policy-making functions in these areas. In any case the number of jobs involved is relatively small and a 'fair share' of them in every region would not go far to solving regional disparities. However, this is to oversimplify the argument, for the main impact of over-centralization falls not in a general manner across the whole of the assisted areas, but more specifically upon the regional capitals whose role needs to be strengthened if the development of the assisted areas is to be enhanced.

Explanations and forecasts

Many studies have been made of the geography of employment and unemployment with the aim of discovering their correlates and, ultimately, formulating models to predict future distributions. So far there has been mixed success; employment tends to be an elusive variable. At the gross regional level growth trends and disparities have been fairly well explained but sub-regional differences – particularly in rates of change in employment – have not been shown to have many (if any) strong correlates. Deterministic models which derive associations between aspects of employment and selected independent variables that are expected to have some influence on these have generally concluded that non-quantifiable and highly specific characteristics of areas and the firms in them are of fundamental importance. Put another way, this means that models based on an assumption that industries are homogeneous and behave identically regardless of location are ill-founded. Moreover, the heterogeneity existing within industries is itself weakly correlated with general geographical variables.

Some evidence of this is presented in Table 7, which is an abstract of the statistical results of a number of studies. All of them found statistically significant relationships, but it is highly questionable whether any of them provides a suitable basis for forecasting the distribution of change, let alone its magnitude or timing. The apparently better results derived from stochastic models of sub-regional change are, in truth, no more satisfactory, for they rely upon assumptions which deterministic models have shown to be unrealistic.

Partial analysis – concerned with particular aspects of employment – has generally been more successful. Industrial movement, which in aggregate terms can be attributed to quite specific variables, exhibits quite regular temporal and spatial patterns; although individual firms still present some mysteries in their locational behaviour, the predictability of aggregate distributions (given assumptions about the future state of the economy and the strength of regional policy) has come close to being established.[15]

Table 7. Summary of statistical results from a sample of studies of selected aspects of employment*

Author and year	Region	Area units	Variables	Period	Correlation (r)
Sant (1967)[8]	GB	74 'cities'	unemployment (%) v. industrial structure	1960–63	0·23 to 0·49
Smith (1968)[9]	NW Eng.	95 areas	unemployment (%) v.	1966	
			(a) change in total employment		0·24
			(b) no. of industrial employees		−0·59
Tulpule (1969)[10]	Greater London		Dispersion of industrial employment v.	1951–61	
			(a) growth of net output		0·55
			(b) investment per capita		0·34
			(c) female participation		−0·34
Hart (1970)[11]	E & W	10 regions	Gross migration v.	1960–61	
			(a) 'gravity model'		0·66
			(b) 'gravity model' plus rate of industrial building		0·75
Gordon (1970)[12]	GB	62 sub-regions	Female activity rates (age adjusted) v.	1966	
			(a) unemployment (%)		−0·62
			(b) average earnings of male manual workers		0·23
Keeble and Hauser[13] (1972)	SE Eng.	112 areas	Change in mfg employment (%) v. male unemployment (%)	1960–66	0·42
			Change in mfg employment (total) v. change in population (total)	1960–66	0·57
Gordon & Whittaker[14] (1972)	E & W	55 counties	Net male migration, aged 15–44 v.	1961–66	
			(a) average male earnings		0·40
			(b) unemployment (%)		−0·34

* All are published in *Regional Studies*.

But this ought to be the case since this is an instance where regional policy has been effective. In contrast, patterns of gross or net migration, whether by age-groups or in total, have been less well explained, as also have sub-regional rates of change in total manufacturing employment.

What are the implications of our poor ability to explain (let alone predict) the distributions of various aspects of employment? One must be to question the basis of our models with, ultimately, the possible recognition that the distribution of change may have few – if any – geographical causes. (This is not to gainsay their geographical consequences, which may be far reaching.) Multi-variate analysis improves levels of explanation, but not sufficiently to permit adequate predictions of either regional systems or, more precisely, of individual elements (places or sectors) within systems. And since the concepts of 'systems analysis' ultimately hang on the behaviour of these elements the implications for this new branch of quasi-scientific research are indeed dire.

Secondly, poor statistical association places greater emphasis on interpretation and a corresponding expansion of room for disagreement which in turn has vital implications for regional policy. A crucial example of this is in the differing importance attributed by Brown[16] and Richardson[17] to the role of industrial structure in determining the economic performance of regions. To the former, 'systematic structural effects seem to have been as important as, or more important than, systematic tendencies for particular regions to do well or badly in all industries together' (p. 146). To the latter, the argument that a region's economic performance is determined by its industrial composition is 'at best, a half-truth ... differential effects may be more important than proportional (i.e. structural) effects' (p. 400). These statements may appear at first reading to be semantically different rather than polarized, but if they are followed through to their conclusions regarding policy then they do seem to lead us in opposite directions. Following Brown the main implication might be the need to concentrate on modernizing the industrial base of the assisted areas. But taking Richardson's line this may be less important than improving urban infrastructure and enhancing the competitive position of firms in the assisted areas. Indeed, if one views these regions in their European context Richardson's case takes on added force.

Employment and regional policy

Attempts to evaluate the impact of regional policy have been made by several authors. Among them they cover a wide variety of approaches but their conclusions generally concur – at least as far as job-creation in the assisted areas is concerned. Where they tend to differ most is in the implications which they draw about the effect of regional policy on the national economy and about future needs for regional development.

Moore and Rhodes,[18] in a series of most important papers, have concluded that regional policy, unlike most other forms of public expenditure, brings about an increase (rather than just a redistribution) in the overall utilization of labour resources which is beneficial to the whole economy in terms of increased employment and output. Further, they believe that the *real* costs associated with regional policy since the early 1960s have probably been negative (i.e. that the Exchequer recouped more than it laid out in the form of grants and loans) and that regional policy may have contributed as much as £400–£500 million to GDP (Gross Domestic Product) during the period 1963–70.

To arrive at this conclusion Moore and Rhodes carried out a series of analyses of the impact of policy on employment, the chief of which was aimed at measuring the diversion of labour demand to the assisted areas. This was done by applying a 'shift and share' analysis to time series of manufacturing employment for 1950–72 in order to compare what actually occurred with what would have been expected to occur if every industry in each region grew or declined at exactly the same rate as its national counterpart. There are problems associated with this technique, not the least of which is the assumption that the gap between 'actual' and 'expected' employment is wholly attributable to regional policy, but the results generally are supported by other studies. Basically, the series for actual and expected employment in the assisted areas ran together until 1963, at which point they diverged radically, following the sharp increase in the strength of regional policy provided by the Local Employment Act of that year. By 1971 this divergence amounted to about 150,000 jobs in the manufacturing sector. Adding in the two industries excluded from the shift and share analysis because they received special government attention (shipbuilding and metal manufacture) yields a further positive divergence of about 10,000 jobs; and adding the estimates for the two smaller assisted areas (Merseyside and south-west England) gives another 33,000. Finally Moore and Rhodes assumed that the divergence in the manufacturing sector would have had induced and indirect effects on the service sector resulting in another 30,000 jobs. Thus the total divergence for 1963–70 came to about 220,000 jobs.

These figures are not divided into regional components and there was no attempt to distinguish between jobs arising from industrial movement and those attributable to the growth of firms already in the region. The latter question has been investigated by Brown[19] using the simple expedient of estimating the number of jobs created in establishments in the assisted areas for which an industrial development certificate was necessary. In the late 1950s this was about 20,000 per year; by the late 1960s the figure had risen to 70,000. The difference (50,000) was then adjusted for the upward national trend in employment of about 12,000 per year, leaving about 38,000 arising from the intensification of regional policy through the sixties. Brown further estimated that less than half of the increase was attributable to industrial movement; the remainder was expansion by firms already in the assisted areas. Using a different approach the present author[20] concluded from a time-series analysis that policy expenditure (at constant, 1963 prices) yielded between 350 and 500 jobs per £1 million of Exchequer costs, and that by the latter half of the sixties policy-induced industrial movement was accounting for 15,000–20,000 jobs per year. Thereafter the situation became more complex as a result of new types of inducement and the possibility that diminishing marginal returns were setting in, giving a new equation between Exchequer costs and the movement of industry.

Thus far the studies reviewed have been concerned with the impact of policy in terms of the creation of jobs and, briefly, in its contribution to the national economy. There are other forms of evaluation, however, which are related to the contribution of regional policy towards reducing regional disparities; this, after all, is its main objective. In addition, there are other questions which are necessarily, if conveniently, overlooked concerning the opportunity costs of regional policy both in detail and as a whole. For example, even if there is a net gain to GDP as Moore and Rhodes argue, it is important to ask at least the following questions: Would a different set of policy instruments having the same Exchequer costs yield a greater benefit to GDP? If there are diminishing returns to regional policy, what is the optimum level of expenditure? Are there different strategies which regional policy might adopt (i.e. apart from industrial movement and direct job creation) which might do more to reduce regional disparities? None of these is directly or easily answered but they – and similar questions – need to be raised frequently in order to evaluate regional policy properly.

Comparing achievements with objectives is a contentious procedure (especially when the objectives are vaguely expressed) but it is unavoidable to conclude that although the instruments of policy – controls and assistance – have been successful, the impact of policy itself has been limited. A large volume of employment was diverted to the assisted areas; and there was a reduction in the rate of net migration from the assisted areas (except Scotland) during the 1960s. But the effects on most indicators of regional disparities were equivocal. The apparent reduction in the ratio of unemployment between the assisted areas and the national average during the 1960s probably had more to do with national levels of demand than with regional policy. This is a cyclical disparity which closes when demand rises. There was also some reduction in the disparities of average earnings but continuing higher levels of demand for labour in southern Britain ensured that this reduction was small. So the position in the early 1970s was a mixed one: in effect regional policy had been a 'holding operation'. Disparities had not been allowed to increase and some major improvements (in infrastructure and industrial composition) took place in the assisted areas. But there remained a gap between achievements and 'objectives'. During the period 1960–70, Moore and Rhodes estimated an additional 800,000–1,000,000 jobs would have been needed in the assisted areas in order to equalize unemployment rates, eliminate net outward migration and equalize activity rates. This was far from being achieved, and given that there is a 'ceiling' on the potential effectiveness of policy instruments, plus the possibility that the assisted areas will have undergone a widening of disparities by the end of the present economic cycle, it is doubtful whether such ambitious objectives will ever be achieved.

Issues and dilemmas

The foregoing review of regional policy leads to pessimistic conclusions, but it may also bring us closer to reality. Industrial mobility is a scarce resource: this was at least implicitly recognized in the 1972 Industry Act which put greater emphasis on the growth of employment in industries indigenous to the assisted areas and subsequent actions (the creation of the National Enterprise Board and additional funds for the Scottish and Welsh Development Agencies) appear to confirm this view. There is a limit to the volume of industry that can be diverted during any given period, and it is likely that this limit can only be reached with rapidly increasing costs. Moreover, the limit can probably only be approached by creating problems for the major source areas, London and the West Midlands, who have become increasingly concerned about the siphoning off of much of their most buoyant sectors. Creating problems in the more prosperous regions may be one way of reducing disparities – though that is questionable – but it is not what regional policy ought to be about.

It would be wrong to read into this an argument against regional policy. The case made by Moore and Rhodes is too convincing for that. But there is an argument that regional policy in its traditional form should be limited and that new variants should be explored. Also, a primary requirement asserted by Diamond[21] is a need to distinguish more clearly between short-term and long-term aims, with the former being concerned with the *rate* of change and the latter with the *direction* and *structure* of change. Diamond argues that continued preoccupation with the short-term role might lead to the 'degeneration of a national policy for the regions into a regional "pressure-group" conflict model' (p. 218) and that in order to avoid this we must consider a longer perspective and provide guidelines for the broad structure and distribution of population and employment.

This is a far from simple task: there is no clear-cut division between long- and short-term objectives and policies. Further, attempting to define practicable guidelines for regional development and employment policy would meet massive political difficulties, not the least of which would be a direct conflict with the pragmatic view of politicians. But what Diamond's argument leads to is the need for a new government inquiry, on a par with the Barlow Commission (and therefore going far beyond the Hunt Committee), whose chief concern would be with questions about the 'quality of life' and its geographical dimensions.

Of course, such questions are being asked continuously and the answers are embodied in a variety of policies and courses of action for the arts, the environment, education, health and so on. There is also at least an implicit recognition that there is no simple equation between jobs diverted to the assisted areas, or their financial contribution to GDP, and the long-term improvement in the conditions of life of either individuals and families or cities and regions. But no attempt has been made to translate this into a long-term view of the direction and structure of regional development. Broadly, there are two possibilities. One is to leave things as they are; to continue with a regional policy geared to actual or expected unemployment disparities. This has been shown to work in the past. But because there are doubts about the continuing capacity for industrial movement, and growing doubts that this is a sufficient instrument of policy, the second possibility takes on added importance. That is, to use regional employment policy to service a wider regional development policy.

References

1. Sant, M. E. C., 'Interregional industrial movement: the case of the non-survivors', in *Environment, Man and Economic Change*, edited by A. D. M. Phillips and B. J. Turton, London, Longmans, 1975.

2. Sant, M. E. C., *The Geography of Business Cycles*, London School of Economics and Political Science, Geographical Papers, no. 5, 1973.

3. Brown, A. J., *The Framework of Regional Economics in the United Kingdom*, Cambridge University Press, 1972.

4. Willis, K. G., *Problems in Migration Analysis*, Farnborough, Saxon House, 1974.

5. Needleman, L., and Scott, B., 'Regional problems and the location of industry policy in Britain', *Urban Studies*, vol. 1, 1964, pp.153–73.

6. Howard, R. S., *Movement of Manufacturing Industry in the United Kingdom*, London, HMSO, 1968; Sant, M. E. C., *Industrial Movement and Regional Development: the British Case*, Oxford, Pergamon, 1975.

7. Westaway, J., 'Contact potential and the occupational structure of the British urban system, 1961–1966: an empirical study', *Regional Studies*, vol. 8, 1974, pp. 57–73.

8. Sant, M. E. C., 'Unemployment and industrial structure in Great Britain', *Regional Studies*, vol. 1, 1967, pp. 83–91.

9. Smith, D. M., 'Identifying the "grey" areas – a multivariate approach', *Regional Studies*, vol. 2, 1968, pp. 183–93.

10. Tulpule, A. H., 'Dispersion of industrial employment in the Greater London area', *Regional Studies*, vol. 3, 1969, pp. 25–40.

11. Hart, R. A., 'A model of inter-regional migration in England and Wales', *Regional Studies*, vol. 4, 1970, pp. 279–96.

12. Gordon, I. R., 'Activity rates: regional and sub-regional differentials', *Regional Studies*, vol. 4, 1970, pp. 411–24.

13. Keeble, D. E., and Hauser, D. P., 'Spatial analysis of manufacturing growth in outer South-East England, 1960–1967. II. Methods and results', *Regional Studies*, vol. 6, 1972, pp. 11–36.

14. Gordon, I. R. and Whittaker, R. M., 'Indicators of local prosperity in the South West region', *Regional Studies*, vol. 6, 1972, pp. 299–313.

15. Sant, M. E. C., *Industrial Movement and Regional Development: the British Case*, Oxford, Pergamon, 1975.

16. Brown, A. J., op. cit.

17. Richardson, H. W., *Regional Economics*, London, Weidenfeld & Nicolson, 1969.

18. Moore, B., and Rhodes, J., *The Economic and Exchequer Implications of Regional Policy*, Minutes of Evidence taken before the Expenditure Committee (Trade and Industry Sub-Committee), House of Commons,

42, xvi, HMSO, 1973; Moore, B., and Rhodes, J., 'The effects of regional economic policy in the United Kingdom', in *Regional Policy and Planning for Europe*, edited by M. E. C. Sant, Farnborough, Saxon House, 1974.

19. Brown, A. J., op. cit.

20. Sant, M. E. C., 1975, op. cit.

21. Diamond, D. R., 'The long term aim of regional policy' in *Regional Policy and Planning for Europe*, edited by M. E. C. Sant, Farnborough, Saxon House, 1974.

Chapter 4
Issues in Transportation

Patrick O'Sullivan

The geographical space in which we act out our lives is not measured along Euclidean lines between Cartesian references but is structured by the ways and charges for transport which we face. This elastic mesh and, thus, where we choose to do things and move, is shaped by political decisions on how and where transport is to be provided. The chief transport issues commanding political attention in the United Kingdom currently concern the extent of the railways' services, the provision of capacity for cars and lorries in towns, and concomitantly, the desirable level of public transport services and prices. These matters dominate many other half-settled or dormant questions on the means of movement. This essay examines the more prominent questions against the background of a wide variety of political and economic considerations.

Transport policy

The goal of transport policy is to ensure the maintenance and development of adequate means of carrying on social intercourse and commerce within and without the nation, counting the cost of doing so in terms of political discontent, possible damage to the well-being of other than the immediate users, as well as of the resources of the land, labour, machines, structures and materials used. The nation's coherence and health depend on the density and continuity of social interaction and trade within its bounds, the ease of access to markets, and the protection of its interests beyond its shores. If we accept this proposition as axiomatic, then it follows that, in order to sustain and deepen national cohesion, it is necessary to provide and keep open channels for contact and exchange between the nation's constituents and between Britain and the rest of the world. Thus, transport facilities and services have seldom been provided without the involvement of the government, and every transport investment and pricing decision becomes a potential bone of political contention. The policy-maker has to decide whether resources should be allocated to particular forms and means of transport on the basis of market requirements or some alternative administrative rationale, made instrumental as a set of predetermined allocative rules, or by the exercise of political judgement. In many instances, the economy's 'invisible hand' or cold, administrative calculation may fail to comprehend the complex, underlying, intangible considerations involved. Only the proximate calculus and will of statesmanship, yielding an arbitrary, albeit well-reasoned political solution, will suffice. The political solution may be a once-off direct investment decision, or the designation of a standard, a regulation, or a prohibition. This is an over-simplification of the choices con-fronting policy-makers, but it may aid our understanding if we examine the major issues in transport in terms of whether the market, administration, or politics is the predominant process invoked in their resolution.

Failure of the market

From an economic viewpoint many transport services display characteristics which deny the efficacy of a market solution in determining the level of their supply.

The long gestation and sheer magnitude of investment in the links and terminals of transport systems have often resulted in direct or indirect government involvement in their inception, since they were beyond the scope of unaided private enterprise.

There is an ingrained popular view of roads as a 'public good' which should be provided and paid for collectively, and there is much sense to this attitude. The objective of pricing the use of roads would be to equate the worth people gain from their use more closely with the costs involved in this use, so as to achieve the best overall allocation of resources. In the case of the road system one of the main costs involved is that arising from congestion, which varies according to time and place. Thus prices would have to vary by hour of the day and location in order to be effective. The administrative and policing costs of collecting charges which reflect where and when people were using roads, and of keeping off the roads those not willing to pay would almost certainly exceed the worth of the gain to communal well-being arising from the equality of use and costs which pricing is meant to achieve.

It is asserted that some forms of transport, because of their enormous initial capital costs and relatively small unit costs of running, enjoy a continually decreasing unit cost as their output expands, and thus constitute natural monopolies. These require strict government control of prices or output to ensure that this power is not abused at the expense of national efficiency. This was the basis for the regulation of railways, which inhibited their flexibility and enterprise well into an era in which they faced stringent competition from lorries and cars. A peculiar convolution of the monopoly control argument, which is powerfully wielded in this country, holds that competition can be wasteful inasmuch as it inhibits the achievement of inherent monopoly advantages, identified as 'coordination' and 'integration'. Additionally, competition is held to be an unstable, and therefore undesirable state of affairs. The prescription arising from these points is that public monopolies should be created by nationalization, or local authority ownership, for the controlled enjoyment of stability of supply, and lower costs with increasing returns to scale. This remedy was applied to public transport in London, and now elsewhere, with little evidence of success to date and little hope for the future. Some socialists would extend the remedy to the whole transport sector.

A further reason for dissatisfaction with the ability of an unbridled market solution to determine the right quantity of transport is the widespread external effects which transport generates – penetrating the dwelling and working space of those not travelling with noise and nuisance, which users are not obliged to compensate for in the price they pay.

Transport needs, politics and planning

The most severe and public transport battles are waged over specific stretches of steel and concrete, which is only right for those directly involved, and usually makes for good news copy. However, this concern with particulars can hinder the practice of good political economy. When the fight is in terms of where to put a third London airport or whether or not to build a Channel tunnel, a Picc-Vic or a ringway, particular solutions to a more fundamental problem often get posed as the problem itself. These might well hide from view possible superior courses of action which are available. The more basic questions in the cases cited are how international air or cross-Channel demands are likely to change and be catered for, and how best to accommodate an evolving pattern of demand for access to work, shops, schools, recreation and social contracts. The most satisfactory answer to the latter problem might be to foster certain locational patterns of activity, or the improvement of telecommunications, in order to reduce the need for physical movement in the longer run. The general objective must be to achieve a socially desirable balance between requirements and provision for the movement of people and goods, given limited resources which could otherwise be used to build houses, make manufacturing machinery or increase the income of pensioners.

People travel and transport their goods from place to place because they judge an excess of benefit to themselves will arise over the cost in money, effort and irritation involved in the act of movement. The benefits arise from the sale of their labour, the production and vending of goods, the consumption of goods and amenities or the enjoyment of meeting or entertainment. The accessibility of a place to various activities via the transport system is mirrored in the rent paid for occupying that location. The inherent disutility of distance in achieving the fruits of production and consumption finds expression in the combination of rent and transport costs involved in overcoming it. In making a choice of where to dwell, work, shop, produce, buy and sell, and what means of transport and route to associate with these activities, individuals may be misinformed about the real resource costs to society involved, or about effects not reflected in the price they pay. Equally the providers of transport may not be informed of such external effects, costly or beneficial, by estimates of the revenue they can achieve. These failures of the market to equate costs and utility occasion public intervention in the allocation of resources. Whether the debate is over the ability of the market to do the job, or over particular or general government decisions, the central issue is the same: what is the best means of achieving the greatest satisfaction of the demand for mobility with the least cost to society? To attack the problem certain technical and analytic skills must be applied to the measurement of both accounted and external costs and benefits and to gauging the size and responsiveness of demand to the price and supply configurations. Economic and design expertise is required for the elaboration of different feasible ways of solving the problem. The selection of appropriate criteria for judging the best solution and the assignment of weights to these by 'experts', however, constitute an imprudent arrogation of political authority. On the other hand, it is perhaps even more reprehensible if political decisions are made, contrary to expert advice, for personal or partisan gain, as opposed to that of the common weal. Ideally, technical and theoretical experts should advise the political decision-makers with suggestions on the alternatives available, the trade-offs involved and measurements of effects. Good decisions are more likely to arise out of a mutually respectful interplay of expertise and political judgement. However, there seems to be an insurmountable barrier to simplicity in this process of problem solving, for both the politician and the analyst, in that the definition of the problem is subject to unforeseeable changes in taste, technology and exogenous circumstances. In the past decade this has been particularly the case in respect of public sensibility to the external costs of transport – noise, smell and disruption of local accessibility. What was previously a minor consideration in decisions over transport investment became a major issue, but waned again as the partly contrary objective of energy-saving loomed larger.

The current pervasive aura of uncertainty has engendered an increase in humility and a shortening in time horizons in the transport planning process, replacing the unbridled confidence and heroic predictions of the last two decades. We are starting to look at what we have and how we might improve it next year, rather than seeking our heart's desire twenty years hence.

Geographical scale

In the sections that follow, more attention is given to the geographical dimension and ramifications of some current issues of transport policy. As in other essays in this book, it seems appropriate to structure the discourse in terms of geographic scale. In proceeding from global considerations to more local issues, however, it is difficult to remain completely objective because of the greater sense of involvement we all share in the things immediately around us.

First, some of the issues over international transport facilities are examined. These mostly concern the location of terminals, airports and docks, but also touch on new links such as the Channel Tunnel. The next band of the transport spectrum relates to longer-distance internal trade and travel, the connections from hinterlands to regional centres and between these – the flows up and down the central place hierachy. The final range of concern on transport matters is that which encompasses the scope of our daily round – the provision for movement to work, shop, school and friends, and to collect and deliver goods. The questions that emerge differ in intensity and accent between rural and urban but not in their fundamental nature, being concerned with catering for private as opposed to public transport. In country areas, apart from those attracting large numbers of weekend and seasonal visitors, there is little call for the expansion of road capacity or parking space and the issue is largely one of how best to provide public transport for those without cars. The urban transport problem concerns the best combination of facilities for car users and public transport, the resolution of which extends itself into questions of urban locational structure.

International transport

The international transport issues which impinge most directly on the majority of our lives concern the location of terminals, docks, airports and access to these. There is an intrusion on some people immediately in terms of the noise and nuisance of planes, trains, road traffic and, indeed, ships. In the longer run they influence the comparative advantage of different parts of the country as sites for industry and thus the availability of jobs and demand for housing and services. The two most public recent conflicts, over whether or where to build a third airport for London and whether to guarantee returns to the Channel Tunnel venture, have been settled by postponement. The political realities, immediate economic circumstances and uncertainty as to the outcome of these investments, suggested that now is not the time to embark on them.

The airport case is instructive inasmuch as the Royal Commission[1] which examined the prospects chose to interpret their charge narrowly and ignored the option of not building a new airport at a specified date in the future – which proved to be the actual outcome. The Minister who briefed the Commission, Mr Crosland, stated that the wider interpretation was open to them. The result of the exercise was a cost–benefit analysis which led the majority of the Commission to favour the building of an airport at Cublington, between London and the Midlands market. This was based on what appears now to be an over-enthusiastic extrapolation of the growth of demand for air travel. This was countered by Sir Colin Buchanan's minority view that the Thames estuarial site at Maplin was preferable as a result of an environmental intestinal sensitivity test, i.e. gut feeling. This selection was endorsed heartily by civil engineering interests with visions of the mountains of muck-shifting involved in a port/airport development. The Prime Minister at the time of the report (Mr Heath) espoused Buchanan's cause, but pressures from Department of the

Environment civil servants forced a review of the Maplin alternative. Growing evidence of a levelling off of air traffic and a change of government resulted in the deferment of the decision.

The analysis of prospects for the Channel Tunnel teetered on the margin of viability, but the deciding factor against pursuing the project seems to have been a Cabinet judgement that the project lacked political appeal and was not a suitable target for commitment when government expenditures had to be seen to be pruned. This choice does have an advantage in that it maintains flexibility of response in a situation fraught with uncertainty in terms of demand, direct and indirect outcomes and technological development of alternative solutions. When you are unsure it is not invariably best to advance. It might well be that the more widespread development of low fixed capital cross-Channel transport by roll-on roll-off vessels, Hovercraft, etc., will reduce the need for concentration of overland traffic, provide a more geographically equitable improvement in accessibility to the Continent and avoid a 'bridgehead' agglomeration of activities in the South-East. The French tunnel terminus would attract activity to an area which has experienced industrial decline and an excess of labour supply. The same political advantage does not accrue to England.

A similar argument in favour of flexibility can be extended to the question of the most suitable dock capacity arrangement for the country. Given that the advantage of containerization lies in rapid turn-around, that containers can be handled without elaborate machinery and that there is an abundance of natural harbours around this island, then there seems no obvious case for excessive concentration of port activity. The development of pontoon docks for roll-on roll-off loading at any state of the tide and barge-shedding catamarans and decked ships implies a minimum of waterfront capital investment and thus wide discretion on points of egress and an ease of responding to changes in demand. By spreading competition for traffic over a wide area there might be significant improvement in efficiency that carried only a small risk of creating utterly immobile excess dock capacity. The fact that concentration of dock activity increases the demands placed on the internal transport system, whereas more widespread access to the sea reduces overland ton mileage, must also be counted in its favour. Such a solution would not, however, gratify the dock union's desire for more wage-bargaining leverage, and is completely against the grain of the Labour Party's intentions to favour the growth of a state monopoly and concentration, as expressed in their transport manifesto.[2]

Internal long-distance transport

The long-standing points of conflict over longer-distance internal trade and travel involve a saga of political intervention in terms of road versus rail competition and of attempts to specify the viable extent of rail and road networks and services.

Direct intervention in the structure of the road haulage sector has been reduced sharply because the Conservative government neglected to execute the quantity licensing provisions of the Labour Transport Act of 1968. Although there is continued pressure from the left for nationalization of road haulage, many would regard the competitive outcome which has emerged as a happy chance, since no obvious scale economies can be detected in road freighting and since other proclaimed advantages of direct control are essentially police and safety matters not requiring ownership.

The most important and unresolved issue concerns the continuing commercial failure of the railways, which can be attributed partly to the collective pressure of BR management, rail unions, and conservationists of various types against any moves to contract the rail system. The prospect of a £1 billion deficit, with a subsidy already equalling revenue and exceeding by a factor of three the outlay of the average family on rail transport, must soon bring home the truth. We will discuss the specific case of commuter passenger services when we deal later with local transport issues; but it is necessary to note here that the implications of the subsidies involved, in terms of the redistribution of income, are disturbing.

In the case of inter-city passenger services, it seems reasonable to postulate that they could be made to break even by a combination of price rises and cost cuts, even if at the expense of thinning out the frequency of services. Covering the current deficit of these services out of the Exchequer is almost certainly shifting resources towards accommodating the better off and those on company expense accounts, away from those who cannot afford to travel regularly by rail. There seems no obvious reason why bigger, less frequent trains with the same reliability should not maintain custom, with improved load factors, given that rail travel is not an impulse purchase but to some degree planned. The result of price increases might lead to a closer scrutiny of the value of the journey as well as of the alternative means of transport available. The effect would not only be some switch to cars and coaches, minute in terms of road capacity, but also a reduction in the number of trips made – which in itself might be no bad thing.

In rural areas it seems so clear as to brook no argument that a generous level of road service to those captive to public transport, in terms of defraying either taxi or bus expenses, could be provided at a cost much less than that of rail services. Yet while we all foot the bill, the rail idolators continue to indulge their necrophilism behind a cloud of charitable intent.

It has never been the policy of governments of either hue to subsidize rail freight operations explicitly, and it has been generally accepted that they should be provided on a commercially viable basis. BR and the railwaymen's unions show signs of discontent with this situation. In BR's 'Reports and Accounts' for 1973, reference was made to a review of 'the future of the freight business in the constrained terms of its *present* wholly commercial remit' (my italics). If this is the case, then the arguments for subsidy require close scrutiny.

The general case for subsidizing provision of a good is that its production is subject to decreasing costs. Economic theory tells us that in order to ensure the efficient allocation of resources between various uses, the cost and revenue from the last unit of output sold should be equal, i.e. that prices should equal marginal costs. If costs are a decreasing function of output, to charge a price that satisfies this requirement would produce insufficient revenue to cover total costs. Total cost is given by average cost of production times the number of units of output. It is obvious that if costs are decreasing as output expands, then the cost of the last unit produced is always less than the average cost of all the previous units produced. It has been argued that a subsidy is necessary in such circumstances to cover the gap between efficient prices, registering the utility of the good for the rest of the economy to note, and the costs of the producer. Some hold that the railways enjoy decreasing costs and are thus subject to this condition, warranting subsidy. There is also an 'environmental' case which boils down to the argument that the balance of negative externalities, such as noise, smell, congestion and accidents, is in favour of rail rather than the road movement of freight, and thus that these could be reduced by encouraging a transfer to rail with a subsidy. Finally, pro-rail interests hold that road freight transport is not required to cover fully the resource costs involved in the provision of its tracks, thus putting it at a competitive advantage over rail, which carries this burden in full. This imbalance would be corrected by awarding rail operations a compensating subsidy.

Taking the decreasing cost of production argument first, it is not clear – the costing of rail transport being extremely complex – that the relationship between output and cost is essentially negative. Evidence from the USA,[3] examining cost and output relationships for railways of various sizes, and for the same railways as output changes through time, suggests that, over the relevant range of output, railway costs for mature systems increase proportionally with increases in traffic. The large, dense north-eastern railways, which are closest in character to BR, exhibited no substantial economies of scale. Joy,[4] in analysing the ailments of BR, insists that railways are not subject to decreasing costs, especially when one examines the way in which costs vary with decreasing output (not necessarily coincident with the way they change as output expands). He holds that a 10 per cent decrease in output could be made to result in an $8\frac{1}{2}$ per cent decrease in costs, if track and signalling costs are reduced appropriately. His contention that it is possible to tailor capacity of a rail route to expected volume and mix of traffic, at least in the long term, and thus that much surplus capacity is avoidable, dents the validity of the decreasing-cost subsidy argument.

The traditional way of covering the gap between the sum of average costs and total revenue has been to discriminate in prices between customers according to how badly they need to use that particular service – i.e. to elasticity of demand – and respectable apologists can be found for this procedure. There is evidence that BR's deficit has arisen in part from unwillingness to do this, even when given commercial freedom. In 1963 the Prices and Income Board revealed widespread underpricing of rail freight traffic. When china clay and gas works coal rates were raised subsequent to this report, there was no loss of traffic to road or water carriers. It is true that BR's present deep difficulty is more a matter of government-imposed restraints on price rises as part of a wider counter-inflationary programme, than of BR's unwillingness to raise prices; nevertheless the suspicion that railway management and workers are more concerned with running a lot of trains on a lot of track rather than running a business is not unfounded.

One major characteristic of freight transport which militates against a subsidy proposal for rail is the evident unresponsiveness of demand to the stimulus of a change in rail prices, or prices in competitive modes of transport. Total demand for freight movement and demand for a particular form of transport is more strongly determined by structural and qualitative considerations than by price. There is no single ideal form of freight shipment, and a variety of facilities have to be used to meet different time, place and quality-specific requirements for movement. The process of adjustment to changes in the price of transport relative to other inputs for total transport demand is a locational one, with an accordingly long time-period for its completion. This is also true for some switches between means of transport. If you want to receive deliveries of gravel by sea rather than rail, coastal rather than inland sources will have to be exploited. Some changes of transport mode require capital investment in loading and unloading facilities and batch-size-related equipment on the part of the customer, which is another inhibition to price responsiveness. Given such inelastic demand, a subsidy to rail freight services will do little to improve the performance of the economy as a whole, and will merely transfer funds from taxpayers to existing rail freight users.

Evidence suggests that the area of active competition between road and rail in Britain is not great. Rail nearly monopolizes iron and limestone traffic, while road carriers have the preponderance of manufactures, food, chemicals and building materials traffic. Coal and coke, scrap steel, oil and aggregates traffic are competed for. Rail merry-go-round coal movements from pit to power station with Coal Board loading facilities are unlikely to switch. This accounts for half the rail coal traffic. Another quarter consists of train load movements similarly insensitive to price changes. The remaining wagon-load traffic might respond to relative changes in road and rail prices. Oil is carried on rail under long-term, inflation-indexed contract prices, and shifts seem unlikely. The traffic most sensitive to rate differences is aggregates, and here BR is trying to capture a larger share of the market at the cost of offering fixed contracts whereby changes can only be increased in line with an inflation index. What few facts are known suggest that in the short term, even where there is active competition, demand for rail freight services is not strongly perturbed by a change in rail freight rates or road rates, i.e., that the ability to take advantage of more favourable prices elsewhere is small.

On both the question of externalities and compensating track cost adjustments, the insensitivity of demand to price would result in little transfer between modes of transport and thus little reduction in the social costs cited. Direct charges to road haulage to compensate for the damage caused would be more efficacious than rail subsidies in achieving a welfare improvement. Nevertheless, the 1968 White Paper on Road Track Costs[5] suggested that the imposition of such a charge would result in a negligible transfer of traffic to rail.

On the externalities question it has been calculated that if half of BR's freight were diverted to road carriage, road traffic would be increased by only 2 per cent, and external costs increased accordingly. The rail network does not have the capacity to significantly reduce the volume of road traffic. The railways carry only 9 per cent of total tonnage and 18 per cent of total ton mileage in the country, and most of the important lines are being used close to capacity already. Moreover, the environmentally deleterious impact of road vehicles is most felt in built-up areas and given that many rail services, and certainly any expansion of traffic, require local road delivery, then transfer to rail would tend to redistribute the nuisance of moving goods from the periphery to the centre, and thus concentrate it.

Proposed solutions to the railways problem coming from outside the industry itself usually involve cutting back the network and services and recommend some form of decentralization into independent profit centres – be they regions or services – along with a separation of track responsibility. Some factions in railway management persist in believing in an investment solution which will make the leap to a golden age of increasing returns to scale. The unions' chief objective is the short-term protection of jobs and enhancement of wage bargaining power, and they are therefore hardly likely to concur readily with any solution that attempts to cure the railways' financial difficulties by clearly cutting it off from Exchequer largesse. If the management is not constrained by commercial viability, subject to specific public payment for socially desirable subsidized services, with penalties for failure to achieve it, then preservation of the status quo or the amassing of plant become the dominant motive. The nonsense of trying to invest your way out of a situation of market stagnation or decline in the face of fierce competition ensues. Like the civil engineer's professional inclination to get a lot of concrete poured, management's inclination to play railways is uncurbed – the attitudes and aptitudes necessary for engineering the graceful contraction of an industry are not very highly developed as yet. Union officials desire to maintain or expand their membership. Nostalgia and innate conservatism bolster the preservationist voice in favour of maintaining the national heritage as arbitrarily represented by the present extent of the rail system. (I must admit an antipathy to the romance of rail. My memories of trains are of dirty, smelly, uncomfortable, erratic things you got on at Paddington and joyfully left at Fishguard some uncertain length of time later. This persuades me that many enthusiasts' love must have blossomed in unrequited longing.)

The construction of a high standard inter-city road network

drawing the nation closer together for car and lorry traffic is an obvious target for austerity cuts in public expenditure. It is also inhibited by local controversy over proposed bits of its extent and their impact on the community, and its peace and serenity. Proposals to reduce the unpleasant impact of lorry traffic on homes and living spaces by designating a limited network to which lorries are confined may well prove prohibitively costly in terms of the nation's freight or police bill, and the building or improvement of a limited number of routes bypassing crucial points of conflict may achieve a satisfactory separation of the interests involved.

There are clearly visible signs of a past geographical misallocation of road investment funds. Some areas where the local political organization has national influence, notably the north-east, have been compensated by both Labour and Conservative governments for industrial stagnation and unemployment by road-building far in excess of any foreseeable demand. It can only be hoped that the impotence of this remedy has been recognized. Quite apart from considerations of geographical equity, it is almost impossible to assess whether the total investment on roads is adequate in terms of the improved efficiency of the entire road system which it brings about. No sound measurements exist to judge the matter on. In practice the question is tackled at the margin of growth of the network, by requiring that each additional piece of road, or improvement to an existing road, achieve a satisfactory rate of return of benefits generated over cost of construction. The benefits are measured in social terms of the time and accident saving projected to result from the scheme. There has been controversy over the way in which time and accidents are valued, but this is essentially settled by ministerial pronouncement. The lower limit of 'satisfactory' for the rate of return is given by the Treasury test discount rate, which all public sector investments are expected to exceed – currently 10 per cent.

Transport for the daily round

Policies governing the transport of people about their everyday business cannot be formulated without regard to the whereabouts and arrangement of the buildings and spaces they occupy for their various employment. The problem of planning our habitat is how best to adapt to continuously changing social and economic requirements, to delete and augment an arrangement of structures, spaces and transport routes resulting from a long and complex technical, market and political evolution.

It is plain that man, his tools, social arrangements and aspirations are inextricably tied up in one another. Faced with a new element to adapt the fabric to, such as the car, it is no good pouring scorn on the ravages caused by the machine without reference to the motives of the man. Not only does the personal ordering of life and *mores* increasingly reflect the mobility which the car bestows, but the extension of car use reflects a desire to be rid of the limitations of the past. For a majority of people the local identity, solidarity and collectivism of the past was enforced by constraints on the ability to travel. Necessity is not totally virtuous. There is an aspiration to a greater degree of individual self-determination. The car has done much to fulfil this desire and change our behaviour and views of one another. The process of change is most advanced in the USA, where the largest number of adults have at their behest the means of getting up and going where and when they will. In terms of perception of the world this has unbound the limited personal geography of most people, formerly restricted to the way between home and work and shops and a walking radius thereabouts, or a few well-known spots connected by corridors of rail, and has thrown open a vision more closely approaching the continuity of the real surface of the globe. The growth of car ownership helps to blur the distinction between cavalier and villager. The advent of two-car households erodes the mobility-dependence of women. In Britain, certain sections of the vocal middle and upper classes seem to begrudge an extension to others of this new form of independence, possibly because it curtails their own formerly unfettered enjoyment of superior mobility. Though prophets may rail at the evils of this creature and the results of its use, there is little prospect of a reversal of what appears to be a universal desire for the freedom which car ownership confers.

Road investment

In the early 1960s the realization of this trend, and the demand for road space it implied, led to Sir Colin Buchanan's analysis[6] of the situation, and prescription in favour of a massive road building programme to accommodate growing demand for car travel to existing town structures. This solution has been discarded of late in a confusion of purposes and emotions. When the flaw in it has been objectively articulated it will be possible to correct the course of events to allow for the error. In the meantime, there has been a tendency towards over-reaction against road building.

As a result of the inertia inherent in the arrangement of homes, shops, jobs, etc., in the major cities in this country – where there is a strong centripetal tendency and a monocentric radial structure which has for the most part evolved in accord with the economics and use of public transport facilities – road building proposals which seek to complement this structure are frequently in competition with high density uses of land. High land costs, constituting one-third of construction costs for primary network schemes, seem to have been the principal cause of the low yields, calculated in terms of gains and losses to society as well as to users, which have been calculated for such investments in inner-urban areas – quite apart from the political dissension they arouse. This does not exclude the possibility that in less concentrated and smaller towns, and in the conurbation periphery with scattered focuses of travel-demand, no practical form of public transport could compare with car travel on even the most stringent social and environmental evaluation. The need in these circumstances is not for channelling flows into a limited access high-performance road network super-imposed on the urban landscape, but for the easier movement of a more diffuse pattern of flows with a multiplicity of local concentrations – essentially for a higher quality 'main road' network. This is for the most part in place already and primarily requires modest improvement of its junctions and the removal of parked vehicles, so as to raise the standard. This may be achieved with small expenditures on signalling, the addition of queuing lanes, clearway designations and the provision of safe crossing points and other protective measures for pedestrians. The only form of public transport likely to attain solvency in such circumstances must use the road network in the form of bus and taxi services. The density of development required to sustain fixed-track mass transport facilities is seldom found, and unlikely to be fostered by land-use planning of anything but the most paternalistic and Draconian nature. Possibly the most constructive way in which the government can intervene is to relax the institutional constraints on entry and pricing which the Traffic Commissioners impose on competition in the bus industry, while maintaining control with respect to safety and financial and technical eligibility to run a service, and to make provisions for a safe and sound extension of taxi services.

Public transport

Considering movements to and within the denser core of cities, only London seems capable of supporting viable rail commuter services. Of employees in inner London, a quarter travel by rail and less than 18 per cent by car. It is more than possible that the current losses of rail passenger and Underground services in London could be met by fare rises. The nature of demand for these services is such that a price rise is not likely to reduce custom to the extent that revenue can never meet outgoings. Long-distance rail commuters are to a large extent middle-class people, owner-occupiers, engaged in management, administrative and clerical occupations, enjoying above-average incomes and more secure employment, who are not going to change home or work places readily. Thirty-eight per cent of professional workers, 25 per cent of employers and managers and 33 per cent of non-manual workers travel to work by rail in London, as opposed to 18 per cent of the skilled manual workers, 14 per cent of the semi-skilled

123

and 14 per cent of the unskilled. Given little or no spare road or parking capacity in the centre, the main impact of fare increases more in line with cost of services would be a small reduction in the amount of rail commuting, a reduction in demand and prices for suburban housing and a general rise in the price of dwellings closer in. In geographical terms the whole effect might be to reverse the present trend towards a 'hollow-centre' distribution of homes and to slow down the rate of growth along the rail radii. The competition for building land and collective increases in journey-to-work costs might lead to a greater dispersal of certain more routine office, manufacturing and service activities to several outlying nodes. The present practice of subsidizing the losses of rail commuter services seems suspiciously like a regressive redistribution of the national output. In effect the particular life-styles of suburban people, who are often in marginal constituencies, are being supported by taxes drawn from the population as a whole.

Traffic congestion

Despite the small amount of road building in major city central areas in recent years, the chaos and seizure through congestion that was feared has not come to pass. Even without traffic management and restraints on the amount of car parking available to end journeys in the centre, an acceptable equilibrium between capacity and use has arisen. This is the queuing solution to the allocation of a fixed supply. Physical management measures which can improve speeds without an offsetting increase in journey distance, or extra difficulties imposed on pedestrians by the severance of their usual paths, are obviously desirable. It seems that delays caused by bottlenecks in the road network are limited in time and spatial extent, and capacities are greater than had been thought. The cost of doing little or nothing where road space is in fixed supply, and not worthwhile expanding in economic and political terms, is not heart-failure for the city. It is the gap between the cost of some socially optimal level of use, where the utility derived by the last user equates the objective costs borne by himself and others as a result of his joining the existing traffic, and the cost of the current queuing solution. The theoretically desirable situation would be achieved by a set of prices specific to time and place for the use of the network. Although the technology is available to achieve this,[7] the cost and possible bitterness engendered by administering it would probably, as we have noted previously, be in excess of the improvement produced. It has aiso been proposed that supplementary licences should be sold, without which one could not use the central area roads, but this would be expensive to operate and police, except when the central area had a limited number of entry points. Singapore, having such a configuration, has in fact instituted such a scheme. This appears to empty the streets of the city during the hours of its imposition in the morning. The evening peak is unaffected and the morning peak occurs just before the time when licences are required. This obviously costs commuters who cannot change their hours of work a lot of waiting time. The peripheral car parks provided for commuters to switch to buses at the licence cordon remain empty. There has been insufficient time to account the advantages and disadvantages of the scheme fully but the World Bank is monitoring this experiment closely. In this country Nottingham instituted a 'ring and collar' scheme, with red traffic lights delaying incoming motorists at peak times as the deterrent, peripheral parking and shuttle buses to the centre. As Nottingham does not have prolonged and serious congestion one would expect only limited benefits, and most of the restrictive aspects of the scheme have now, in fact, been abandoned. Many provincial centres will only have dire traffic problems if their own excessive estimates of future central area employment are realized. If the forecasts of central area office employment of all local authorities in the country are added up, the total is many times the most ambitious projection for the country as a whole. Many urban governments evince an inordinate eagerness to suffer the sorrows that go with their peculiar vision of greatness – a core full of clerks in office blocks.

It is unlikely that a subsidy to public transport would produce any significant effect on road traffic; the major determinant of car use is car availability. Availability itself is determined much more by increases in people's incomes than it is by changes in the cost differentials between modes of transport. The advantages of the car for more diffuse circumstances seems so far in excess of anything that public transport can offer that even free public transport will not cause a return to the bus. Price reductions and service improvements mostly attract people who would otherwise have stayed put or walked. The most important factor in a motorist's perception of the relative advantages of the car over other means of travel is the availability and price of parking. Parking charges which reflected the cost of the land used, in terms of what someone else would be willing to pay to obtain it for shop office or residential use, would in most central areas bring about a level of demand and network performance not far removed from the socially desired optimum.

Policies of inaction, apart from some minor adjustments to the present system, are sadly denigrated. Such policies are frequently the result of political paralysis, yet they can be an explicit, reasoned response to a given situation. It usually takes considerable political courage to offer a more humble approach, especially when the problems are perceived to constitute a crisis. By not engaging in dramatic changes, however, one can maintain the ability to adapt flexibly to new circumstances, and there is less need to make pretentious forecasts about the future state of things. If we sensibly hesitate to hazard a projection of total national population and GNP twenty years hence, never mind levels of various activities and the distribution of population, it would appear foolish to go into the details of how an unknown total is housed and transported. And yet concrete plans for the radical restructuring of cities are based on such projections. Cautious incrementalism has much to recommend it as a strategy for urban transport planning.

Many observers would hold that London has achieved a congestion equilibrium at a tolerable speed level and certainly without utter chaos. It is debatable whether this situation results from the degree of parking restraint and management exercised or whether it would have arisen in any case. In judging the efficiency of the present situation against the possible results of more stringent restraint, such as road pricing or supplementary licensing, the implications that arise for different sections of the community must be taken into account. It can be argued that rationing of a fixed supply by a queue results in a progressive redistribution of welfare, whereas price rationing is regressive – the lower-income groups valuing time less highly in terms of money than the rich. In addition, the imposition of penalties in time rather than money terms may be more effective in reducing the peak of congestion by spreading out the time at which people travel, since it will most strongly affect those who value their time highly. People with lower incomes, who value their time less highly, are mostly governed by fixed work hours, whereas higher income, managerial and supervisory jobs often allow a greater degree of discretion about when the work day starts and finishes.

The planning and finance of local transport

Along with the reorganization of the Local Government Act of 1972 there was to be a new dispensation for the planning and finance of local transport facilities. This came into effect in 1975/6. Former specific grants for roads, public transport infrastructure, rural bus services, rail service subsidies and for the purchase of new buses, were replaced by a unified grant from central government. This encompasses current as well as capital expenditure, public transport as well as roads. Some part of this payment is absorbed in the needs element of the rate support grant. Any transport expenditure above a threshold level, defined by a general formula in terms of population and type of area, is met by a supplementary grant. In the early years of operation this will cover 70–75 per cent of the expenditures by local authorities, but will be reduced to 50 per cent by 1980. To obtain the supplementary grant together with sanction for any loans they wish to float, county councils must submit Transport Policies and Programme (TPP) statements to the Department of the Environment every year. This annual package, including road, public transport infrastructure, vehicle purchase and operating subsidy outlays, along with traffic and parking management schemes, is framed in a five-year expenditure rolling programme for the county. This in turn must be geared to a local transport policy strategy with a ten to fifteen year horizon. The whole should, of course, bear some resemblance to the intentions stated in the county's land-use structure plan. This constitution certainly conveys the notion of the opportunity cost of various transport expenditures to county councils in a most telling fashion. The long-run benefits of investment must be weighed against the immediate relief of subsidies. Traffic restraint and management become clear alternatives to pouring concrete. Inasmuch as the procedure decentralizes local transport policy, it allows for a better adjustment to unique local needs and circumstances. Policy formulated at the national level can trample roughshod over these. After the first couple of rounds of this procedure, however, central administrators still appear uncertain as to how much detailed control can safely be relinquished to local sovereignty.[8]

All in all this set of more immediate and down-to-earth in-struments of government appears as a healthy antidote to the thinking which the transportation/land-use planning scheme, with its grand strategy for twenty years ahead, engendered. They encourage the good husbandry of what we have rather than neglectful dreaming of great days to come.

Conclusion

In conclusion, it may be objected that I have addressed the issues in terms of demands and not needs, and thus ignored specific questions of equity between parents and children, men and women, workers and pensioners, the healthy and the disabled, as far as ability to travel is concerned. The provision of transport facilities is not a keen enough weapon to bring about any prescribed change in family arrangements, even if one accepts the inequity in what exists. But in any case, the chief disadvantage from which people suffer is a lack of wealth. It would be more efficacious and more in accord with the dignity of those currently deprived to tackle that directly and leave it to them to choose whether and how they travel.

A further objection which might be levelled at this essay is that it pays insufficient attention to the depredations that certain forms of transport wreak on the environment. 'The environment' can be defined as the world as it exists in isolation from man, and therefore, all of man's activities and artifacts may be seen as undesirable blemishes on the face of nature. On the other hand, the definition of the environment might include man, and thus all of his acts and creations are in some way 'natural' and cannot be decried on these grounds. Obviously the word is not really very useful, and we risk getting into a philosophical tangle when we talk of causing 'harm to the environment'. In evaluating the relative merits of various transport proposals we are concerned with the direct and indirect specific impacts on the well-being of the various members of society, including those who will use the facility and those who will not. In response to an increase in popular sensitivity to noise, smell, dirt and danger, every effort is being made to incorporate the external effects on non-users in cost–benefit analyses of transport projects. The physical measurement of noise, air pollutants and visual intrusion, and the prediction of levels of these associated with various traffic volumes on roads of different configurations, say, is fairly well developed. Thus it is possible to judge between different transport proposals to meet the same need for movement, for example, a sunken or elevated profile for a particular piece of road. The alternatives can be compared in terms of the numbers of people affected by undesirable levels of the various intrusive effects, for example within a certain noise contour line about the road. Any difference in costs between options examined can be judged against the external effects one at a time. A value judgement can be made of the relative importance of the various effects and their values can be turned into standardized scores, weighted and summed to produce a composite environmental score for each option. But only a politician has the credentials to do this and impose on society decisions made on that basis. Even this exercise falls short when the decision concerns different projects in different places. In such cases values in common units, i.e., in terms of money, have to be applied to the measures of intrusion, the benefits to users and the cost involved, if a comparable trade-off or rate of return is to be estimated. This implies putting a money value on external impacts. This is the stumbling block. One possible recourse is to look at the preference which people reveal in the market, e.g. the difference in house prices which can be attributed solely to the degree of shelter from noise. It is very difficult to separate one attribute like this in the housing market, especially when by definition it relates inversely to access to main roads. Observations of house price differences often suggest private reactions to noise quite at odds with the current conventional wisdom on the value of quiet. Results gleaned by asking people how important peace and quiet is to them are of little use either. Those in quiet locales proclaim it very valuable and those near major roads register indifference. The gap between perception and substance presents additional confusion. The main pollutant from motor vehicles is carbon monoxide, which has a deleterious effect on health and is imperceptible, while the diesel fumes and smoke from lorries are relatively innocuous, but are the occasion of much public outcry. It seems that the difficulty of arriving at sensible and generally acceptable costs for peace, quiet and clean air means that they cannot realistically be included in cost–benefit calculations. The evaluation of the undesirable external effects of transport operations must remain a matter of political judgement and in some cases the question has been or will be resolved by the legislation of minimum acceptable standards for design of vehicles and routes, hopefully made with the cost of achieving these clearly in mind. There is as yet no theory or method available to social science enabling such questions to by-pass the political process.

References
1. Royal Commission on the Third London Airport, *Report* (Roskill Report), London, HMSO, 1971.
2. 'Transport Policy: The Report of a Study Group', *Socialist Commentary*, April, 1975.
3. Meyer, J. R., Peck, M. J., Stenason, J., and Zwick, C., *The Economics of Competition in the Transportation Industries*, Cambridge, Mass., Harvard University Press, 1959, chapter 3.

4. Joy, S., *The Train that Ran Away: A Business History of British Rail, 1948–1968*, Shepperton, Ian Allan, 1973, p. 153.
5. Ministry of Transport, *Road Track Costs*, London, HMSO, 1968.
6. Buchanan, C., *Traffic in Towns*, London, HMSO, 1963.
7. Ministry of Transport, *Road Pricing: The Economic and Technical Possibilities*, London, HMSO, 1969.
8. Considerable support, at least in principle, is given to the extension of local authority controls over transport planning in the recent government White Paper, *Transport Policy*, Cmnd 6836, London, HMSO, 1977.

Chapter 5
Issues in Retailing

Ross L. Davies

The business of shopping has changed dramatically in the last twenty years, from the point of view of both the retailer and the consumer. There have been enormous upheavals in the methods and organization of retailing, especially since the introduction of self-service techniques on a wide scale and the proliferation of supermarkets. There has been the development of cash-and-carry forms of wholesaling, leading in turn to the formation of voluntary trading groups for small independent retailers (such as Spar and V G), the expansion of mail-order trading, the emergence of super-stores and discount houses, and most recently the inception of trade centres and trading marts. Collectively, these innovations have led to an increasing integration of the distributive trades and a blurring of the traditional distinctions between wholesaling and retailing. There has been a general escalation in bulk-merchandis-ing practices to achieve economies of scale, and an increase in the corporate sizes of multiples or chain companies as well as the physical sizes of stores. The corollary of such growth, of course, has been a decline in the number and trading strength of the smaller, traditional activities, particularly the retail markets and corner stores.

On the consumer side, there have been commensurate changes in shopping habits and travel patterns. Most noticeable has been the reduction in frequency of short, daily shopping trips for small quantities of convenience goods and the greater emphasis on once or twice-weekly bulk-buying expeditions. This has occurred partly because of the growth of female employment and partly because of the increase in personal mobility and the acquisition of freezers.

The general rise in disposable incomes has also allowed for a greater total expenditure on shopping and particularly on durable goods and luxury items. Clear preferences have been expressed for the new forms of precinct and enclosed shopping centres which have further encouraged a greater trend towards family participation in shopping, especially on Saturdays. Perhaps the most significant factor affecting retailing itself, however, has been the overall shift in the pattern of population in the post-war years. The movement of people from the inner city to the suburbs has left behind a legacy of out-moded trading conditions in the older urban areas while creating vast new reservoirs of purchasing power in outlying housing estates.

In view of these spatial and other changes one might have expected to find some clear areas of conflict or controversy between consumers on the one hand and retailers on the other. In fact, however, the instances of direct and serious confrontation between them have been relatively few. This is not to deny that there have been periodic outbreaks of dissatisfaction, particularly over the prices and quality of goods; but in the main, there has been considerable public acquiescence to even the most undesirable consequences of retail change. The main reason for this can probably be attributed to government intervention, which has contained the main forms of abuse and worst excesses to relatively low levels. In acting so vigilantly on the consumer's behalf, however, various government agencies have also tended to be identified as working against the whole process of retail change. It is therefore in the relationship between these government agencies and certain retail firms that most of the confrontation over retail change has occurred.

Apart from its introduction of special taxation procedures (such as the former Selective Employment Tax and present Value Added Tax), central government has sought to extend its control over the retail system in two main ways. First, it has actively encouraged the formation of a variety of consumer advisory bodies. These are expected to watch out for unfair trading practices, identify areas in need of more local shopping support, help in the settling of individual grievances and the like. Many of

133

them have now been subsumed under the general auspices of the National Consumer Council, which it is hoped will eventually command the same degree of importance in reflecting consumers' views that the Trades Union Council and Confederation of British Industries do for other sections of society. In addition the Department of Prices and Consumer Protection enacts legislation and formulates policies specifically designed to protect consumer interests, especially in the matter of the prices and quality of goods. In recent years, of course, this has led to the allocation of heavy subsidies to various producers, particularly of foods, and to restrictions on the level of price rises, which are subject to careful review.

The second form of government intervention is to be found in the planning field. Local authorities are empowered with the same kinds of development control that they exercise in the case of other land uses; but, in addition, central government calls in for its own scrutiny all those proposals for new suburban shopping facilities that exceed 100,000 square feet (9290 square metres) in size. (Between 1972 and 1976 notification had to be given of any shopping centre above 50,000 square feet.)[1] Since local authorities are also themselves increasingly developers of shopping facilities, the new Community Land Act and Land Development Tax provide them with further powers to mould the emerging retail system to their own ends. These extensions of locational and management controls are particularly contentious. To date, both local authorities and central government have taken a cautionary stance in permitting new developments and most effort has gone into renovating the traditional pattern of shopping facilities. Now that the main period of central area reconstruction is over, however, there is still the question of what forms of new growth will be accommodated in the future and what part will be played by the private retail sector.

There is no other country in the western world which exercises such stringent planning controls over the retail system, particularly in terms of curtailing market pressures for a greater amount of decentralization of trade. While other countries have provided similar levels of consumer safeguards and in some cases given stronger powers to consumer protection agencies, their influence over the spatial distribution of retailing activities has been markedly less than in Britain. It is this spatial intervention that has led to most conflict between retailers on the one hand and government agencies (or 'planners') on the other; and hence it is essentially a set of spatial issues that form the subject of this essay. There are three particular questions that we might most profitably consider:

1. To what extent have various planning authorities been justified in concentrating new retail investments into traditional city centres rather than permitting the development of new forms of suburban shopping facilities?

2. What have commercial redevelopment programmes achieved with respect both to central area reconstruction and to the revitalization of other parts of the inner city?

3. How can the problems of smaller businesses and the weaker elements of the distributive trades be alleviated while accepting that planning policies must provide for an efficient and modern system of retailing?

The debate over decentralization

The process of suburbanization is a world-wide phenomenon, but at its most conspicuous in North America. There the massive shifts in population concentration have been accompanied by extensive changes in the retail pattern, such that considerably more shopping is now undertaken in the suburbs than in the traditional centres of cities. Since there has been little planning control over this decentralization of retail trade, vast new 'out-of-town' shopping facilities have been allowed to compete with the central area and collectively their impact has led to its deterioration and decline. Some serious problems have thus emerged over the spatial inequalities in quality levels of shopping facilities. In essence, a highly attractive, convenient and modern set of shopping centres has grown up in suburban areas to serve the needs of a relatively wealthy middle-class population; while in the inner cities, a poorer, older and predominantly coloured population has been left with a legacy of outworn and inferior shopping facilities.[2]

The experience of North America represents an extreme case of what happens when there is uncontrolled growth, and its importance here lies in the fact that it is often taken as showing the sorts of consequence that might follow from an expansion of suburban retail trade in Britain. By contrast, however, the experience of other countries, particularly in western Europe, provides examples of how a more limited amount of decentralization can be accommodated without such deleterious effects. In various planning climates, from France to West Germany and Sweden, large numbers of superstores and hypermarkets have been allowed, although large new suburban shopping centres have generally been restricted. Essentially, a distinction has been made between those new shopping facilities providing convenience goods and those that might compete with the more specialized functions of city centres. The result has been a considerable increase in overall suburban shopping with little decline of traditional centres except in the case of surrounding local shops.[3]

The debate over decentralization in Britain therefore needs to be considered against the background of the types of shopping development that are likely to be involved. A wide assortment of proposals has been made both for centres and individual types of store. For simplicity we will distinguish here between three kinds of centre: 'out-of-town' centres, 'edge-of-town' centres, and district or neighbourhood centres; and three kinds of store: hypermarkets, superstores and discount houses. The characteristics of each of these are given in Table 8. It is the 'out-of-town' centres and hypermarkets which have drawn most controversy because these are both large developments that tend to occupy green-field sites and are most likely to have radical effects on traditional patterns of trade. The district or neighbourhood centres and discount houses are generally the most acceptable forms since these can be integrated into the existing hierarchy of shopping provisions. In between are the 'edge-of-town' centres and superstores which in many ways constitute compromises

Table 8. **Different types of suburban shopping facilities**

A. Shopping centres

  1. *'Out-of-town' shopping centres*
complexes of shops dominated by variety stores or department stores
vary in size from community-level centres to regional-level centres
serve catchment areas of 50,000–250,000 population, mainly car-borne
shoppers
occupy green-field sites on the outskirts of cities, alongside major routes
usually enclosed centres with a mall form and extensive car parking

  2. *'Edge-of-town' shopping centres*
complexes of shops dominated by large supermarkets or variety stores
principally oriented to convenience trades rather than specialist trades
serve catchment areas of 25,000–100,000 population, mainly local groups
occupy green-field sites or vacant land on the edges of large housing
estates
usually enclosed centres on smaller scale to 'out-of-town' centres

  3. *District shopping centres*
similar in size, functions and catchment populations to 'edge-of-town'
centres
greater emphasis on convenience trades and units for local shops
greater orientation to shoppers walking from surrounding housing
estates
occupy positions in the middle of housing estates within the built-up area
usually open-air precinct developments with limited amount of car
parking

B. Free-standing stores

  1. *Hypermarkets*
large 'hangar' like structures, ranging from 75,000 to 250,000 square feet
combine food trades with wide range of cheaper household goods
may incorporate individual units, such as a bank, hairdresser, restaurant
occupy green-field sites on the outskirts of cities, alongside major roads
often stark appearance, extensive car parking for mainly car-borne
shoppers

  2. *Superstores*
variations in size, but typically range from 25,000 to 75,000 square feet
greater emphasis on either food trades or household goods

Table 8 – contd.

resemble either giant supermarkets, variety stores or discount houses
occupy both green-field sites and off-centre locations in built-up areas
sometimes integrated with shopping centres but with extensive car
parking

3. *Discount houses*
variations in size, but typically range from 10,000 to 25,000 square feet
greater emphasis on bulk household goods and domestic appliances
often occupy older premises, abandoned warehouses and factories
usually sites within built-up areas, some fairly inaccessible
sometimes poor appearance and décor resembling wholesaling establishments

---

between the extremes. 'Edge-of-town' centres are more akin in
their functional role to district centres in providing mainly convenience goods, but their location will not necessarily be confined
to the middle of housing estates and could include accessible
points alongside main roads in the outer parts of cities. Similarly,
superstores are more like giant supermarkets than hypermarkets,
although their trade need not necessarily be in foods but could
include the cheaper range of household goods as well.

So far, no large 'out-of-town' centre in a proper sense has been
permitted in Britain. Applications for regional shopping centres
at Haydock Park (between Liverpool and Manchester), Stone-
bridge (between Coventry and Birmingham) and Cribbs Causeway
(outside Bristol) have all been refused after extensive public
inquiries.[4] A single exception perhaps is the Brent Cross regional
shopping centre in Barnet (at the junction of the M1 and North
Circular) which exhibits most of the design characteristics of
'out-of-town' centres although it is located within the built-up
parts of north London and hence has been alternatively conceived
as a new strategic town centre for this part of the metropolis. To
date, four hypermarkets have been permitted, at Caerphilly,
Telford, Eastleigh and Irlam, but more than ten further applications have been turned down over the last three years. More
relaxed views have been taken towards 'edge-of-town' centres,

examples of which are to be found on the outskirts of Peterborough (Bretton) and Northampton (Weston Favell) and towards super-stores (such as the Gem outside Nottingham, and Fine Fare outside Aberdeen). Many modern, enclosed shopping centres that act essentially as new suburban and sub-regional focuses, how-ever, have been built as the town centres of new towns and extensive housing estates (such as the Galleries at Washington and Shopping City, Runcorn); likewise, many large superstores, such as the Woolcos and Azdas, have formed the nucleus of new town shopping centres or even taken sites in traditional town centres. Discount houses and district shopping centres have, by comparison with other developments, been allowed to flourish throughout the urban areas of our largest cities.

The prevailing planning attitude towards new suburban develop-ments in Britain has therefore been heavily restrictive, with most discrimination being applied to the car-oriented, free-standing shopping centre and hypermarket. It would be misleading, how-ever, to characterize all planners as sharing this view, since there has been a growing voice of dissent, particularly amongst those advocating a greater decentralization of the convenience trades. Similarly, retailers are by no means united in their opposition to the restrictions. While most supermarket chains have pressed hard for more scope in suburban locations, several of them have argued in favour of limited 'edge-of-town' developments rather than penetration of green-field areas; and many of the specialist High Street retailers have been against any significant amount of decentralization whatsoever.[5]

The main arguments

There are essentially three main arguments involved in the debate over decentralization at the present time:

1. There is a set of economic considerations wherein lower operating costs for retailers and hence potentially lower prices on goods for consumers have to be measured against the erosion of trade in other localities and the possible creation of blight con-

ditions. Suburban locations are clearly attractive to large-scale retailers because of the greater amount of space available, the ease of access for both consumers and delivery vehicles, the generally lower building costs incurred, and the close proximity to other elements of the distribution system (namely warehouses and redistribution centres) that can be achieved. It is argued that the greater business efficiency that can be attained can lead to price reductions on goods of up to 10 per cent (on national averages), besides providing shoppers with a greater choice of goods and a more congenial shopping environment. The establishment of a large new suburban facility will inevitably lead to the capturing of trade from existing and mainly smaller shops, however; and in certain cases, may even lead to loss of trade from a traditional town centre. Many councils and planning departments are particularly sensitive to this because of the amount of public investment that might already have been channelled into providing local shopping needs and redeveloping the traditional town centre. The counter-argument is therefore essentially one of protection rather than antipathy to a modern form of shopping.

Not unexpectedly perhaps, claims over price advantages and over trading effects have both tended to be exaggerated and often disputed by various research findings. The real benefits in lower prices have to be considered against the additional costs which may be incurred in visiting a suburban store, where these include not only journey costs but also the outlay in purchasing storage facilities for bulk produce, together with their running costs. It has been found that the impact of a new superstore or hypermarket falls hardest on the small branch outlets of the multiples rather than independent corner stores;[6] and many retailing firms are so confident of having only a minimal effect on town-centre trade that they continue to retain their own branches there even when opening a larger suburban facility.

2. A second area of contention concerns the threat to the environment which large-scale suburban developments might pose. This involves not only the premises themselves but the amount of traffic which they would be likely to give rise to. Traffic considerations are important because of the possibility of over-

loading suburban roads in the course of alleviating bottlenecks in other parts of the city. Without a considerable road widening and improvement scheme, bottlenecks might simply be shifted from one point to another. While much has been made of this argument by planners, however, the same degree of opposition does not seem to have been met by other categories of land use (namely wholesaling and industry) which have been more actively encouraged to decentralize. There are clearly differences in the volume and character of flows to be considered here, but the possibility of linking certain kinds of retail development to new wholesaling and industrial areas does not appear to have been fully explored. Potential conflict between shoppers and heavy lorries has been raised as one form of objection, but this is a problem that can surely be resolved in the way it has on a much larger scale within the central area.

The possible links that might be drawn between certain kinds of retail development and outlying wholesaling and industrial areas are worth examination in a further context, that of the extent to which suburban shopping facilities can or should be allowed to penetrate green-belt land. This is an issue which has been vigorously argued in planning inquiries, where planners have taken the view that both hypermarkets and 'out-of-town' shopping centres are likely not only to take up much valuable space because of their large size but also to spoil the character of the countryside by their (mainly poor) physical appearance. Developers have then tried to counteract these points by suggesting that many pockets of dereliction within the country side could actually be improved by the presence of shopping facilities, especially if strict standards in appearance were laid down, and that the employment opportunities created by these developments might well lead to a general upgrading of the locality. There is no doubt that in many conurbations excessive urban sprawl should be checked; but at the same time it seems that green-belt protectionist policies have been more strictly adhered to where retailing is in question than for most other categories of land use.

3. The provision of new suburban facilities on a much larger scale than is now usual would, however, be interpreted by many

planners and various consumer pressure groups as discriminating against the poor, the elderly and other minority sections of the population. Since these people are predominantly confined to the inner areas of cities, they would not have the same benefits of access as younger, more mobile, middle-class consumers. Moreover, the growth of extensive suburban facilities might lead to a serious deterioration in their own local provisions. These potentially inequitable effects, however, need to be considered against the background of other retail changes. The inner areas, by virtue of their proximity to the city centre, are likely to suffer proportionately more from the effects of redevelopment schemes and the building of new 'in-town' shopping centres than they are from 'out-of-town' or 'edge-of-town' developments. Even in the middle and outer parts of cities, local shops remain just as much in danger of closing because of the competition of large new stores coming into the existing urban market as they do because of developments in the suburbs.

Local authorities have rarely worried about the social inequalities resulting from their own 'in-town' shopping developments, but continue to use these arguments as a major reason for curtailing decentralization. Recently the principal criterion for refusing to allow a Tesco superstore on the edge of Swansea was that it would 'result in a material reduction in trade in local shops and some would be forced to close. People without cars, especially old people, would be seriously inconvenienced.'[7] Research into the shopping patterns of the elderly, however, has indicated that these are by no means a homogeneous group; and, indeed, in some cases evidence has been found that they are often more likely to travel further than younger people because of their greater amount of free time and the availability of free or cheap bus passes. There is no doubt that superstores appeal more to the younger, family-based households, but the elderly are often prepared to foresake their local store loyalty for visits to the central area. Within the older age band, however, there is obviously a difference between those people who remain fit and well and those who are seriously incapacitated. It is the minority who are effectively housebound who are most in need of care and attention. They have difficulty visiting even local shops, but few suggestions have been made about improving their situation.

The way ahead NO

The debate over decentralization in Britain has been going on for more than ten years and unfortunately has not been as constructive as one might have hoped. Instead of a healthy exchange of ideas and the reconciliation of different needs, there has been too much antagonism between retailers and planners, with the taking up of firmly entrenched positions. The debate has not been helped by a surfeit of emotion and confusion over the semantics of the new developments involved. As in many other aspects of urban society in Britain, there has been too much confrontation and not enough action – at least in a forward or positive direction.

The loser has ultimately been the consumer. The bulk of the population remains heavily constrained in its choice of shopping facilities and is effectively restricted to two kinds of centre: the city centre for specialized or comparison goods and the neighbourhood centre or local parade for convenience items.[8] In certain localities, of course, superstores and other new developments have been introduced, but these are not always in the most ideal locations and still represent the exceptions to the general case. For most suburban residents, the main form of modern provisions has been the open precinct district centre, the equivalent of older inner city ribbons but designed to be safer and easier to approach. While this modern form of traditional concept has no doubt made travelling to shops easier, its material effect on the actual economic and social functions involved has been small. Prices of goods remain high because of the difficulty of achieving scale economies in small, separate shop units; the variety or range of goods remains equally limited, often with too much duplication; goods have to be hauled around without the use of trolleys or store buggies; there remains the discomfort of shopping in bad weather conditions (except in the cases of enclosed district centres); untidiness and vandalism are difficult to control when the upkeep falls to the local authority; the main visual impact on the shopper is usually one of concrete and bricks rather than of the internal decor of the actual shops.

It needs to be made clear, however, that we are not advocating here a complete relaxation of planning constraints such that new types of suburban development can be established at will. We are concerned with providing a greater degree of choice in situations where this can be sensibly accommodated. There are certain rules of thumb that may be used in this decision-making. First, there are only a limited number of sites throughout the country as a whole in which large new 'out-of-town' shopping centres could conceivably be built. These are around the major cities and conurbations and ideally should be linked to potential growth areas. The commitment already made to city-centre redevelopment schemes, however, and the prohibitive costs involved in this scale of development mean that it is likely that few if any will actually be built in the next decade. Secondly, the case for a greater decentralization of convenience trade is stronger than that for more specialized needs, hence applications for 'edge-of-town' centres should primarily be adjudicated on the basis of their intended functional role. In many cases, these might well resemble in form the conventional district centres; but in others, a small cluster of independent shops may well be dominated by two or even three very large establishments. Thirdly, the most worrying features of hypermarkets, by comparison with other types of superstore, are their preferred location in green-field sites and their enormous size. The two features are inextricably linked, such that the potential penetration of rural areas looks far more damaging in the case of a large proposal than a small one. Restrictions on the overall size of permissible developments would reduce not only the environmental threat but ensure competition within only one part rather than the whole of an urban market. Fourthly, superstores and discount stores need to be considered much more in terms of their compatibility with, rather than difference from, traditional neighbourhood shopping centres. In functional terms, many of them provide the same kinds of goods as a series of small, independent stores, but with these arranged under one roof rather than in separated units. A deliberate integration of these into the hierarchy of shopping facilities within the city would ease the pressure on alternative sites which is now being felt. This positive arrangement in the provision of more special-purpose sites could then be matched with more restrictive policies towards the use of vacant buildings in inner city areas.

Besides these changes in planning outlook, there are certain other requirements that need to be met. The whole procedure for vetting applications for new developments has got to be made more efficient. Not only are there substantial delays in adjudicating cases (the Brent Cross centre took fifteen years to be finally settled), but considerable sums of public money are spent on the preparations for public inquiries (that often go over the same lines of argument) and other problems that might be of equal or even greater concern tend not to be scrutinized with the care they really deserve. Much of the research evidence on which decisions are based is derived from forecasts using a gravity model approach, the statistical and theoretical validity of which is now seriously questioned.[9] It would seem more profitable to undertake broader comparative research (showing how various retailing innovations change people's behaviour) that would then be applicable to a wide variety of situations. Above all when looking to the future needs of consumers it seems essential to work out a spatial commercial policy that is forward-looking rather than retrospective, and makes special provision for the accommodation of new developments rather than simply tacking them on to the traditional hierarchical retail system. This means having a much more coordinated approach to future regional and sub-regional needs while letting individual authorities work out their own requirements.

Commercial redevelopment programmes

In contrast to the procrastinations over the amount of decentralization of retail trade that should be allowed to take place, there has been a quiet but radical transformation of shopping facilities in the inner areas of British cities. This has involved the redevelopment of city centres and of the myriads of local clusters of stores in the so-called twilight zone. Curiously, despite the enormous sums of public money used, there has been little argument over the desirability and aims of these programmes. This is due partly to the general recognition that these areas have long been in need of renovation and partly to the fact that those changes which have been made have often been incorporated into other redevelopment schemes (involving the clearance of houses and warehouses and the building of new roads, etc.) which in themselves have commanded more attention or drawn more controversy. Even so, the record of achievement in terms of the improvements which have been made is not very impressive and a number of issues can be identified which need more thoughtful attention in future.

City-centre shopping schemes

The initial stimulus to city-centre redevelopment came from the bomb damage of the last war when many cities, most notably Coventry, Plymouth and Southampton, were in serious need of physical reconstruction. The complete obliteration of large parts of the central area in these places allowed for experiments in the separation of vehicles from pedestrians and the planning of a more orderly arrangement of retail land uses. As economic conditions improved and the precinct concept of shopping evolved, more and more cities embarked on comprehensive redevelopment programmes, prompting the publication in 1962 of a series of guidelines by the Ministry of Housing and Local Government and the Ministry of Transport on how these policies should be carried through (see Figure 9).[10] Subsequently, in the late 1960s, new types of enclosed shopping centre began to be built instead of the open-air precinct forms; and the construction of inner ring-roads and urban motorways allowed for the banning of traffic from the traditional High Street.

The general principles embodied in these city-centre shopping schemes are difficult to fault. They provide a much safer and usually more congenial shopping environment for the bulk of the population. What can be criticized, however, is the rather arbitrary way in which many new centres have been built and their frequent lack of attunement to local business needs. These short-comings are manifested in a variety of ways, but most noticeably through their poor design and the difficulties developers have faced in getting units let. From the consumer's point of view, there has usually been a significant increase in the number of specialist chain shops, but shops which offer a rather standardized range of products and lack the individuality and character of those in unplanned shopping streets.

Several different kinds of developments can be recognized, however, each of which has met with varying degrees of success.[11] First, there is a limited number of large new regional shopping centres which we might consider to be the 'in-town' equivalents of large 'out-of-town' centres. These include both the extensive open-air shopping precincts of new town centres (such as Coventry and more recently the Whitgift Centre in Croydon) and extensive enclosed shopping centres (such as the Victoria and Broadmarsh centres in Nottingham and Eldon Square centre in Newcastle). They normally contain more than 500,000 square feet (46,450 square metres) of retail floorspace and serve as a replace-ment for or substantial addition to the traditional High Street. Secondly, there are a variety of smaller precinct and enclosed shopping centres that we might liken to outlying district and 'edge-of-town' centres from the point of view of the shops they contain and their importance relative to other centres. They are typified by the precincts of the town centres of new towns and the new enclosed Arndale centres. They vary from 50,000 to 250,000 square feet (4645 to 23,225 square metres) in overall size and may serve as sub-regional centres. Thirdly, there are various kinds of small-scale development that constitute planned accretions to the city centre but have often grown up in a piece-meal way as small plots of land have become vacant. These may be in the form of open or enclosed malls but usually contain a group of small units that cater for a particular sector of trade, such as office workers or teenagers. They may be seen as analogous to neighbourhood centres in outlying areas; but there are few parallels to super-stores, hypermarkets and large discount houses which, in an

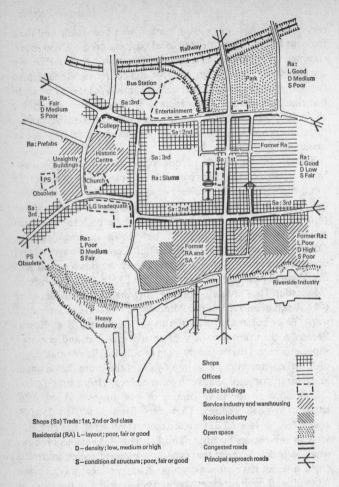

Shops (Sa) Trade : 1st, 2nd or 3rd class

Residential (RA) L – layout ; poor, fair or good

                D – density ; low, medium or high

                S – condition of structure ; poor, fair or good

Shops	
Offices	
Public buildings	
Service industry and warehousing	
Noxious industry	
Open space	
Congested roads	
Principal approach roads	

9 Typical planning guidelines for city-centre redevelopment schemes in the 1960s.

(a) An appraisal map for identifying the major problems

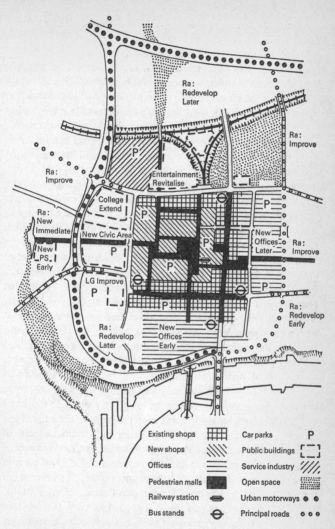

Legend:

Existing shops	⊞	Car parks	P
New shops	⫽	Public buildings	⌐¬
Offices	≡	Service industry	⫽
Pedestrian malls	■	Open space	⋯
Railway station	⊖	Urban motorways	● ●
Bus stands	⊖	Principal roads	○ ○ ○

(b) A blueprint summarizing the extent of new proposals

inner city context, have their equivalents in the surrounding frame rather than the central core of the city.

There are issues which can be raised with respect to each of these forms. The most contentious are the new large regional shopping centres which add considerably to the specialized retailing stock of the city. These have been questioned not so much in terms of the quality of their design, which generally speaking has been quite high, but for the rationale behind their development, given the enormous impact they have. The impact can be felt in three different ways. First, because of the overall increase in the size and importance of city centres in which they are found, surrounding town centres at lower levels in the regional hierarchy find themselves depleted of trade and likely to suffer from closures and commercial blight. These deleterious effects may be experienced not only in traditional town centres but also in those which have themselves undergone a degree of redevelopment. Even if the competitive effects are not severe, they hinder any growth potential that might be there. Thus, while the Eldon Square regional shopping centre will no doubt bring considerable benefits to Newcastle, it will have a severely depressant effect on the new town centre at Gateshead and other redevelopment schemes within the Tyneside conurbation. Secondly, within the city centre in which the regional shopping centre is built, there are radical shifts in the centre of gravity of trade, leading to a considerable upgrading of certain shopping streets but also a substantial decline in those which suddenly find themselves in an off-centre location. Such shifts in the centre of gravity of trade are most severe when a regional shopping centre is built on the edge of the central area away from the High Street and traditional axis of pedestrian flow, and the effect is compounded by the movement of many of the larger stores into the new centre itself and even in some cases the re-location of a department store. The effect is felt throughout the central area, for the introduction of one of these schemes completely upsets the finely tuned balance of trade that has grown up through relatively free market forces over a long period of time. The third type of change that causes concern is the growth in the dominance of chain stores or multiples at the expense of smaller independent stores. Smaller stores are effectively penalized in two ways: through the loss of sites when an area is cleared to make way for a new regional shopping centre, then through inability to go into the new scheme because of the high level of rents that must be paid. This leads to fewer personalized stores and a reduction in the variety of services and unusual trades.

Given the fact that most of the 'in-town' regional shopping centres have been developed by the local authorities themselves (in a partnership arrangement with a property company) it seems remarkable that they have been allowed to go up with a minimum of public scrutiny and fuss. The potential effects of an outlying superstore or hypermarket are small compared with what these giant city-centre schemes can do. This is not to suggest that their development has been wrong. On balance the advantages they bring in terms of improved shopping conditions for the urban population outweigh their disadvantages; but the problems they bring about are substantial ones and deserve more serious consideration than they have hitherto been given. Fundamentally there should have been a closer regional control over the post-war evolution of the hierarchy of town centres and the relationships between different redevelopment schemes.

The lack of a regional policy towards redevelopment schemes has meant that most towns and cities have tried to promote their own shopping importance and growth, leading to a general over-provision of retailing stock. At the same time, the larger centres have gained in commercial strength at the expense of smaller ones. Much of this is due not to the single effect of a large new regional shopping centre but to the cumulative effect of smaller precinct and enclosed centres. The net benefits of many of these schemes are dubious because of duplication of existing stores and a lower level of environmental standards. Some schemes have been abject failures (such as the Elephant and Castle Centre and the Tricorn Centre in Portsmouth) combining a poor design with an inappropriate location. The majority, however, have emerged as rather uniform, monotonous concourses with the same types of stereotyped chain store, adding little variety and pleasure to the actual business of shopping. The slight advantages in safety and weather protection (in enclosed centres) are probably counter-acted by the loss of small specialist traders forced out through their competition. Exceptions include several of the Arndale Centres which, whilst perhaps lacking imagination and finesse, usually look bright and cheery and have considerable consumer appeal.

Redevelopment in the inner city

Redevelopment programmes outside the city centre have mainly been concerned with removing commercial slums and reducing the surfeit of small marginal businesses to be found in the inner parts of cities. Few people would quarrel with the underlying need to modernize the retail system in areas where there has been a substantial decline in trade. The arguments arise over the scale and apparent impartiality of clearance schemes and the form which new shopping centres take.

It is impossible to quantify the amount of change which has taken place in Britain. Surveys undertaken in the USA, however, indicate that more than 100,000 small businesses have been dislocated through redevelopment schemes in that country since 1950. Since only about one third of these have managed to start up again, we must question whether the rate of enforced closure has been excessive. Detailed case studies undertaken in Chicago suggest it has not, given the high rates of liquidation to be found in areas unaffected by redevelopment.[12] As many as one third of all new businesses in the inner parts of American cities fold within the first two years of operation and the average life-span for all new businesses is only about seven years. However, even if redevelopment simply intensifies what is already happening, it is inevitable that certain healthier businesses become casualties when they might otherwise have survived. It is this inequality in localized situations and the lack of compensation (both in monetary terms and the provision of appropriate new sites) that is of most concern.

The types of business most seriously affected are the small independent traders. These face difficulties in moving to new locations because of the high rents incurred in new shopping centres. The chief beneficiaries of the new local shopping centres in fact tend to be the chain companies or multiples, especially supermarkets, which can often quickly establish a monopoly of trade in redeveloped areas. Many businesses, particularly those engaged in services and repair activities, however, find the form of the new local shopping centres unsuitable to their needs. These are businesses which have grown up along main roads so that they can be accessible to passing motorists from various parts of the city as well as drawing from a local surrounding population. The new shopping centres which replace these ribbon developments tend to be sited off the main roads and in concept are designed to meet local domestic shopping needs rather than the more specialized and occasional requirements of people passing through.

Places available for typical ribbon activities are rapidly disappearing. In view of the problems of congestion, safety hazards and commercial blight, it seems desirable to clear away or reduce the extent of the existing ribbon development. Few planners, however, have been prepared to concede the need for building new special-purpose facilities to cater for those businesses which will continue to be displaced. These might take the form of new service plazas or planned strips which retain close proximity to main roads but where the availability of off-street parking is much improved.[13] As it is, most car-oriented service activities are being squeezed into a few remaining sites around the edge of the central area, where the seeds of future problems of disorder and decay are now being sown.

The problems of local shopping

Several of the issues we have described in connection with the debate over decentralization and the inequities of commercial redevelopment programmes relate to declining provision for local shopping and to problems of small independent traders. These warrant a further, separate consideration for they have perhaps commanded more attention and raised emotions higher than any other subject in the retailing field. The background circumstances are generally well known.[14] There has been a substantial reduction in the number of small local shops throughout the urban area, primarily because of the competitive effects of chain stores and the inability of independent traders to generate sufficient profits in an era of increasing operating costs and shrinking markets. These difficulties have been exacerbated by planning interventions in two ways: through redevelopment programmes in the inner city, with the sorts of consequence we have already discussed; and through restrictions on the number and type of new locations permitted in outlying areas, which effectively consist of only local parades and neighbourhood shopping centres confined to the middle of housing estates.

The overall reduction in numbers of small shops is not in itself of major concern to the majority of consumers for they have been primarily responsible for this state of affairs. Apart from a sentimental attachment to such shops, what worries them most is the disappearance of certain more specialized or unusual trades which they would like to have available for occasional needs. These businesses often provide a range of goods that the multiples will not supply because of limited demand. There are certain sections of the population, however, who are clearly more dependent than others on the presence of a wide assortment of local shops; and it is with these groups in mind that various policies to prevent any further significant decline are now being discussed. Such groups include the elderly concentrated in the inner city and women with small children on outlying housing estates.

Two different schools of thought appear to be emerging, nevertheless, on how the market conditions for small independent traders can be improved. The first is in favour of a greater degree of local authority support, whereby certain types of shop might be given rent subsidies in new shopping centres or preferential treatment over chain stores in the allocation of sites. An extension of the change-of-use orders might also prevent more desirable and essential local shops from being converted to service establishments and non-retailing activities. The second school argues for a reduction in state interference and the promotion of an atmosphere much more conducive to self-help within the business community itself. Changes envisaged would include a relaxation of planning and building controls, allowing smaller businesses greater freedom of choice over new locations and the premises they use, and a revision of the tax laws, particularly regarding VAT. These diametrically opposite viewpoints obviously have political undertones and are difficult to reconcile; but it may be that compromise solutions can be worked out at least with respect to the spatial considerations. There could, for example, be a general loosening of planning constraints as a general principle throughout the city as a whole, but a tightening of controls in specific localities where protective measures are clearly called for.

These possibilities need to be examined in the context of the different requirements of different kinds of shop, however. To date, most sympathy has been shown for the problems of the corner shop or the traditional counter-top establishment engaged in the convenience trades. This is because they are felt to play a valuable social as well as economic role within a community. There are a number of other businesses, however, which could justifiably claim that they face more intractable operating difficulties and have been systematically discriminated against by local authorities. These include many of the services found in ribbon developments that we have mentioned before and also a set of more dubious traders concentrated in the 'twilight' zone. Table 9 gives some examples of community-based, car-oriented and twilight-zone businesses, and of the categories in which they might be placed.

For instance, among the community-based activities, a further distinction can be drawn between those which are essentially remnants of an outdated, historical form and those which show signs of modernization and innovation. The former are for the most part owned by an elderly couple; they survive in an area of declining population, depend on independent wholesaler deliveries for their stocks, and continue to engage in a high degree of personalized selling. While a great deal of nostalgia is associated with such shops, it is these which are most vulnerable to future decline and the most difficult to assist in a practical way. What we might regard as the more progressive shops, however, are those that have

Table 9. **Examples of different types of small business**

	Goods	Community-based Services	Car-oriented	Twilight
Convenience	corner shop	launderette	newsagent	second-hand
Specialized	hardware	optician	car accessories	antiques
Traditional	draper	shoe repairs	café	tattoo shop
Innovative	boutique	hair stylist	motel	sauna
Essential	chemist	post office	service station	charity shop
Acceptable	off-license	fish and chips	public house	social club
Questionable	pet-foods	betting shop	junk yards	sex shop

Source: Davies, R. L., 'Planning Solutions to the Problems of the Small Shop', *Town and Country Planning*, May, 1976.

a more expansive business outlook, have sought to penetrate new local markets, utilize the services of cash-and-carry depots or voluntary wholesaling groups, and introduce more efficient selling techniques. These can be more easily helped through a variety of measures, such as the building of cheaper premises, the provision of additional storage space, assistance in obtaining credit facilities and even, in some circumstances, by rent relief.

While these measures might provide temporary or short-term relief to the business difficulties of certain local shops, the more fundamental need is usually an improvement in their locations. Considerations of location vary throughout the urban area but some brief generalizations can be made here to indicate the nature of the problems involved. First, although the number of local shops to be found within the central area is small, there is nevertheless a group of activities which is oriented to localized demands; for example, cafés and newsagents serving office workers, people waiting in bus stations, etc. It is clearly desirable that in central area redevelopment schemes these services are given scope to re-locate in buildings and positions appropriate to their use. Secondly, within the inner city, much greater sensitivity must be shown to the community loyalty built up around certain stores. This means that local shops must be much freer to integrate with new housing schemes than has hitherto been allowed. Ideally, these would include many so-called twilight activities such as second-hand shops, which are often particularly important to immigrant groups. Thirdly, in the middle parts of the city, there are serious problems of accessibility to and parking around traditional shopping centres, especially those which grew up in the inter-war period at road junctions. Since the surrounding population is increasingly more mobile, at some stage in the future improvement must be made to the existing facilities or alternative sites must be provided. Finally, in the outer suburban tracts of the city, certain local shops might benefit from being located on the edges rather than in the middle of new housing estates. This would give them the chance to capture passing motorized trade as well as serving the adjacent neighbourhood. It should even be possible to conceive of new forms of centres: perhaps single superstructures resembling superstores but with the interior compartmentalized into independent units.

The risk that goes with a general relaxation of planning controls, of course, is that there will be a lowering of environmental standards. Given the current conditions to be found within most new local authority shopping developments, however, we would judge these effects to be relatively slight. A further consideration is that any significant locational shifts that emerge might hamper those who are relatively housebound or strongly dependent on nearby local facilities. This problem could and ought to be met by an increase in home-delivery services.

Conclusion

There have been two predominant areas of concern in retail planning during the last two decades: the need to redevelop the outworn parts of the inner city; and the need to provide new shopping facilities in the rapidly growing suburbs. These two requirements are clearly interrelated, for an overall balance has got to be created between the total amount of new floorspace added and the total population which is being served. Instead of pursuing these problems together, however, each one has been made the subject of a separate policy, with the result that they have been viewed as a choice between alternatives: either we have a continued concentration of retail investments in city centres or a widespread dispersal into suburban locations. The consensus response within planning circles has been to bolster up the traditional system. It could hardly have been different given the fact that a choice had to be made.

Now that the main period of central area reconstruction is over, however, and the economic climate makes it unlikely that there will be any more large 'in-town' shopping centres built in the near future, it seems an appropriate time for a more comprehensive planning approach to be adopted giving more scope to the decentralization at least of the convenience trades. This has clearly got to take account of the needs of small businesses as well as the larger chain companies and provide a modern and attractive local shopping environment for both the mass of middle-class consumers and more disadvantaged minority groups. It should also recognize the claims to new locational settings of a wide variety of retail services, particularly those which have been the major casualties of redevelopment schemes. The coordination and integration of these different requirements into a single commercial plan may need some new concepts both in terms of the spatial organization of shopping for the future and in terms of the individual forms that shopping centres or store clusters take. We need a design framework which enables us to relate hypermarkets and superstores to the traditional hierarchy of shopping facilities, and some imaginative blueprints for what the modern counterparts of ribbon developments and street parades should be.

What consumers have really lacked in the emerging retail system to date is an air of enjoyment and comfort in shopping, particularly for convenience goods. They have been provided with too limited a range of dull and stereotyped shopping facilities that do little to remove the drudgery and boredom involved in the routine aspects of shopping. Now that the planners have expanded their ranks, have more control over wider territories and have almost completed the task of removing the worst of the commercial slums, let us hope that we shall see more enlightenment in their policies and greater flair in the physical design of their schemes.

References

1. Department of the Environment, *Out of Town Shops and Shopping Centres*, Development Control Policy Note no. 13, London, HMSO, 1972.
2. Simmons, J. W., *The Changing Pattern of Retail Location*, Department of Geography, Research Paper 92, University of Chicago, 1964; Cox, E., and Erickson, L. G., *Retail Decentralisation*, Bureau of Business and Economic Research, Michigan State University, 1967.
3. MPC and Associates, *The Changing Pattern of Retailing in Western Europe*, Worcester, 1973; NEDO, *The Distributive Trades in the Common Market*, London, HMSO, 1973; International Geographical Union, *Commission on Applied Geography Symposium Papers*,

'Urbanisme Commerciale et Renovation Urbaine', University of Liège, 1975.

4. Evidence concerning the effects of these centres is contained in: Bristol City Planning Department, *The Cribbs Causeway Out-of-Town Shopping Enquiry: A Report of the Proceedings*, Bristol, 1972; Manchester University, Department of Town Planning, *Regional Shopping Centres in North West England*, part II, Manchester, 1966.

5. Different viewpoints are expressed in: a special issue of *Built Environment*, vol. 2, no. 2, 1973; Sainsbury, T. A. D., 'Retail Store Location', *Estates Gazette*, vol. 224, Nov. 1972, pp. 803–5; Freeman, H.B., 'The Case for the High Street', *Estates Gazette*, vol. 221, March, 1972, pp. 1501–3.

6. Lee, M., and Kent, E., *Caerphilly Hypermarket Study, Year 2*, Donaldsons, 1974; Thorpe, D., and McGoldrick, P. J., *Carrefour Caerphilly: Consumer Response to a Hypermarket*, Manchester Business School, Retail Outlets Research Unit, 1974.

7. Reported in *Planning Newspaper*, October 1975. See also Lee, M., and Kent, E., *Planning Inquiry Study*, London, Donaldsons, 1976.

8. Davies, R. L., *Patterns and Profiles of Consumer Behaviour*, Department of Geography, Research Series no. 10, University of Newcastle upon Tyne, 1973.

9. Openshaw, S., 'Insoluble Problems in Shopping Model Calibration when the Trip Pattern is Not Known', *Regional Studies*, vol. 7, 1973, pp. 367–71.

10. Ministry of Housing and Local Government and Ministry of Transport, *Town Centres: Approach to Renewal*, London, HMSO, 1962. See also, Holliday, J., *City Centre Redevelopment*, London, Charles Knight, 1973.

11. Jones, C. S., *Regional Shopping Centres: Their Location, Planning and Design*, London, Business Books, 1969; Darlow, C., *Enclosed Shopping Centres*, London, Architectural Press, 1972.

12. Berry, B. J. L., Parsons, S. J., and Platt, R. H., *The Impact of Urban Renewal on Small Business: The Hyde Park-Kenwood Case*, University of Chicago, Center for Urban Studies, 1968.

13. These ideas are elaborated on in Davies, R. L., 'A Conceptual Framework for Commercial Planning Policies', *Town Planning Review*, vol. 48, 1977, pp. 42–58.

14. Kirby, D. A., 'The Decline and Fall of the Smaller Retail Outlet', *Retail and Distribution Management*, vol. 2, no. 1, 1974, pp. 14–18; Unit for Retail Planning Information, *Local Shops: Problems and Prospects*, Reading, 1976.

Chapter 6
Issues in Recreation

Reg Hookway

Speculation about recreation is fraught with difficulty. Patterns of recreation activity, or indeed inactivity, reflect both our personal abilities in using leisure time, and the social, geographical and economic circumstances within which we live. Individual tastes are extremely varied and may change dramatically during a lifetime, as new interests replace old ones. And when, as now, we live in a period of rapid social and economic change it is unwise to assume that past trends will continue.

The pessimists say that in a competitive world, with more and more constraints on the availability and price of food and non-renewable resources, we in Britain will be so hard pressed to provide for our survival that leisure time and recreation activity will decrease. Others, however, paint a very different picture. They see advance in our technologies and sciences bringing even further freedom from the time constraints of work, and a new age of leisure on the horizon.

Whatever the answer, the use of the available time will inevitably be constrained by the dominant geographical facts, that our mainly urban population in Britain is large in proportion to the land area available, and that we live in a maritime location with a mild, wet climate. If we want reliable winter ski-ing with the strong possibility of calm, sunny weather, or a fortnight's summer holiday with warm sea-bathing and with the near certainty of hot sun from cloudless skies, then, obviously, we must travel to other lands.

In this essay attention is first focused on our basic need for recreation and the opportunities there are for the fulfilment of that need in Britain. Key issues to be examined are: How much time will we have for recreation? How will we spend that time? How will conflicting interests be resolved?

The need for recreation

Recreation is a basic human need, the satisfaction of which is generally accepted as necessary to our physical and mental health. It is a component of the way of life of all human societies, primitive as well as advanced. The amount of time available for recreation is conditioned by the nature of the society in which the individual lives, subject to the primary need to devote time to procuring the basic means of survival. For example, the more advanced the society by western standards, the wider the range of recreational pursuits which can be followed. But in advanced industrial societies, with many working on production lines or on routine clerical tasks, there is a separation of work and leisure into almost different compartments of life. This is less clearly discernable in societies of agriculturalists and craftsmen. The modern worker may choose recreation interests of quite different character from his work: interests which are a counter to industrial noise, to the rhythm of the machine, to the presence of too many people or, alternatively, to loneliness at work. Painting, pottery, gardening, for example, are ways of releasing creative energies which may be suppressed by modern work systems and environments.

Participation in many types of recreation activity can be related to the satisfaction of basic human needs. We express the physical reality of living through the enjoyment of food, drink, exercise, colour, sound, form, space. Hunting, now of little relevance to the provision of food, continues in field sports, coarse and sea fishing, and riding. Games of all types, and much sport, have components of challenge, competition and achievement which have long been regarded as basic to the preparation of individuals and groups for war and probably commerce as well. Furthermore, the need for spiritual and aesthetic recreation is fundamental to religious practice, to conservation (which can be regarded as a modern 'religion') and to most of the creative arts.

Man's social need is expressed in certain group practices. Many recreation activities are carried out within the family or in clubs; others involve much greater public participation, as in football matches or horse racing. The fact that we enjoy listening to and watching others is the basis of most passive and spectator activity. We enjoy being with others in crowds: on plazas and promenades, on crowded beaches or in a park. Whether very young or very old we seem to be attracted to the pleasures of 'playing' with others in play groups, teams, bridge drives, orchestras, choirs, old people's clubs and group outings of all sorts, ranging from Sunday School treats to professional or union conferences or study tours.

There has been a remarkable persistence of certain types of recreation activity and interest over the centuries. As average wealth has increased and technology developed, and as government has taken on more responsibility for the provision of recreation facilities and services for us, what was once the prerogative of the powerful and rich can now be enjoyed by most people.

The minstrel and the jester have progressed from private palaces to public theatres and, in this century, to the sitting-room. Indeed, they are available wherever one can carry the portable radio, television or tape player. We summon our entertainer, our adviser, our friendly voice, by the pressing of a switch. There are parks and pleasure grounds in town and country, in which we can enjoy open space designed to offer vistas and colours in the different seasons. They may not be outside our front door as they were in the days of the palace or mansion, but they are usually not very far away. Our libraries are public ones, with an immense choice of books. We have public art galleries and museums, public tennis courts and other facilities for games. And many of us seem to enjoy most of all the benefits of having our own 'carriages' to provide for our pleasures as well as our work. On the roads, and through the air, they can take us quickly and comfortably to the pursuit of our leisure interests: indeed the active use of the vehicle, and the time spent on caring for it, is a recreation in itself.

Recreation resources in Britain

The range is so great that it is not easy to list and classify the recreation resources and services available to the individual or group, either spatially or in terms of quality. Nor is it possible to provide a complete summary of the vast range of recreation interests or activities followed by individuals and groups. Some are designed expressly for the refreshment of the mind, as are cathedrals, churches, galleries and concert halls. Others, such as dance halls, sports grounds and swimming pools are designed for physical recreation. Facilities may be multi-purpose – the lido which is also a reservoir; the schoolroom used for teaching or evening leisure pursuits. They may be designed to facilitate the use of natural resources: the seashores, cliff tops, and inshore waters which are Britain's great playground, the rivers and lakes, the woods and mountains. Some facilities may be man-made, such as slipways and steps, car parks and moorings; services such as wardens and rangers, beach and mountain rescue teams may be provided. And of course our railways, roads, power-supply and water-supply systems, police, ambulance and medical services are as integral to the pursuit of our pleasures as they are to our commerce and industry. If the electric power supply engineers decide to strike then factory lathe and hi-fi are both silent, and there is no light for the office or the television screen. We even imitate nature, with ice rinks and plastic ski slopes, climbing walls and heated swimming pools. There are very few recreation interests that cannot be pursued somewhere in Britain.

Many of the recreation resources and assets we tend to take for granted are envied by those in countries elsewhere in the world. Certainly this can be claimed for our footpath system and the right of access to nearly all our foreshores. It is frequently claimed for our pubs, perhaps the most popular of all our recreation resources, our theatres, television and radio services, our town parks and public library service. In contrast, however, our facilities for athletics and gymnastics may not be as plentiful or of such high standard as in some other countries.

We are progressively creating new physical resources, for example leisure centres, sports stadia and country parks, to meet increasing demands. Technical advances, such as colour television and hi-fi in the home, sub-aqua equipment and hang-gliding kites, enable us to enjoy recreation activities beyond the experience, if not the imagination, of our forbears. Technical developments have dramatically increased the use we can make of some facilities. Man-made track and play surfaces can resist the wear and tear which may destroy grass. Floodlighting and covered facilities counteract winter conditions of darkness, cold and wet, and by reducing physical discomfort with better water and wind-proof clothing the enjoyment of walking, climbing and sailing in winter has increased substantially. The rubber 'wet-suit' enables the water skier or the surfer with his malibu board to enjoy winter as well as summer activity.

Thus in Britain we can identify a great commitment of resources and skills to recreation: evidence of a considerable amount and a wide variety of recreation activity. This is the basis from which issues in recreation can be examined, and assessments made of possible future change. The most important of these is the element of time: time for leisure within which recreation activity will take place.

How much time will we have for recreation?

The time available for recreation in Britain has increased drama-tically in the past century. There are a number of factors behind this growth. The slowly increasing average life span, brought about by better medicine, diet and living conditions, has given more people, in retirement, more years free from the constraints of work. Compulsory holidays, and in particular holidays with pay, have added considerable amounts of leisure time to millions. The weekend is now more than the 'day of rest'; it is commonly two days. The hours worked each week, and in particular the daily amounts, have decreased dramatically, though in recent years the rate of decline has been slower. The years of 'work' are fewer through the raising of the school leaving age for all, and because a greatly increased proportion of people is receiving higher education.

Different considerations apply for that large group of workers who are out of work. (At the time of writing this is nearly 1¼ million, larger than at any time since the war.) We have a deep social conscience about the dehumanizing and economically wasteful effects of unemployment, and make considerable efforts as a society, to provide both work and support for those in need. But in terms of leisure time the unemployed can be counted with those on holiday and retired.

The writer would be foolhardy to suggest that the housewife, who is not in paid employment, is other than a slave to labour for all the waking hours. That said, one of the conspicuous features of the post-war period is the contribution that household equipment and 'convenience'foods are making to her leisure time. For increasing numbers they combine to reduce the time taken to acquire and prepare food, and to create and maintain a home. Innovation in marketing and retailing, in food packaging, dehydration and freezing, and the widespread adoption of fridges, freezers and other kitchen equipment provides some release from work. So do gas and electric fires, central heating, vacuum cleaners, washing machines and detergents and a multitude of other household aids. If many of these advantages are restricted to the more privileged, women of all social classes find they need to spend less time on the care of their children than did past generations, because of the general tendency to have smaller families.

More time has also been made available for recreation activity by reason of improvements in personal mobility and transportation systems. For those with cars the time taken for journey to work, shopping, and school and the time spent in travelling as part of recreation activity, may be much less than for users of public transport, and indeed, as any user of the motorway system will appreciate, may be much less now than was a comparable car journey in the past.

The constraints on leisure time

But what of the future? What are the present constraints on the time available for leisure, and the possibilities for changing them? There is little to be learnt from existing data. For a society with a substantial time and resource commitment to recreation it may be thought surprising that there are not authoritative statistics showing how much time is actually devoted to leisure within the varied social and age groups in society, and what we do in that time. How else, it may be argued, can one formulate the policy and investment decisions which might be expected to be associated with the increasing commitment of public resources to recreation? Private investment has its commercial roots and operates to make a profit, being prepared to risk capital to do so.

Data is limited, in range and value, and whilst we can draw on some user trends and the benefits of experience, we have neither a sufficiently comprehensive framework nor the degree of detail necessary over a long period of time to use statistics as a base for anything other than the broadest of judgements. In 1974 there were 53·4 million people in Great Britain. Of these, 24·6 million were gainfully employed. Let us say that they worked an average 43 hours a week for an average of 48 weeks in the year. There may be more precise figures, but these are sufficient to illustrate the general conclusion that of the 468,000 million hours or so of living in Britain in 1974 (53·4 m. × 365 days × 24 hours), the time spent in gainful employment absorbed only some 51,000 million hours (24·6 m. × 43 hours × 48 weeks), or approximately 9 per cent of the available time.

Of course the remainder is not leisure time within normal understanding of the phrase. Even the abnormally wealthy man, whose every want is met and who may be considered wholly leisured, still has to spend time sleeping and feeding, dressing and washing. These personal needs are as much a constraint on the free use of our time as is the work we need to do to provide for our food and well-being. Furthermore we cannot change this time constraint to any substantial extent.

We also need shelter and family care, and all that goes with the home in our society and culture. There were 18·5 million households in 1974, and whilst, for reasons given earlier, the time and labour involved in running them and caring for the family has been much reduced for millions, caring for the home is still a demand on time. As our housing stock improves, and as the aids to easier living become more widespread, so more time will become available. For example, the transfer of half an hour a day from household care to leisure time as the home becomes better equipped would be a realistic goal. If it happened, the extra amount of leisure time available would be some 3,500 million hours a year: not large when compared to the 51,000 million hours spent at gainful employment, but a large figure nevertheless.

A final major time constraint is that of education. The discipline of school hours, and the more self-imposed time disciplines of formal adult education, involved 11·6 million people in 1974: a very substantial commitment of time. And even discounting part-time education for the purposes of enriching our leisure time, there is an additional substantial time involvement in part-time education which may increase individual capabilities at work and in running the home. It is almost inconceivable that our society will choose to reduce its commitments to education principles and systems. We cannot look for more leisure time from this source. So except for changes through increasing ease in looking after ourselves and our homes, it will be through reductions in the amount of time we work that any substantial changes in the already substantial amount of leisure time will have to come.

What then is the potential for change in the amount or the periods of time we work? Will we have to work more to maintain present standards of wealth, thereby losing some leisure, or can we have more leisure and more wealth? These extreme alternatives hide a variety of further options. As indicated, it takes only 9 per cent of available time to produce the resources to sustain our life and well-being in these islands through the mechanism of gainful employment. Only a proportion of this is spent in producing goods. Much employment is in services, and some is in the leisure field itself. Employment in the social services does much to enhance the quality of life in Britain. Arguably we accept it as more beneficial to society as a whole than would be the greater volume of leisure time which would be available for society to devote to leisure, if such services were not met out of taxation revenues. But they are, and whilst a very full use of recreation time can be had at little cost (with extra money tending to be spent on luxuries such as specialized equipment, more exotic holidays and expensive entertainments), if we want better social service, full employment and better living standards all round, including more resources to spend on leisure pursuits, we need to earn more wealth or make some radical changes in our social structures and attitudes.

Is this happening? It seems that we are not as content as we used to be with our ways of working. The failure of many people to get job satisfaction (particularly from assembly-line work) has led to many suggestions for change. One remedy (adopted in some car factory operations in Sweden) is to restructure the pattern of working. Another is to reduce the time constraints on work, through such techniques as flexible time keeping, which is of course much easier in an office than on a production line. A third option is to alter the time cycles of working where appropriate. For example, the boats of Trinity House, which safeguard our shipping lanes and the approaches to ports, now work through fortnightly cycles at sea, with two crews, one on duty and one off duty. The boats, expensive in capital and operational costs, spend more time at sea and are thus more efficiently used. The crews spend more time working on operational duties, because the weekly journey to and from port is eliminated. But their time on duty is, in total, decreased. Another example is the air-line operator whose staff have agreed to take their holidays in the winter months when work pressure is low. They get a very long paid holiday – nearly three months. The operator does not have to take on extra staff or pay overtime through the busy spring to autumn months. The general effect is an increase in leisure time without losing income.

How much, in consideration of human as well as organizational interests, shall we be able to alter the traditional time-table and structure of work? Are we, as some believe, rather slow in adjusting to new opportunities created by sophisticated machines? Are we at a disadvantage because of our own conventional thinking about recreation time, such as weekends off work and holidays in August? These are times when costs are highest and recreation resources are under heavy pressure. Shall we change our jobs more frequently with longer leisure breaks between jobs? Shall we have more sabbaticals? The choice, probably as never before, lies within ourselves. Shall we choose more leisure time rather than more wealth?

The whole subject may be influenced by more intangible issues. Is the work ethic, which was so strong a force in Victorian Britain, giving way to other values as some of the fears about earning a living are removed by social provisions, pensions, unemployment and supplementary benefit, for example? Many analysts think it is and are ready to demonstrate this with a whole variety of economic indicators. If so, is there a strong recreation ethic developing and what horizons will this lead us towards? What, in relation to the figures for gainful employment, could these possibilities lead to?

Let us look again at two fairly extreme hypotheses. First, let us suppose that the same labour force as in 1974, 24·6 million, had six weeks' holiday each year (the present average in Sweden) and a 35-hour working week instead of 43. The time commitment to work then becomes $24·6 \text{ m.} \times 35 \times 46 = 39,600$ million hours approximately. Compared to the present 51,000 million, this would be a 22 per cent decrease in working time for the labour force which is clearly substantial. This does not imply, however, a commensurately large increase in the total amounts of leisure time throughout society, because it would involve less than half the population.

Secondly, what would happen if workers retired five years earlier, say reducing the labour force by approximately 10 per cent, with a limited reduction in weekly working of, say, 2 hours to 41 hours, and an extra week's holiday? The time commitment to work then becomes $22·2 \text{ m.} \times 41 \times 47 = $ some 42,800 million hours, compared to the present 51,000 million hours. This would give a 16 per cent decrease in working time for workers but, again, much less of an increase in the volume of leisure time for society as a whole. If from the first hypothesis we add a predicted 11,400 million hours less gainful employment to 3,500 million hours less time caring for homes, then the total extra release of time to leisure is 14,900 million hours approximately, or just over 3 per cent of available time. In essence, there are clear, finite limits to the future increase in leisure time even if technologies, or the evolution of a recreational ethic, are to lead to dramatic changes in our life styles.

But, of course, the release of such volumes of time from fixed constraints would have heavy and probably quite unpredictable effects on recreation activities and resources. The housewife with more time to indulge her own interests, because caring for the home is less time-consuming, would probably still have to adapt those interests so that she could provide meals or meet children from school. The husband, with an extra week's holiday, may well alter the leisure activities of a whole family by taking them away from home on, say, a camping holiday.

Thus the possiblity of extra leisure time, beyond the large amounts we already have, raises a whole chain reaction of un-certainties. The questions range from those related to our capacities as individuals to use leisure time to the effects of changing tastes, pressures on existing resources and the whole spectrum of recreation activity.

How will we spend that time?

Our capacity to use leisure time, and the vast range of recreation facilities and services available, depends on a variety of considerations and circumstances. Those which relate to age, physical abilities and general health can confine some activities, mainly physical, to relatively short periods of the life-span. Our spiritual, emotional and intellectual needs for recreation also vary at different times of the life-span, either in a short or long cycle. They are related to factors such as our general educational background, both formal and social; our training in the use of recreation time, which can involve a wide range of cultural and sport pursuits; and our experience of different types of recreation, which is not the same as a training in recreation.

It is obvious that where we live and the time we have available for recreation are major influences on what we do. These lead to different patterns of activity related to the permanent home and the working week, the weekend, and the holiday home. It is also obvious that the amount of money available to pay for things such as transport, equipment, club fees and charges for accommodation will have a considerable influence on choice of activity.

Finally there is the less tangible factor of motivation, the drive to do things. Collecting, following a political ambition, seeking a circle of friends, seeking physical exercise, natural competitiveness, are all examples of drive toward recreation activity.

Thus the patterns of recreation activity followed by any one individual may, and do, change erratically over quite short periods of time. But the numbers participating in most recreation activities, accepting that they are subject to periodic surges of fashion, demonstrate more stable trends. At least, those concerned with recreation believe so and it is a premise on which much investment is based. As has been mentioned, we are short of reliable and comparative leisure data, particularly in the field of informal recreation. Though it is difficult to develop information systems quickly or to persuade those in charge of censuses and surveys to include many questions relating to recreation, there is likely to be a steady increase in the small amount of data available. But general knowledge gives us some information.

For most of us the home is the main leisure centre. The recreations of reading, listening, viewing, playing cards and other games, receiving, talking and dining with friends, and caring for and enjoying pets, dominate indoor use. The living-room is the main indoor playground; our music room, our library and our study. But great numbers of us now have our own private outdoor playground too. It may be a tiny patio, in which to sit in the open air in summer, or else a personal pleasure ground of lawns, herbaceous borders, rose beds, clipped hedges and the vegetable plot and greenhouse. For millions these gardens, large and small, are both a joy, a place for self-expression and pride, and outdoor space. The fulfilment from them is one reason why we have a much lower ratio of second home/summer house ownership than do people in other European countries. For those without gardens, or with small gardens, the allotment may fulfil a similar function.

Whether our leisure needs get as much attention in estate,

house and garden design as they should is debatable. It can be argued that there is sufficient variety in the property market to cater for people's different tastes. On the other hand there has been so little change in internal house layout over the last quarter century that one could suggest we have been extremely short-sighted in our vision of how existing houses will be used as leisure centres in the longer-term future.

Since most of us live in urban areas it is not surprising that most purpose-built facilities for recreation are found within towns and cities, with the scale of provision closely related to population size: the high-cost facilities occurring only in the larger cities, or alternatively in the resort towns which specialize in meeting heavy recreation demands. People are gregarious. We enjoy our pubs, dance and bingo halls, cafés and restaurants, cinemas and theatres. We are attracted in large numbers to watch horse racing, football, rugby, athletics, and riding. More frequently, and still in large numbers in the big cities, we use our museums, galleries, theatres and concert halls. We use our schools for study, crafts and physical exercise in the evenings. For physical recreation, though it may be that we are less zealously active in competitive sport and games than are some others, there is a wide range of public and private facilities to enjoy – swimming baths, squash and tennis courts, golf courses, pitches and tracks and many new sport and leisure centres. Our cities and towns are also places for much outdoor informal recreation. Walking and looking at shops, buildings or people, or exercising a dog, tend to take up a lot of leisure time; though the people of many European countries, and particularly those with less variable and wet climates, probably make the casual stroll in the town square or promenade more of a feature of their lives. On the other hand our grassy urban parks, urban commons and river banks are a great attraction, and where in towns there are rivers or lakes or canals to fish and boat in, then, except in the few places where bad pollution remains, they are intensively used. Arguably, most of our leisure time outside the home is spent in the town or city where we live or spend our holidays; for most of our holiday accommodation is in towns.

The older and larger holiday resorts along the coast and inland were mainly a product of the railway age. The rail link remains of importance to them, even though much holiday-making is based on the use of the car. At most coastal resorts, built on a summer holiday demand, the main asset is still the beach, that marvellous, self-cleansing, normally self-rehabilitating resource where the most ebullient energies of small boys can be gently absorbed. But they now have covered leisure facilities as well so that, like inland resort centres, they are places to which people will go for recreation. Thus they will have leisure facilities, whether built or open space, on a greater scale than the industrial or commercial centres of similar size from which many of their visitors come. This can be of great benefit to the day tripper from a wide catchment area. But the big provincial cities with their concert halls, theatres, parks and sports grounds are great leisure centres, and the greatest of all our holiday resorts and leisure centres is, of course, London. With its immense flows of foreign as well as domestic visitors supplementing the activities of its own residents and supporting the best of our leisure facilities and services, it is also the main centre of television and radio broadcasting, which help so many others to share those recreation activities.

But while a large proportion of holiday leisure time is spent in buildings, even more is spent out of doors. For the great majority, the summer holiday is based on the informal enjoyment of that wide variety of environment where sea and land meet. Our coastline is truly our greatest national playground, with its extent, the variety of its form and the services to support its use – for day recreation as well as holiday-making. It imposes a dominating spatial influence on holiday recreation in Britain. It offers us the natural resources of beaches, cliffs and rocks to explore, waters to paddle and bathe in, to surf on, to fish and to enjoy in boats in our millions. We do so from hotels and boarding houses, from holiday camps and caravan parks, from the homes of friends or relatives, or people doing 'bed and breakfast', and, as mentioned, from our own homes on the day trip. Nobody lives more than ninety miles from the sea and there is a daily tide of humanity using our developed and undeveloped coastline. This tide is small in winter, with slight weekend surges. There then follows a small peak at Easter, a decline, another peak over the spring bank holiday, and then a rise to the great crowded, rumbustuous flood of July, August and early September, before the rapid drop back to the low levels of winter. This is the classical British seasonal pattern of holiday-making. It is, of course, also the seasonal pattern of traffic in the holiday areas; less exaggerated where there is a large retirement population within close driving range, but made extremely acute on summer Saturdays by our habit of starting and ending holidays on that day. Expenditure in these areas is even more seasonal, for prices increase with demand. It is from the expenditure over some twelve to sixteen weeks of the average holiday season that the costs of the built facilities and services needed by the holiday-makers have to be defrayed. The long summer holiday seasons of the Mediterranean countries, or the two-season resort areas of the Alpine region, have a very different economy. It is a reflection of ingenuity and entrepreneurial skills that in the holiday camp and the self-catering caravan camp we have been able to blend low capital investment accommodation with an acceptable form of holiday-making. If the appearance of much of our coastline has been dramatically changed and, by most considered judge-ment, sadly impaired by the caravans, chalets and tents of these self-catering holiday-makers, this must be set against the pleasure given to millions of them, the probable benefits to their health and well-being, and the general enriching of their year. But the effect of the seasonality of our holiday habits is that they are relatively high cost. The reasonable price of a luxury twin-bed-with-bath, three-meals-a-day, fortnight package in Spain, with sunshine and gaiety thrown in, is more easily explained by the long season than by slightly cheaper labour. For well over half the time, indeed in many parts of this country for over two-thirds of the time, the holiday beds which cater for the mass demand are empty.

Resorts during their 'off-season' have an air of emptiness or abandonment. Places are closed and shuttered, or almost empty of users. Car parks look windswept and wasteful, and those services which must be able to cope with the peak periods of demand begin to wind down. The police, ambulance and medical

175

services, postal and newspaper workers and indeed all who cater for others in shops, restaurants and pubs, can relax. The facilities which have cost great sums to build, such as rail, road, parking, water-supply and sewerage systems are used well below capacity.

The question of how to alter the patterns of our holiday-making is at the heart of much tourist planning. 'Weekend breaks', 'Away-days', and special packages for the retired are all success stories. But the economic, and indeed social, inefficiency of our short domestic holiday season remains a great challenge. If our leisure time increases, can we make domestic holidays in the off-peak season more attractive?

Some of our holiday accommodation is in the inland country-side, as opposed to coastal countryside. But despite the fame of the Peak District, the Dales and the Roman Wall, Snowdonia in Wales, the Cotswolds, the Chilterns, the Downs and the New Forest, the number of bed spaces in these places is relatively small. Only on the Thames and the Broads in boats, and in the Lake District in hotels, boarding houses and caravans, is there a substantial inland residential tourist industry.

The number of cars visiting such areas of the countryside, however, is very high. The enjoyment of the countryside on the day visit, from home and from holiday base, has grown rapidly. Many surveys have shown that most people will typically spend about one hour travelling, or thirty miles, for the day trip. For half-day or after-work journeys it is less. Of course the distance may be increased where there is ready access to motorways and fast roads outside the towns. If we are not going to the coast it is to the view points, to country parks, to the scenically attractive country and, above all, to the rivers, lakes and other inland bodies of water to which the crowds are attracted. 'Water is a focal point for recreation' was one of the truisms set out in the great *Outdoor Recreation Review Commission Report* produced in the United States in the early 1960s.[1] The numbers involved are huge. There is the same seasonal and weekend pattern of pressure on the inland countryside as on the coast. In many respects it produces the same range of problems: of investment, of pressure on resources, of coping with peak traffic.

The demands for participation in the traditional sports of the countryside – game fishing, shooting and hunting – continue to be heavy, though they have become an expensive recreation. There are other sporting activities – cross-country running, riding, orienteering – but a very substantial majority of us enjoy our country pleasures informally. We walk, picnic, watch birds, enjoy flowers, visit places and generally savour the life and character of an environment very different from the sort of area we live in.

However, unlike urban recreation, most of which takes place in buildings or on spaces specially set aside, much of our country recreation involves a secondary use of land. Some is potentially in conflict with the production of food and timber from our limited land area. To seek to resolve such conflict we are developing systems of planning and management for countryside recreation. These can be related to three primary objectives. The first is to secure a greater intensity in the use of existing resources (the most valuable of which is the footpath system) without prejudicing the character of wildlife interest of the resource, by managing the land, the visitors to it, and their vehicles and equipment, with much greater efficiency. The second is to develop recreation as part of a multiple use of land and water which have previously been restricted to a simple use; a right of access to much open country through negotiated agreement, or to water reservoirs through management policy changes, are the main examples of this. Thirdly, we are creating new resources – new 'honeypots' as the country parks have been called – from derelict land and water areas, the parks of old houses, downland view points, cliff tops and woodlands, where there was no public use previously or where new investment has enabled a greatly increased use to be made.

There are other objectives, secondary perhaps in terms of priority rather than importance, concerned with enhancing the quality of the enjoyment of the countryside. We seek to instruct the visitor through promotion of the Country Code, through interpretive displays and publications, through guided trails, farm open days and other techniques. We seek to improve the quality of services by better training, and to improve the quality of facilities by better management and design. The involvement of local government authorities in that work increases rapidly. But such public activity is substantially supplemented by voluntary movements. Although primarily conservation-orientated, through organizations such as the National Trust, the County Naturalist Trusts and the Royal Society for the Protection of Birds, the scale of support and the rate of growth of the voluntary movements are remarkable. Conservation was earlier referred to as a spiritual recreation, and it is as though huge numbers of people are expressing, in their support for national parks and nature reserves ('Islands of hope', as they are referred to in the title of an American book) the devotion, concern and willingness to work which must have supported the growth of the early Church.

We pursue these objectives within a framework of statutory designated areas. To protect scenery, we have our National Parks, Areas of Outstanding Natural Beauty and Heritage Coasts. To protect wildlife, we create national and local nature reserves. We protect archaeological monuments and buildings by a variety of conservation orders and management. The designations are backed by administrative arrangements and grants for both public and private owners, to provide the facilities and services needed to care for large numbers of visitors. On a commercial basis some fascinating things have been done. Many of the private pleasure grounds of great houses are now pleasure parks, adapted for use by the public, with museums and shows, displays of exotic animals, and rallies for cars and machinery. A few receive up to a million paying visitors a year.

All that has preceded this, our need and time for recreation, our capacity to use that time, the recreation resources and constraints of our homes, our cities, our holiday resorts, our coasts and countryside, provide a basis for identifying the issues and challenges ahead. But the way ahead is not a clear one. It is our capacity to use recreation time, and the motivations behind it, that makes recreation so diverse and so unpredictable. The availability of money for recreation, or more correctly the propensity to spend money on recreation, is obviously a tremendous influence on it, particularly on holiday-making. National economic well-being must be a dominating influence on the future structure of recreation; because it will widen the options available to individuals, it will enable the providers and managers of resources to do more and it will support more training for recreation. But more recreation must increase the danger of conflicts with other important social and economic issues in society. To reduce these conflicts in future we shall require greater intervention by public authority in decision-making about allocation of resources.

How will conflicting interests be resolved?

Recreation is not regarded as an important party political issue in Britain, despite the importance of leisure time in our life-style, the bewildering diversity of recreation facilities, organization and services, the importance of employment and capital investment in leisure, and apparently the values we place on it (both tangible in terms of expenditure and intangible in terms of attitudes). Party manifestoes are content with a few bland phrases about support for the arts, or sport or National Parks: depending no doubt on who was on the drafting committee. It does not yet seem to be 'meat' to be growled over at party conventions, as is employment or education, or housing or defence: even though estimates of spending on leisure, however rough, link closely to spending on housing and defence. Nor is it yet more than that 'cloud, no bigger than a man's hand' at the great Trades Union Congress.

But the interest of central government in recreation is clearly growing. For example, in the 1960s and early 1970s it led to the commissioning of a variety of reports, such as Wolfenden's on sport,[2] Albemarle's on the youth service,[3] Pilkington's on broadcasting,[4] Russell's on adult education,[5] Sandford's on National Parks;[6] and there has been the recent – a first ever – Select Committee of the House (of Lords) on Sport and Recreation.[7]

In the last decade, on the recommendation of various White Papers, central government has established promotional bodies on countryside conservation and recreation, sport, tourism and the arts. These bodies have powers to distribute grant aid and advise local government, clubs or private entrepreneurs on how to do things. The objective is to provide more facilities, better information, better services and higher standards, to meet growing demands, and to reduce conflicts between the recreation interests and between recreation and other interests.

Major government organizations are involved. There is promotion by the Department of Education and Science of the youth service and adult education; by the Department of the Environment of visits to the ancient monuments and historic buildings it manages; by the Forestry Commission of the use of the public woodlands which it manages; by the British Waterways Board for its canals, etc. The departments and agencies carry out research and conduct studies to provide a basis for better planning and management. They have assembled a wide range of knowledge about recreation, and demonstrated a need for trained and specialist staff which universities, polytechnics, art and agricultural institutes are seeking to meet. New academic disciplines and new professional organizations are also appearing.

The interest of local government in recreation is also growing. There has been a considerable increase in the range of activities undertaken by those authorities with a long tradition of providing parks, libraries, baths and places for assembly. Most local government authorities at metropolitan, county and district levels took the opportunity of local government reform in 1974 to set up leisure departments, either under that or some comparable name. The objective was to coordinate, harmonize and thereby improve services. The by-product is that local government, and central government through its agencies, is developing a new range of professionals in the public services who should be in a position to resolve the conflict of interests of which we have been speaking.

The financing of new recreation facilities and services is a major area of potential conflict. How do we determine the respective fields of interest of commercial forces and public services for leisure? How do we find the resources for more public authority provision?

Of course central government has a strong indirect economic interest in recreation. It takes much revenue from tobacco, drink, gambling, motoring and leisure equipment. It is interested in foreign earnings from tourism, in leisure travel on the railways, in employment that relates to leisure. There are signs that it realizes the importance of promoting recreation as a source of physical and mental well-being. We cannot assess this precisely, but we do know that the cost of our medical services is heavy, and physical and mental sickness are an awful blight on the lives of many of our citizens. We do not know much about the relationship of recreation opportunity to social stability.

Society does not yet, through consensus or political leadership, seem to have clear policy goals for leisure. There are now few aspects of recreation entirely free from a government connection or the power of governmental influence, particularly through taxation; but there are different policies, for different parts of recreation, within different parts of government.

Meanwhile a whole range of important questions remain unanswered. Should existing policies be based on the meeting of demand or of need? It can be argued that it is the under-privileged of the inner city areas who are most in need of the benefits of countryside recreation. But the demand comes from the wealthier car-owning groups. Sports centres, even those accessible to under privileged groups, are mainly used by middle-class family groups and so are many of the art, cultural and educational leisure services. Is this the effect of greater social, intellectual, educational and financial development? How much emphasis should be given in education to preparation for leisure? How much training in leisure activity? How will present horizons be changed by new ideas and new technologies?

Conclusion

Little that is going on in the world today leads one to believe that our urban industrial societies are stable. Indeed, wise and sober counsel, drawing on the increasing knowledge of animal behaviour under confined conditions, questions whether the human animal might not behave even more ferociously if our institutions, our disciplines, our patterns of life come under too much stress. The main threats to this stability are held to be the problems of uninteresting work, unemployment, poverty, crime and violence. How much of a counter to these factors of unrest would be created if more emphasis was given to that greater part of our lives and time devoted not to work but to leisure.[7] More meaningful leisure activities and a wider acceptance of a 'right to recreation' could reduce the significance to us of 'work', and of affluence for its own sake. In leisure, a way of life reflecting more clearly our basic needs and higher potential as human beings could be better realized than, so far, we have been able to achieve in our work. This is perhaps the great and dominating issue in our urban society. It may be our one life-line.

References

1. Outdoor Recreation Resources Review Commission, *Outdoor Recreation for America*, Washington, Government Printing Office, 1962.
2. Central Council of Physical Recreation, *Sport and the Community*, 1961.
3. *The Youth Service in England and Wales. Report of the Committee appointed by the Minister of Education*, London, HMSO, 1960.
4. *Report of the Committee on Broadcasting*, London, HMSO, 1962.
5. *Adult Education: A Plan for Development. Report of a Committee of Inquiry*, London, HMSO, 1973.
6. *Report of the National Parks Policies Review Committee*, London, HMSO, 1974.
7. *First and Second Reports of the Select Committee of the House of Lords on Sport and Leisure*, London, HMSO, 1973.

Chapter 7
Issues in Housing

Town + Country Planning + urban theories

A. A. Nevitt

Introduction

In this chapter a broad examination is made of housing issues and the reasons for government interventions in housing markets. An attempt is made to set housing into a wide socio-political, economic and legal context because it is the author's belief that 'housing' as a subject area reflects all the strengths and weaknesses of a society. It is not an 'industry' which can be analysed simply from an economic viewpoint. If housing is restricted in this way, it degenerates into a study of a commodity like 'hotel rooms' which can be considered in terms of short-run equilibrium prices. If it is viewed too much from the legal side, it becomes little more than a catalogue of statutes, and their interpretation through case law. A sociological approach is equally one-sided as costs are neglected and the possibilities of satisfactorily enforcing good practices by legal methods are seldom considered.

Housing appears by its nature to be a subject for which an intra-disciplinary approach to study is essential. The challenge of maintaining a balance between the various disciplines is very great, and in this essay little more has been done than to point to the complexities and inter-relationships found in the housing field.

Housing shortages

If it be sensible to refer to *the* housing problem it is because a shortage of dwelling space appears to be so inevitably associated with both economic growth and progress towards a more socially just society. The shortages which have arisen during periods of economic growth have been well documented[1] by economic

183

historians and their magnitude and periodicity have been examined by economists[2] whose major interest was in trade cycles rather than housing. In more recent decades with the growth of government interventions in housing markets, the focus of interest has shifted from cyclical studies to an examination of the influence of income distributions and the operation of the filtering process.[3]

The earlier trade cycle studies tended to emphasize the physical aspects of supply; existing stocks and the annual flow of new construction occupied the centre of the stage while the very heterogeneous flows of population from one household unit to another and from one income category to another tended to be treated as a rather ill-defined backcloth to the more measurable changes in physical stocks. In contrast, income-distribution studies tend to treat the physical stock as a flexible resource which can be divided into a multitude of different dwellings of very varied standard, in accordance with the demands generated by the constantly changing locations and incomes of the population.[4]

These two approaches represent different concepts of the way in which housing markets operate and constantly reproduce shortages. Trade cycle models, and their modern equivalent the credit cycle, conceptualize 'housing' as a physical entity very much like other tangible goods which are subject to the laws of demand and supply, and the major characteristic of the housing commodity is given as its high capital costs of production relative to almost all other consumer goods. An important secondary characteristic is the physical limitation on the supply of land, which reinforces imperfect market conditions and gives rise to the payment of monopoly rents. In these models variables identifying credit availability and rates of interest play a dominant role in determining supply costs and bringing supply and demand into equilibrium.

Given this concept of housing markets it will be obvious that if credit is restricted for any reason, the supply of new houses can be expected to fall and the sale of existing houses at going prices to become more difficult. The availability of credit may be regarded as a barometer of the internal health of an economy and the external shocks to which nations are subject. Thus, if an economy has been experiencing a period of rapid economic growth which has led to rising employment, profits and wages with a consequential deflection of goods from exports to home consumption, interest rates may rise in adjustment to a balance of payments deficit and thereby restrict house-building activities. Wars, which traditionally impose a deflection of credit availability as governments increase the quantum of national debt, also have immediate and constricting effects upon house construction.

Econometric studies of housing starts, interest rate movements and aggregate credit supplies have shown that there is a close association between credit availability and house starts. It is from these studies of housing markets that the links between increasing local economic activity can be observed (the development of Glasgow in the nineteenth century for example), and increases in demand for dwellings via increases in wages and profits. Increases in demand cannot be expected to correspond exactly with the start of a trade cycle 'upturn', since rising wages must be fully established and some migration occur before rising demand for more, and better, housing space begins to manifest itself in an increase in effective demand. When that moment arrives builders respond by increasing house starts and incidentally increasing demands for labour in the expanding locality. With the passage of time economic variables change; the development of new factories comes to a halt as supply outruns demand for the output of the manufacturing sector and/or interest rates rise to intolerable levels. At this stage in the trade cycle the supply of new houses will start to fall well before all the housing need generated by the original and migrant populations of the expanded locality has been met.

This gloomy picture of the way in which housing markets operate explains why the housing conditions of the urban working class deteriorated during the century following the industrial revolution. The growth of housing shortages was not due to a particularly low average rate of building, but to the fluctuations which occurred in the trade cycle. The downturn of a cycle caused bankruptcies amongst builders and houses could only be sold at reduced prices which did not cover the costs of construction. In free market situations there was a tendency for peaks to occur simultaneously in the number of vacant properties *and* the number of households which were overcrowded.[5] The overcrowding was caused by the sudden drop in the incomes of wage earners and the high vacancy rates were a symptom of the imperfections of the market. The 'stickiness' of rents has been discussed by Turvey[6] as an aspect of rent determination in profit-maximizing market situations; it is also important in connection with the very considerable imperfections introduced into housing markets by discrimination in favour of tenants able to produce references attesting to their rent-paying ability and other desirable social characteristics.[7]

Turning now to the second concept of housing markets, we start, not with a house as a physical structure of bricks and mortar, but with 'housing' as a collection of intangible legal rights which give access to land and the buildings, or parts of buildings, thereon. These rights of occupation are saleable and each individual in society has either an indirect or a direct natural right (a right by virtue of absolute physical necessity) to occupy some land however small. (An example of an indirect right is that which is available to children as a result of the duty falling on parents to support their offspring.) The value of the security of a legal right to occupy a piece of land depends upon the income and wealth of each purchaser and shortages are caused by unequal distribution of incomes, which in extreme conditions means that some people have no income, and others have barely enough for the smallest and most inadequate forms of shelter.

In this model of the major characteristics of housing markets, the cause of housing shortage is found not only in the maldistribution of incomes and wealth, but also in legal ignorance. For the great mass of any national population 'law' and custom are hopelessly confused; illiterate people may migrate from ancient village settlements where each individual obtains shelter by well-established social usage to modern urban settlements in which custom no longer holds sway and the acquisition of legal forms of tenure are beyond their reach, not only because of poverty but also through illiteracy and general ignorance. The populations of shanty towns and squatters' enclaves in developing third-world countries are examples of the great social problems which arise when property ownership and occupation rights are not available to a large substratum of society.

It will be clear that while these two concepts of the housing market are profoundly different they explain the same phenomenon of housing shortage. In the 'physical' concept, changing money incomes play an important role in determining changes in demand; in the 'right to occupation' concept, it is recognized that income distributions change over the trade cycle and, at the crest of each cycle, the dispersion of incomes is more favourable than at any other time, and higher incomes and full employment generate effective demands for the subdivision of land and the construction of additional dwellings. The two schools of thought therefore use the same variables and reach much the same conclusions with respect to the analysis of markets. However, they differ considerably in terms of the policies they recommend for overcoming the shortages which are the outcome of their respective models. On the whole, the supporters of the physical model think that shortages may most readily be overcome by (*a*) the removal of fluctuations in the price and availability of credit, and (*b*) a reduction in market imperfections such as monopolization of building materials production, unionization and limitation of skilled manpower, and the reduction of barriers to the acquisition of land.

The 'right to occupation' school stresses the importance of (*a*) redistributing incomes and wealth, and (*b*) the introduction of legal forms of protection (e.g. statutory statements of tenants' rights, rent controls, the establishment of a public health housing inspectorate), and (*c*) the provision of dwellings by non-profit making organizations. Like so many public and academic controversies, these two views on the causes of housing shortages appear on close examination to be like the opposite sides of the same coin. If the whole is to be understood, both sides must be taken into account. In a sense, the 'right to occupation' approach is prior to the 'physical' approach, because it contains within the model the social objective of providing adequate housing (hence an adequate income and adequate tenancy laws) for everyone;

the 'physical' approach only explains one of several reasons why this objective has so far been unobtainable.

Regional variations in standards

Since incomes, and until very recent years, credit availability have varied from place to place, both standards of housing and the relative extent of housing shortage vary from one locality to another. Cities which have been particularly subjected to local industrial specialization (mining, shipbuilding and textiles, for example), over long periods of time, reflect trade cycles in booms and slumps of house-building activity more dramatically than cities or regions which derive their income from a wide range of industrial and/or commercial activities. Since present urban environments are largely a reflection of the earlier history of a locality, housing conditions retain the imprint of earlier decades of industrial strife, unequal opportunities and incomes, and national and local housing policies, long after the reasons which gave rise to the differences have ceased to exist.

Despite the great social, political and economic importance of local distributions of incomes we are still profoundly ignorant about them. A detailed examination of data from the Family Expenditure Surveys for the period 1957–72 by Roberti[8] gives a crude measure of the very wide differences which exist between one region of the United Kingdom and another. Roberti divided the size distribution given by FES data into income deciles and examined the characteristics of households within each decile. I have averaged his data for the three years 1970–72 to obtain some idea of the household income variations which operated over that period. Figure 10 shows the results for the two regions of the UK (Greater London and Northern Ireland) which represent the extremes of wealth and poverty. The graph is drawn on the assumption that if incomes were distributed similarly in all regions, each income decile would have the same proportion of population. Thus, according to FES data, Greater London contained 12·39 per cent of the total UK population of households; each decile might therefore be expected to contain approximately 12·5 per cent of

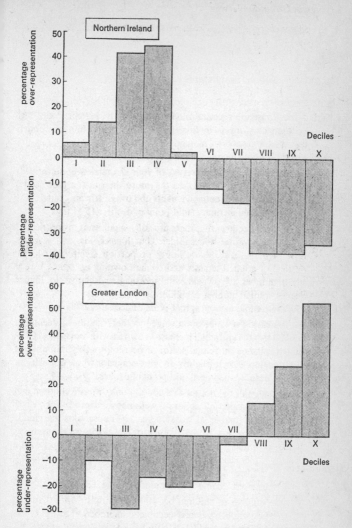

10 Distribution of household incomes by income deciles, 1970–72

Major characteristics of households in each income decile
Notes to Figure 10

Deciles

I Most households contain only one elderly person. Very few children or workers in this decile. High proportion of council tenants and owners owning outright.
1972 household income at mid-point of decile, £9·37 p.w.

II Households mainly composed of retired married couples. Still very few children or workers but more than in the first decile. High proportion of council tenants and owners owning outright.
1972 household income at mid-point of decile, £15·51 p.w.

III A marginal decile in that there are still a significant proportion of elderly and retired householders, but households with workers now in a majority. A declining proportion (relative to lower deciles) of council tenants and owners owning outright. A very small number of owners with mortgages. Relative to higher deciles, a small number of children.
1972 household income at mid-point of decile, £22·78 p.w.

IV An increasing reliance upon wage incomes, continued decline in council tenants and small increase in owners with mortgages. Continued reliance on rented sector of housing market. Number of children increase, to slightly above average for whole population.
1972 household income at mid-point of decile, £29·75 p.w.

V More than half the households contain one or more children and the total number of children well above average for whole population. Number of workers per 100 households marginally above average for whole population. Majority of households living in rented accommodation, but proportion owning with a mortgage increasing rapidly both over time (from 1963–1972) and relative to lower deciles.
1972 household income at mid-point of decile, £35·96 p.w.

VI Largest number of children per 100 households. More than half of the householders owner-occupiers. Number of workers per household just exceeds 1·5. Number of dependent adults and children per 100 households higher for this decile than any other.
1972 household income at mid-point of decile, £41·96 p.w.

Notes to Figure 10 continued

VII These two deciles contain more children than the average of the
& whole population but only an average number of dependants
VIII (adult plus children) as more than half the households contain
a working married woman. The majority of householders are
owner-occupiers and the proportion of council tenants appears
to be falling over time. In these two deciles households containing
three or more workers become significant (more than 10 per cent
of the total).

VIIth 1972 household income at mid-point of decile, £48·49 p.w.

VIIIth 1972 household income at mid-point of decile, £56·40 p.w.

IX There is a substantial drop in the number of children per household, a large majority of married women work and there are, on
average, just over two workers per household. Middle-class
occupations of more significance than in lower deciles. A higher
than, statistically, expected proportion of this decile group is
resident in the Greater London area.

1972 household income at mid-point of decile, £68·70 p.w.

X Households in this decile contain more people and workers than
other deciles, but fewer children and adult dependants. Many
more of these households are resident in Greater London than
would be expected if they were distributed according to their
proportion in the national population. This reflects the relatively
large proportion of professional and managerial occupations.
A large proportion are owner-occupiers but there is a small
proportion of council tenants which does not appear to be
declining over time, in spite of the predominance of white-collar
workers. Married women in this decile are slightly less likely to be
working than those in the eighth and ninth deciles.

1972 household income at mid-point of decile, £99·84 p.w.

Source: *FES Reports* 1970–72

London households. However, an examination of the data shows
that over the 1970–72 period only about 9·5 per cent of the lowest
income decile households were Londoners and there was therefore
a shortfall in the representation of this group in the bottom decile
of about 24 per cent. On the other hand, in the top decile Londoners
were over-represented by almost 53 per cent. In Northern Ireland
the opposite situation occurs: the lower half of the deciles had an

over-representation of households, while the upper half was severely under-represented. The graph shows that the one distribution is almost a mirror image of the other.

There are three main reasons for these differences in income distributions. First, there are variations in demographic characteristics amongst local populations that have often been determined by long-term patterns of inward and outward migration, but can sometimes be produced by long-term differences in birth and mortality rates. Secondly, there have been short-term differences in rates of unemployment. These differences are a reflection of the industrial structure of different regions and the natural advantages of different localities. Thirdly, there have been substantial differences in economic activity rates. These relate both to economic and social factors and have tended to change very slowly over time. When local employment opportunities for one sex are very low, migration of either men or women leads to a considerable imbalance of population with consequent changes in the demand for dwellings, not only in the exporting, but also in the receiving area, where accommodation for single people who are predominantly of one sex may cause local market difficulties.[9]

Occupational differences in conjunction with differences in employment opportunities and industrial structure also cause differences in the distribution of income between one region and another. For instance, in London the high proportion of households found to be in the tenth decile group is explained by the relatively high number of persons employed in the professional, administrative, executive and managerial occupations (see Figure 8). It is only in Greater London and the rest of the South-East* regions that households are over-represented in the tenth decile. The North, Yorkshire/Humberside, East Midlands, East Anglia, South-West, Wales and Scotland are all under-represented in the tenth decile to a greater extent than in any others. The regions most over-represented in the first decile are the North, Yorkshire/ Humberside and the East Midlands; Wales is most over-represented in the sixth decile and Scotland in the third.

* These are the standard regions for statistical purposes as defined in the *Abstract of Regional Statistics*, 1972.

As this essay is on housing issues, our central concern is not with the equity of these differences in regional distributions; indeed, insufficient evidence has been presented to allow a considered judgement on the degree of social justice attained. The differences must, however, be taken into account when considering the outcome of economic markets for dwellings. Given the costs of building a minimum standard dwelling (relative to the average income of occupiers), we know that in Britain new houses will not be built by private enterprise for people with incomes below the sixth decile and, if land costs are included, only potential customers from the top two income deciles are likely to be adequately served. These decile groups are over-represented in the West Midlands, Greater London and the rest of the South-East, and builders may therefore be expected to build fairly heavily in these areas for the private sector. *Per contra*, in the North, Wales, Scotland and Northern Ireland less can be expected from the private sector.

It will be noted that the above conclusion does not depend upon the existence of a physical shortage of dwellings. It is based upon the assumptions that costs of building differ less from region to region than income distributions owing to similarities in the cost of capital, raw materials and the wage rates of building operations, and that the demand for new dwellings can only be made effective when the income of households is sufficient to cover the costs of construction. This view of the operation of a free-enterprise market in dwellings represents the backcloth against which government interventions occur to remedy 'shortages'. In the first part of this essay it was suggested that shortages arose out of credit cycles and unfavourable distributions of income. In this discussion of regional differences in income the general discussion has been brought down to a rather more micro level, in which it should have become apparent that at each stage in a credit cycle the local impact of housing market operations will differ markedly. In the northern region, for example, where the distribution of income is very skewed towards the bottom five deciles, a building boom could be expected to start later than one in the South-East and come to an end sooner. Thus, relative to the number of lower-income householders, there would be fewer second-hand houses into which poorer households could filter, as the better-off people took advantage of the boom and moved to new homes. With each succeeding generation, assuming that the unfavourable distribution of income remains, the relative shortfall of modern houses would increase. In areas where income distribution was more favourable, for instance in the South-East, a relatively greater supply of new houses and a more active use of the filtering process would occur as house-building booms lasted longer and the exceptionally high proportion of better-off people vacated houses into which poorer people could move.

These purely economic aspects of housing markets generate different political and social attitudes. In many localities the income distribution is such that approximately 60 to 70 per cent of the residents can afford to buy their own houses; social and political attitudes then seem to harden into an emotional defence of owner-occupation as the most satisfactory form of housing provision. When incomes are not favourably distributed, demands are generated for government intervention in housing markets and the provision of financial aid and/or the public ownership of dwellings. These socio-political attitudes have created the conflicts over housing policies which have been such a characteristic of British politics since the industrial revolution. Unhappily, those who debate housing issues seldom realize how large the differences are in the regional distributions of income, and how a solution which is relevant to one distribution may be totally inappropriate to another.

While such regional comparisons are useful indicators of spatial variations in income, they are, however, less meaningful as a framework for pursuing corrective policies than studies undertaken at a more local level of inquiry. Greater London, for example, should at least be divided into the sub-localities defined by the Metropolitan boroughs; similarly, Northern Ireland is too heterogeneous a region to be a useful unit for market analysis. Nevertheless, it is hoped that the importance of, and variation in, income distributions has been established in the above discussion.

Government intervention in housing markets

Governments intervene in housing markets for four quite separate and distinct reasons. They are given below in order of their importance in the housing field, although the ordering may not necessarily accord with their macro-economic or political importance.

1. The creation of property rights[10]

Rights to real estate (land, buildings, fishing rights, etc.) require government definition. If the 'ownership' of land is simply thought of as like the ownership of carrots or cloth, most modern urban problems become insignificant and the solution to the problems that remain are found in manipulation of market supply and demand curves. But from time immemorial land has been regarded as a special good which may not be freely bought and sold, because of its general association with ideas about the 'common good'. At its simplest, this meant that the possession of land was associated with certain duties and the failure to perform these duties could lead to forfeiture. In modern times it has meant that the uses to which land may be put are strictly controlled by society through the implementation of 'plans', both wide-ranging structural plans and the more specific approvals which must be obtained by landowners before the demolition, enlargement or new construction of buildings.

A second important feature of the occupation of land is that enforceable agreements are made, which by their nature relate to the future fulfilment of certain obligations. This places upon governments not only the duty of providing Courts of Law, but also of laying down such rules as may seem appropriate to guide the decision of judges. From a general concern that the occupation rights of one individual should not be undermined by trespass, or the taking away of natural light, support, or water supply by a neighbouring land owner, governments have in the post-feudal age gradually extended their patronage and protection to those who have been regarded as 'defenceless' or in a weak bargaining

195

position. These protections range from the imposition of minimum building standards which reduce the dangers of fire or collapse of buildings, to the protection of the interests of widows.[11] The best known of these protective groups of statutes are those relating to public health in housing and the Rent Control and Regulation Acts. Recent interventions of this kind are to be found in the statutes which prohibit discrimination in the housing field on the grounds of sex or race.

When all the protective statutes are considered as a whole it seems very likely that on balance they have marginally increased the demand for dwellings and have quite radically reduced the supply. This follows from the costs involved in the protective statutes, which fall primarily on the suppliers of dwellings whether they be landlords or builders. Soundly constructed, low-density houses built to Parker Morris space and heating standards[12] will quite obviously cost more to construct than very high-density jerry-built tenements with insufficient natural light and only primitive plumbing and heating equipment. Similarly, if rents are controlled below market levels, the return to landlords will be lower than other non-controlled market investments and landlords will attempt to shift their investments to alternative outlets and thereby reduce the supply of rented accommodation.

This consequence of governmental creation of property rights has been mitigated over the last century by government-organized increases in supply. These two aspects of housing policy should always be seen together but are all too often divorced. When, for example, under the Rent Act 1974 furnished tenants were given security of tenure, it was quite clear that this would create a 'shortage' of furnished lettings, and strictly speaking the protection should not have been given without the introduction of complementary arrangements for meeting the shortfall in supply.

2. Government aids to the disadvantaged

Until very recent years the major method of rectifying unfavourable distributions of incomes has been through the mechanism of social security payments. These benefits have had a major impact on households in the bottom two income deciles. These two deciles are primarily composed of retired single householders (the lowest decile), and retired couples, the sick, unemployed and one-parent families (the second decile). In the nineteenth century it was these two groups of householders who were particularly vulnerable to the most acute forms of poverty and to eviction. Today they are able to retain their homes because of the availability of social security.

As to the supply of dwellings the main thrust has of course been through the provision of 'public' subsidized dwellings by local authorities. This public provision has been complemented by a variety of government actions which have safeguarded the supply of private enterprise dwellings for the richest half of the population. These include:

1. The enforcement of standards of financial management on building societies.

2. Grants to building societies so that interest rates may be kept below market rates or to encourage the purchase of pre-1919 houses (formerly rented).

3. The abolition of taxation on the imputed rental income of home ownership while retaining the taxpayer's right to deduct mortgage interest from gross income before calculating taxable income.

4. The provision of mortgages to owner-occupiers by local authorities and the provision of improvement grants to owners and private landlords.

5. The exemption of the residential home from Capital Gains Tax.

6. The sale of local authority dwellings to 'sitting tenants' or newly married couples at a substantial discount from the market price.

7. The designation of land by planners for housing for owner occupiers and the utilization of public powers of compulsory purchase to acquire development land on which owner-occupied houses may be built.

When these seven major forms of assistance to the wealthier

sections of the population are combined with local authority building for the poorer groups, it may seem strange that housing shortages still persist. There are, however, two problems which have so far frustrated government attempts to eradicate shortages created in past generations and to prevent new ones from arising.

The first problem relates once again to the uneven distribution of income within any one town or locality, and the differences between localities. If the figures for Northern Ireland and Greater London are reconsidered it may be easier to understand this stage in the argument.

In Ireland, the exceptionally high proportion of low-income households means that the supply of local authority dwellings may have to reach about 65 per cent of the total before all individuals unable to purchase a house on the terms and conditions laid down by building societies have obtained satisfactory rented accommodation. (Note that in Northern Ireland, 63 per cent of households had less than the UK median income in 1970–72.) If the assumptions are made that each local authority house is subsidized, capital for the building programme is borrowed at market rates of interest, and that the occupiers of local authority dwellings are the poorest 65 per cent of the population, and therefore by definition are unable to afford to pay full-cost rents for their dwellings, the cost of supplying these dwellings (in relation to the relatively small number of people rich enough to pay taxes to meet the subsidies) is bound to be high. Furthermore, public housing is, by definition, in competition with all other government expenditure (education, health, defence, etc.) for funds. In theory, if only 20 per cent of a population required public housing, a stock of this size might be supplied over a period of approximately twenty years; but, with a requirement for a stock representing 65 per cent of the total, a much longer period (about fifty years) is required. Moreover, to achieve this, it is necessary to have political approval for a constant building programme, which must be planned and executed efficiently. However, in practice, as costs of provision rise, and historical circumstances and attitudes to social deprivation change, building programmes also change, and before sufficient dwellings have been provided for a poorer than average region, changes in subsidies and building starts have been introduced and have perpetuated shortages. This 'stop and go' aspect of public housing politics was well described by Churchill in 1921 when he wrote of the collapse of the post-1913 building programme, that until April 1921 determined efforts had been made to accelerate the programme, but by August

we had cast aside our housing policy and were vehemently directing ourselves to 'anti-waste', building operations were everywhere curtailed and new ones prevented, local authorities who in the preceding quarters had been lashed to the utmost exertions were now whipped off and ordered to shut down.[13]

Turning now to the housing consequences of an income distribution such as the one portrayed in the graph for Greater London, a rather different aspect of the difficulties of housing markets and the allocation of government assistance may be examined. Because of the relatively high incomes which can be obtained in a capital city and other major commercial and industrial centres such as the Birmingham/Coventry complex, there is a very high demand for land in these centres. Acute competition for what is available forces up land prices and (relative to those prices) the position of householders in the bottom four income deciles may become even more acute than the position of similarly placed people in regions where sluggish demand results in low land prices. To meet the needs of all the low-income householders in the Greater London region it may therefore be necessary to have at least 40 per cent of the total stock in the public sector. It is difficult, however, to attain this overall figure because of the wide variations in income distribution within such large cities. On the one hand, some of the outer London suburban authorities are able to satisfy their housing needs from a relatively low stock which meets the requirements of elderly people with minimal pension incomes and the needs generated by a relatively small proportion of unskilled manual workers. On the other hand inner boroughs, with a traditional predominance of manual workers, can only overcome housing shortages if virtually all individuals have access to subsidized housing. In a third, mixed type of authority, where the very wealthy and very poor live side by side, the conflicts between private owner-occupation and public provision develop into something akin to open political warfare. This is because of the exceptionally high costs of provision in these localities and the political pressures which arise in marginal constituencies where people of different socio-economic classes live in adjacent neighbourhoods.

The overall high costs of providing dwellings and the experience of irreconcilable political pressures have made it impossible for London to achieve a balance between supply and demand which is sufficient to avoid major shortages. Given the constant growth and decline of individual households, the mobility of workers, the deterioration of particular dwellings and the re-utilization of land as one use becomes obsolete and a new one is required, it would be utopian to expect a perfect match between dwellings and households; but the imperfections of the London relationship between supply and demand would appear to be unnecessarily great, and to stem from an unwillingness to share the available land supply in an equitable fashion.

The second major factor which inhibits government attempts to increase supply and protect the interests of lower income groups is the simple, but very real and much neglected physical shortage of convenient land, building materials and skilled labour. By convenient land is meant land which is both conveniently located and fully provided with public services (roads, drainage, etc.). The limited supply of such land means that new dwellings can often only be provided by clearing away old ones; this in turn means that many of the dwellings built by local authorities are only replacements rather than net additions to the housing stock. Later in this essay the question of whether *all* the houses demolished in slum clearance and urban renewal programmes should have been demolished will be discussed, but here it must be established that there could not have been a large-scale development of local authority housing unless a large number of old dwellings had not first been pulled down.

3. Regional and physical planning policies

The disparity between regional levels of unemployment and the quality and quantity of the stock of social and industrial capital has for long been a matter of considerable concern to British governments. Many different policies have been introduced to counteract the tendency for regional disparities in income and employment to widen over time as the industrial structure of the nation changes. The data already given on regional distributions of household incomes show the relative lack of success of these policies in so far as the primary purpose was to achieve equality of opportunity for the people of different regions. However, notwithstanding the limited success of the policies of subsidizing industry and employment in development areas, regional policies, taken with central government methods of subsidizing local authority expenditure on social capital and current expenditure on local services, have had a significant impact on the housing standards achieved in the poorer regions. In the absence of a policy designed to achieve at least some element of territorial justice,[14] housing standards could be expected to reflect the total range of incomes; that the housing conditions of the British people are much more narrowly dispersed than incomes, is primarily due to the attempts of British governments over the period 1919–76 to direct housing subsidies to those areas in which social distress was greatest, and to impose national standards which were for the most part determined by reference to physical needs rather than the economic ability of tenants or local tax payers to pay the costs.

The determination of physical standards appears to have been an amalgam of the urban philosophy which under-pinned nineteenth-century developments of model villages and garden suburbs, public health regulations, road widths and traffic requirements, and perceptions of the role of the home in the life of a family and the varying needs of the members of each family.[15] The high ideals which motivated many of the politicians, town planners and architects responsible for laying down housing standards were, unhappily, not always realized in the design and execution of housing projects. The lack of success seems to have been due in large measure to a lack of commitment to the full social objectives involved and to pathetically low levels of architectural aesthetic imagination. The absence of egalitarian ideals led many councillors to accept the view that local authority houses and flats should be differentiated from private sector dwellings, and in some cases should be so markedly different that any casual passer-by could identify the 'public' and 'private' houses and associate the former with the worst part of town and the latter with the best.

The lack of architectural talent is more difficult to explain. Part of the problem may lie in the fact that, from the earliest development of council housing, estates tended to be large and the constant repetition of a few simple designs tended to create a sense of visual boredom and inferiority. An alternative explanation, frequently put forward by the architectural profession itself, is the method by which central governments have controlled the capital cost of council housing programmes and in particular the ceiling costs which are imposed by Whitehall. There can be little doubt that the method of subsidizing council housing has had a very deleterious effect on local decision-making processes because it splits the responsibility for the design and costs of a particular project between central and local government and each may blame the other for failures. But pure ugliness and the error of building very expensive high-rise flats for families accustomed to life in terraced houses cannot be blamed upon a mechanism of cost control; and at the risk of being regarded as unwisely provocative it seems fair to say that some of the failure of British housing policy over the last fifty years has been a reflection of British class divisions and poor architectural work.

The regulation of land use and the determination of housing densities may be an important exception to the criticisms made above. An examination by Glen Drover[16] of the planning densities laid down in London and New York suggested that in London a very much more egalitarian view prevailed than in New York, where planners appeared to follow the market. In Britain, regulations relating to density appear to have been used much more consciously to counteract market forces and to cut off the peak of high densities which competition for central city land generates in a market situation. However, it still seems true to say that, in Britain, council dwellings are likely to be built to a much higher density than most private enterprise housing.

The relatively low densities imposed on new developments in Britain are a reflection of the British preference for single family houses with gardens. This preference has found expression in the Garden City movement and the development of new towns in the post-war period. These traditions have been strengthened by other planning motivations such as the designation of green belts and the preservation of open space. These town planning regulations have undoubtedly increased the opportunity for many people to enjoy a pleasant environment which combines many of the desirable features of both town and country. However, they have also contributed to the problems of inner city areas in two main respects. First, they have diverted social expenditure on schools, roads, etc., to outer areas and away from city centres. Secondly, they have tended to draw away the younger, richer and more mobile section of the population particularly those associated with the fifth to ninth income deciles. This leaves the lowest income groups in the first to the fourth income deciles confined to the inner areas of cities where their combined purchasing power is too low to remedy the environmental deficiencies accumulated over a century or more.

The issue which is raised by this discussion of regional and physical planning policies is the distribution of resources to territorial areas. In a mixed economy social investment must include both public and private investment activities and if governments wish to equalize housing and environmental standards over the country, they must not only direct public investment to the most deprived areas but also seek to match the private investment carried out in prosperous regions.

So far in this essay I have analysed housing markets with the use of a very simple market model which assumes that income levels determine demand functions and that supply is a production function determined by the cost and availability of land, credit, capital equipment, raw materials and labour. This model has been fully reflected in the stress I have given to income distributions. If, however, we are to obtain a more rounded understanding of the way markets function, social behaviour must be explicitly introduced into the market model. This might be done by introducing the concept of market imperfections which place constraints upon market forces and create shortages which cannot be justified in terms of a physical absence of productive factors. One example of such an imperfection is the discrimination against coloured immigrants which was fairly widespread in the late fifties and sixties.[17]

HOUSING PREFERENCES AND THE PRESERVATION OF COMMUNITIES

It is important that demographic statistics should be collected and the structure of housing demands be monitored in a way which relates household characteristics (size, age of head of household, race, etc.) with incomes *and* people's housing preferences. Housing preferences have been much neglected in the development of social indicators of housing stress. Many of these indicators place far too much emphasis upon the easily measurable physical characteristics of houses, for example, the availability of prescribed amenities, or the age of the houses. Such indicators tell us little, if anything, about the quality of the stock of dwellings and nothing about its improvability and/or desirability. Similarly, statistics which measure rates of occupation and 'indicate' levels of under-occupation disregard the economic demand for space and the association which exists between space occupied and the general quality of domestic levels of living.

More satisfactory groups of social indicators can identify neighbourhoods of housing stress where government intervention is required. However, such indicators cannot be dealt with in isolation from the reactions of householders or the officials whose function it is to remedy housing shortages and maintain and improve environmental standards. This means that if a central agency collects statistics relating to housing conditions nationally, these statistics should not be elevated to the status of social indicators until they have been subjected to local examination and tested against local knowledge and housing aspirations. The refinement of social indicators is a long and painstaking process in which the concepts of housing stress or housing need are gradually clarified by repeated attempts to make accurate identification of local conditions. Thus, if census material is used to identify enumeration districts of special need, it is not sufficient to know from the data that these districts differ from others; it is also necessary to know whether local people regard the identified districts as being in need of special assistance and the form that the assistance should take. Technically, if sufficient effort were made it should be possible by an iterative process to refine indicators to an extent which would make it possible for central governments to respond to changes in local conditions as they arose. At present this is not possible because such indicators as we have are very imperfect measures of housing stress and because they are unrelated to any model of the way urban markets operate. They therefore give no guidance on the types of solution which might be applied to the problems being measured.

The divorce between problems and solutions might be illustrated by reference to the controversy which has arisen over rehabilitation versus urban renewal. Much of the controversy appears to be due to different focuses of attention. When Lionel Needleman[18] drew attention to the weaknesses of a subsidy system which led to widespread demolitions, he was stating little more than the ancient truth that every economic decision should be taken in the light of local circumstances and current factor prices. The subsidy system limited the range of choice open to local decision-makers largely because subsidies were given for *slum clearance*. Local authorities therefore had an incentive to renew rather than to rehabilitate dwellings.

This would be a demonstrably absurd subsidy policy if it were both contrary to the wishes of the inhabitants and uneconomic in the sense that after improvements had been made to the old houses these would have provided dwellings as satisfactory as, but at lower cost than, newly constructed ones. It does not follow from this, however, that there is a conflict between rehabilitation and renewal; on the contrary, it suggests that both options should be used where appropriate and that 'appropriateness' must be judged by both economic and social factors. The measurable economic factors are the influence of interest rates on decisions to invest in assets with varying life spans and the relative costs of renewal and rehabilitation. The social factors are less easily measured. When a large area is redeveloped, the surrounding neighbourhoods suffer from the dereliction and the disruption which accompanies population loss. Individuals are often reluctant to move and may agree to do so only after great protest; shopkeepers lose their livelihood; and owner-occupiers feel doubly deprived when they have to move, as they both lose their family home and a valued capital asset. Relatively few of the hardships caused by large-scale redevelopment projects are fully compensated for or indeed could be; it is therefore very important that they are only imposed upon people when there are very clear benefits to be obtained by the removal of existing urban structures. The debates on these issues, and the increasing organization of local pressure groups against radical urban renewal programmes, have focused attention on the vulnerability of urban structures to irreversible ecological damage and to the importance of regarding urban complexes as living organisms which should be gradually and sympathetically developed towards a more perfect state, and not subjected to violent surgery which destroys both the social and economic well-being of the inhabitants.

4. Monetary and fiscal policy

The impact of the combined monetary and fiscal instruments of macro-economic controls is of course of paramount importance in housing markets. All industries must continually adjust their activities to changing macro-economic environments and can be encouraged to expand or induced to contract by changes in money supply (via credit availability and interest rates) or taxes imposed upon profits, the factors of production, or the commodities produced. Of all industries, however, housing seems to be the one most seriously affected by changing economic environments and particularly by sudden shocks to the credit or tax structure.

The great expansion in the money supply over the 1970/71 to 1974/5 period is now generally acknowledged to have caused a wholly inefficient inflation in property prices and a catastrophic increase in interest rates. According to the House of Commons Expenditure Committee,[19] over this period £1000 million was added to government expenditure on housing which had not been foreseen at the time when government expenditure plans were made. An essay on housing issues is not the place to consider these matters in any detail, but it is appropriate to draw attention to two essential consequences of credit mismanagement. The first is that it is particularly disruptive of housing markets, the second that it creates economic hardships (via income redistribution from non-wealth holders to wealth holders) which require counter-balancing fiscal measures. These measures may in turn have an adverse affect on housing markets.

Fiscal policies affect housing via the level of direct taxes, and indirectly housing policies affect the total revenue to be raised through taxation. Until the Second World War housing was considered to be of particular importance because rent constituted the largest single item of expenditure in family budgets; but this is not so today, when the largest item of expenditure is direct taxation (national insurance contributions and income tax). The growth in housing costs and taxation over the period 1959–72 is given for a one-child family with an income at the mid-point of the fifth income decile, in Figure 11. Incomes have been computed from FES Reports[20] and a one-child tenant family with a sole earner has been selected for examination since this is fairly typical of the household structure of the fifth decile income group. The estimated housing costs have been based on the net average rents charged by the LCC/GLC for inter-war two-bedroom flats. The rent is therefore fairly 'low' for London, but is more or less in line with provincial rents.

The income of the selected household lies at the 45th percentile (the mid-point of the fifth income decile) and represents a typical semi-skilled manual wage earner's position. If all households containing non-working adults were extracted from the data, and only employed heads of households placed into the distribution of incomes, the selected family would be at approximately the

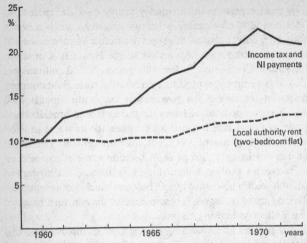

11 Taxes and rents as a percentage of gross incomes of one-child families with incomes at the 45th percentile of household (UK) incomes

35th percentile. The family may therefore be regarded as relatively poor both in relation to the whole UK population, and to the population of workers.

The unsubsidized housing costs for such a family were approximately twice as high as the rent charged, but if tax is taken as 'given' and rents were to double, the effect on any family would have been that about 45 per cent of its income would have been allocated to direct income taxes and housing; to this figure about 8 per cent should be added for general and water rates, leaving approximately half the family's income for all other expenditure.

No one familiar with the budgets of these households would expect them to be able to purchase all necessary food, fuel, clothing etc. if they retained only half their gross wage for these items.* Housing costs have therefore been subsidized more and more heavily as taxes on incomes have risen. It may be thought

* In 1970 the 45th percentile income was £1,540 per year; if income tax, NI contributions, net rents and general and water rates had absorbed 50 per cent of this income, the family would have been left with £770 for all

absurd to keep rents below economic cost levels and impose taxes on families enjoying housing subsidies, and indeed it is a highly inefficient 'Mad Hatter's Tea Party' combination of policies. It has been allowed to occur for a variety of reasons, most of which relate to the inefficiency of government systems of decision-making.

From the above, the manner in which taxation policies affect housing subsidies should be clear. Few people could have afforded to be owner-occupiers in the last fifty years if some reduction in tax had not been made available to those buying houses. The concessions which have been made to owners (infrequent valuations for Schedule A tax on the imputed rental value of their homes, and the abolition of this tax in 1961) has had the effect of eroding the tax base and raising the rate of taxes in general, with the burden of taxes falling on tenants in particular. This makes it more difficult for tenants to pay the cost rent of their dwellings and subsidies to this sector have increased with tax burdens; this has in turn raised central government taxes and local rates, making it still more difficult for individuals to pay for their housing.

---

other expenditures. The SBC weekly benefits (from November 1970) were £8.50 plus £1.80 for a married couple with one child aged five to ten. This SB income of £10.30 per week (approximately £536 per year) could be supplemented by a long-term addition of £26 per year and the disregard of small capital sums owned by recipients. In real value terms the benefit was further increased by eligibility for means-tested schemes such as free school meals and exemption from prescription charges. Added together this gives an estimated real level of living roughly equivalent to an income of around £600 per year. From the given workers' income of £770, net of taxes and housing costs, approximately £100 should be deducted for work expenses (transport, union dues, meals away from home, work clothes, etc.) giving the working family an income of approximately £70 per year or 12 per cent more than the real level of living of similar non-working families on SB. The question of whether or not this would be too low a differential is of course a matter of opinion; however, SB levels are commonly regarded as very low indeed and many families living at this level have the utmost difficulty in keeping their expenditure in step with their income.

In setting council rents well below the level necessary to cover costs of supply, local authorities are tacitly acknowledging that their ordinary tenants cannot afford to pay half their income on taxes and housing, and as taxes cannot apparently be reduced house rents have been kept low and thereby offset some of the 'burden' of taxes.

Once a circular system has been generated it is very difficult to break into it and inhibit the feed-back effects. However, taxes now fall on even the poorest working families and it might be possible to lower taxes and simultaneously increase rents. An adjustment of the tax relief on interest paid by owner-occupiers might be made as part of a package deal between government and people. The state might agree to manage the money supply more effectively so that interest rates would be tolerable; owner-occupiers would then accept as a quid pro quo that tax relief on mortgage interest was an inefficient method of subsidizing housing.

From this very brief discussion of the housing issues raised by monetary and fiscal policies, it may be thought that British housing policies have been operating in an environment in which failure was certain. A recently published book was given the title *Housing: the Great British Failure*[21] and much comment in British housing literature would suggest that this is a widely held opinion on the record of events. This seems not only an unduly pessimistic view, but also an inaccurate one to the extent that it cannot be supported by the evidence and it lacks all sense of historical perspective.

In order to end this essay on a more cheerful note, data is given that shows the distribution of British households by tenure and income deciles. From Figure 12 it will be clear that over 90 per cent of British households are living in 'protected' sectors of the market of one sort or another (as owner-occupiers, local authority tenants, members of housing associations and other privately rented 'controlled' or 'regulated' properties) and less than 7 per cent still use the least satisfactory sector in which the tenancy of the accommodation is either a short-term furnished letting, or is tied to the employment.

The move from an almost totally unprotected market condition to the current situation has occurred since 1918; this is a remarkable achievement which has involved a massive transfer of property rights from the few to the many, and has taken much of the anxiety from the lives of both working- and middle-class people over the ways and means by which homes can be retained in times of old age, sickness, unemployment or short-time working.

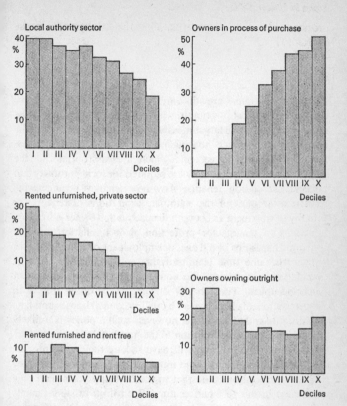

12 Tenancy by income decile, UK, 1970–72

Those who decry this achievement because it has not yet covered 100 per cent of the population appear to yearn for a utopian existence and seem unaware of the very real problems involved in raising the number of dwellings by even a few percentage points; others condemn the achievement because of its apparent high costs and the many inefficiencies, stop-go policies, political disputes, and absurd fiscal policies which have made the success so far achieved more expensive than was necessary. But these expenses and stupidities apart it would seem unwise to condemn all the progress which has been achieved with such difficulty and immense effort.

Conclusions

Many housing issues are still unresolved, and we may now have reached a historical position in which further progress cannot be made without a much larger measure of national agreement on the principles upon which housing policies should be based. New forms of tenancy agreements which are appropriate to the members of a modern society are required for local authority and housing association tenants. Any new tenancy arrangements must take account of the legitimate aspirations of tenants for equality of treatment as between themselves and owner-occupiers, the needs of tenants for protection against inflation and the economic hardships of old age, unemployment or marital failure; but at the same time tenants' rights and aspirations must be evenly balanced against the equally legitimate aspirations of owner-occupiers. Theoretically one means of doing this is to convert all tenants into owners by selling council houses and flats to sitting tenants; in practice, however, such a policy is unlikely to provide a long-term solution to the housing difficulties of low-income householders who will have to buy their way into the market. There seems to be no more reason to suppose that they will be in a position to do that in the next fifty years than they have been in the past half century. Even if all existing tenants were to become owner-occupiers within the year, new families formed subsequently would regenerate a tenant sector of the market. Given income and wealth inequalities a more lasting solution than the idea of a straight shift to individualist forms of owner-occupation may be the development of new leasehold systems of tenure which give tenants a right to participate in management decisions and some share in the equity of the property they occupy.

A second major issue which is still unresolved is the relative priority which should be accorded to housing in the complex structure of a modern welfare state. Housing must perforce compete with all other forms of public and private expenditure and as more and more people become satisfactorily housed we may expect a diminution in public commitment to the declining proportion of ill-housed families. Unlike the social services of health or education, housing is not a social service which is universally available to all who are defined as being in need and the priority accorded to the service fluctuates from year to year; if these fluctuations are not reduced in magnitude there are bound to be recurrent housing crises with consequent short-term responsive policies that generate long-term disruption of housing cost structures and permanent deterioration in the chances available to low-income householders to obtain good-quality accommodation at a price they can afford.

References

1. See for example, Ashton, T. S., *Economic Fluctuations in England 1700–1800*, London, O.U.P., 1959; Thomas, Brinley, *Migration and Urban Development: A Reappraisal of British and American Long Cycles*, London, Methuen, 1972; Mumford, Lewis, *The City in History*, London, Secker & Warburg, 1961, and Penguin Books, 1973.
2. See particularly Lewis, J. Parry, *Building Cycles and Britain's Growth*, London, Macmillan, 1965; Cairncross, A. K., *Home and Foreign Investment 1870–1913: Studies in Capital Accumulation*, Cambridge University Press, 1953. For an econometric analysis of housing markets, see Whitehead, Christine M. E., *The U.K. Housing Market: An Econometric Model*, D. C. Heath Ltd, 1974.
3. See for examples of this approach Muth, Richard F., *Cities and Housing*, Chicago, University of Chicago Press, 1969; Reid, Margaret Gilpin, *Housing and Income*, Chicago, University of Chicago Press, 1962; Grigsby, William G., *Housing Markets and Public Policy*, Philadelphia, University of Pennsylvania Press, 1963.
4. Glass, Ruth, *Newcomers: The West Indians in London*, Centre for Urban Studies Reports No. 1, London, Allen & Unwin, 1960; *Report of the Committee on Housing in Greater London*, Milner Holland Report, Cmnd 2605, London, HMSO, 1965.
5. Lewis, J. Parry, op. cit., p. 137.
6. Turvey, Ralph, *The Economics of Real Property*, London, Allen &

Unwin, 1957, Chapter 3; Cullingworth, J. B., *Housing in Transition*, London, Routledge & Kegan Paul, 1963, p. 16.

7. Burney, E., *Housing on Trial*, Oxford University Press, for the Institute of Race Relations, 1967; Tucker, J., *Honourable Estates*, London, Gollancz, 1966; Rose, E. J. B., and others, *Colour and Citizenship: a Report on British Race Relations*, Oxford University Press, for the Institute of Race Relations, 1969; Karn, Valerie, 'Retiring to the Seaside: A Study of Retirement Migration in England and Wales', University of Birmingham Ph.D. thesis, June 1974; Karn, Valerie, *No Place That's Home: A Report on Accommodation for Single People in Birmingham*, University of Birmingham, Centre for Urban and Regional Studies, 1975.

8. Roberti, Paolo, *The Distribution of Household Income in the U.K. 1957–1972*, Working Papers series published by Centre for Studies in Social Policy, 1974.

9. Greater London Council, *A Strategic Housing Plan for London*, Consultation Document, 1975; Nevitt, Della A., 'Towards a Greater London Housing Strategy', *London Journal*, vol. 1, no. 1., May 1975.

10. Partington, Martin, *Landlord and Tenant*, London, Weidenfeld & Nicolson, 1975.

11. Report of the Committee on *One-Parent Families*, Finer Committee, Cmnd 5629, London, HMSO, 1974; see part 6, Housing.

12. Ministry of Housing and Local Government, CHAC, *Homes for Today and Tomorrow*, Parker Morris report, London, HMSO, 1961.

13. Cabinet Papers, CAB 24/128, C.P. 3345, 28 September 1921.

14. Davies, Bleddyn, *Social Needs and Resources in Local Services: a Study of Variations in Standards of Provision of Personal Social Services Between Local Authority Areas*, London, Michael Joseph, 1968.

15. Hall, Peter, *Urban and Regional Planning*, Penguin Books, 1974.

16. Drover, Glen, 'London and New York: Residential Density Planning Policies and Development', *Town Planning Review*, vol. 46, no. 2, 1975, pp. 165–84.

17. Rex, J. and Moore, R., *Race, Community and Conflict: a study of Sparkbrook*, London, Oxford University Press, 1967.

18. Needleman, L., *Economics of Housing*, London, Staples, 1965; Sigsworth, E. M., and Wilkinson, R. K., 'Rebuilding or Renovation', *Urban Studies*, vol. 4, no. 2, 1967, pp. 109–21; Needleman, L., 'Rebuilding or Renovation?, A Reply', *Urban Studies*, vol. 5, no. 1, 1968, pp. 86–90; Needleman, L., 'The Comparative Economics of Improvement and New Building', *Urban Studies*, vol. 6, 1969,

pp. 196–209; Sigsworth, E. M., and Wilkinson, R. K., 'Rebuilding or Renovation: a Rejoinder', *Urban Studies*, vol. 7, 1970, pp. 92–4; Sigsworth, E. M., and Wilkinson, R. K., 'The Finance of Improvements: a Study of Low Quality Housing in Three Yorkshire Towns', *Bulletin of Economic Research*, vol. 23, no. 2, 1971, pp. 113–28.

19. First Report from the Expenditure Committee, 1975–76, *The Financing of Public Expenditure*, vol. 1, London, HMSO, 11 December 1975, HC 69–1, paragraph 8.

20. Roberti, Paolo, op. cit.

21. Berry, Fred, *Housing: the Great British Failure*, London, Charles Knight, 1974.

Chapter 8
Issues on Need

Bleddyn Davies

The rate of growth of expenditure on personal social services was 10 per cent a year at constant prices between 1968/9 and 1974/5, and for some years after the new social services departments were established in 1971 it averaged 14 per cent per year. These rates of growth have raised the expectations of providers and consumers alike.[1] Current expenditure by local authorities rose by three fifths between 1971/2 and 1975/6; but the programme of current expenditure presented in the White Paper on public expenditure of February 1976 provides for a growth between 1975/6 and 1979/80 of only 10 per cent.[2] The White Paper asserted that this would be 'sufficient to cover the current costs arising from capital investment and to maintain existing standards of service to those groups in the population ... whose numbers are increasing ...' but for 'no general improvement in standards of services'.[3] Meanwhile central government is attempting to prevent local authorities from raising their expenditures by more than the amounts which it has stipulated. In particular, the Department of the Environment Circular 45/76 states:

The Government ... now wish to make it clear to individual authorities that the 1977/8 Rate Support Grant settlement will be made on the basis of the expenditure figures set out in the public expenditure White Paper ... The Government will assume that any excess resources authorities will receive in 1976/77 above the necessary to finance expenditure in accordance with the public expenditure White Paper ... has been put to balances and so will be available to finance expenditure in 1977/8. This additional source of revenue will be fully taken into account in setting the level of grant for 1977/8.[4]

In other words, local authorities will be fined for 'overspending' in 1976/7 a sum equal to that overspending, by means of a reduction in the Rate Support Grant for 1977/8. This is real pressure to keep down local spending. It reflects the most important implicit assumption of the Layfield Committee on Local Government Finance:[5] that it is essential to curtail the growth of local government expenditure. The year 1976/7 is the beginning of a new era.

Political pressures are such that the expansion of services whose budgets have grown fastest is likely to be curtailed most, irrespective of the rate of growth in consumer demand and need. Moreover, central government estimates of the costs of providing services at a constant standard (especially costs of new services) tend to be conservative.[6] Perhaps the personal social services are the most vulnerable. Yet their high rate of growth has been mainly due to a faster rise in demand than for other services. This growth in demand has been caused partly by social and demographic trends, partly by the provision of services which have helped define a need in the minds of potential recipients, partly by the improved standards of provision which have done something to kill the disrepute of their Poor Law origins, and partly by changes in the way old problems and the possible solutions to them are perceived. Of these factors, the demographic are the easiest to quantify. The rise in the proportion of the population in the age group that makes most demands on the personal social services, that aged seventy-five and over, will continue; numbers will have risen by one-fifth in the decade to 1981 and more than a quarter by 1991. However, population projections by themselves provide an inadequate basis for forecasting needs and demand. Though there will be an increasing number of elderly people in situations where they could receive service, at least by current standards, the increase in demand itself is very sensitive to a number of factors – the degree to which the medical services provide social care as a by-product of health provision, the housing conditions or levels of real income, which play a large part in determining people's capacity to do without services, and the degree to which families are able and willing to provide care for elderly relatives. This sensitivity results from the low proportion of the aged dependent on services; only one out of ten persons aged seventy-five and over and one out of twenty aged between sixty-five and seventy-four now receive any kind of domiciliary personal social service. If there should be a reduced willingness to provide informal care, demand for services might increase considerably. For instance, one in two men and two out of three women aged seventy-five and over, living in private households, claim that they suffer from long-standing illnesses.[7]

There can be little doubt that the social consequences of economic setbacks will increase the need and demand for the personal social services. Some of the relationships between need (and demand) for such services and prosperity are predictable: for instance, the relationship between mental hospital admissions and unemployment is well known.[8] Higher rates of unemployment and larger numbers in poverty will impose additional strains on families that are now just managing to cope without external assistance. The family breakdowns that would be caused by the increased strain would result in larger numbers of child-batterings, the separation of parents and the acceptance of some of their children into care. Higher rates of juvenile unemployment could result in higher rates of delinquency.

In the circumstances, social resources must be used to their maximum effect. This means holding – indeed if the White Paper assumptions are accepted, cutting – the provision in those authorities which are now best provided with services in relation to their needs, so as to allow development in those areas in which provision is least adequate. It also means finding ways of ensuring that the areas with greatest need are not deprived, in order to safeguard the budgets of services whose protagonists have more political power in local authorities (or, for that matter, the central government). Yet the Layfield Committee recommends more local autonomy. Some of their assumptions are discussed in Section I. Without territorial need indicators, a more efficient allocation cannot be developed. The need indicator is discussed in Section II. Section III assesses whether sufficiently valid and reliable need indicators can be constructed to provide a more equitable territorial allocation of resources.

Territorial justice and local autonomy

In this essay, the term 'social justice' implies 'to each according to his need', and 'territorial justice' implies 'to each area according to the needs of the population of that area'.[9] If perfect social justice prevailed, there would, by definition, be territorial justice, but between areas one could have a distribution of welfare that met the statistical requirements for territorial justice without attaining a socially just distribution between individuals: perfect territorial justice is a necessary but insufficient condition for perfect social justice. However, greater territorial justice does not necessarily lead to greater social justice. Since ethical propositions concern individuals and primary social groups, not the large and changing populations that inhabit areas, our real concern is with social rather than with territorial justice. But unless there are large variations in the efficiency of authorities in allocating resources between individuals, and unless these variations in efficiency are correlated with need (but there is little sign of this), improvements in territorial justice are almost certain to lead to improvements in social justice. Therefore the assessment and monitoring of territorial justice is of profound importance to those interested in securing greater social justice. Likewise, a considerable insight can be gained into the effectiveness of government policies in promoting social justice by studying their past record of achievement in extending territorial justice.

The degree of territorial justice within any community has been measured by examining the degree of inequality in the ratio of indicators of output to indicators of need – or, which comes to much the same thing, the degree of correlation and relative inequality of the two indicators. (Neither is precisely equivalent to an operationalization of the cost–benefit criterion of territorial justice, which would be the equalization, between areas, of the ratio of benefit to cost for an additional unit of 'intervention resources'. However, no way has been found for estimating this directly from the data available, though it is reasonable to assume that it is highly correlated with the measurement procedures actually used.) The most likely source of error in judging the degree of territorial justice is the crudeness of most need indicators and the use of indicators of input and performance as proxies for indices of output.[10]

The national standard policy-paradigms that are the basis of the need indicators are only one form of ideology that may legitimately influence the amount of local service provision. Apart from specifically local citizen ideologies, the local incidence of nationally important political ideologies also affects the issue. No survey evidence exists which allows us to determine the influence of these national political ideologies on local populations. Perhaps the best available data on which to base an indicator is the local electoral success of national political parties, though such indicators are even more approximate than indicators of need and output.

The Layfield Report[11] recommended a localist model of central–local relations. So that they should clearly bear the primary responsibility for decisions about spending, local authorities would enjoy greater powers of decision than hitherto in such functions as education, social services, transport and housing, where central government influence is at present strongest. There would be freedom from government intervention unless there was some precisely specified national interest at stake. The central government's ability to secure greater territorial justice would be greatly limited. As it became possible to measure output and the necessary costs of achieving it – fields of research whose importance the Layfield Committee stressed – the central government could set minimum standards. But these would be much lower than average standards. 'Greater local discretion implies that the standard and extent of local services and the local taxation required to finance them could vary more widely than they do now between areas of differing social composition', though the Commission thought that 'very wide disparities' would be unlikely to develop – an optimistic opinion supported by only a few sentences of argument.

Is the Layfield Committee correct in thinking that greater territorial justice can still be achieved with an expansion of local autonomy? If Layfield is wrong, the consequences for social justice could be profound; since local authority expenditure not only constitutes a large part of the 'social wage', but also has great multiplier effects on local levels of income and employment (hence the growth and decline of areas). Perhaps we can best test the Layfield argument by mobilizing evidence to answer three questions. (1) Is there evidence to show that the present system, which gives authorities less autonomy to vary spending than Layfield proposes, allows the need-generating characteristics of the population within a given area to be a major and pervasive influence on levels of output? (2) Is there evidence that the local strength of national political ideologies has a powerful effect on these levels? (3) If neither of these have much influence can we argue nevertheless that local authorities are sensitive to citizen preferences, even where these preferences are unrelated either to policy paradigms or to factors that differentiate left from right at the national level? The answers to these questions should influence our attitude to the proposal of a fundamental shift to local autonomy as set out by Layfield. The Layfield proposal is one which entails too many risks for it to be accepted lightly. It is for those who support it to provide evidence that these are not real dangers.

1–2. The influence of paradigm implicit needs and political ideologies

The first two questions can be taken together.

The impact of area variation in the incidence of needs, judged by the nationally standard criteria of the policy paradigm, can be assessed by examining the results of statistical models 'explaining' variations in indicators of output. So can the impact of local adherence to the ideologies associated with the main national political parties. The greater the positive impact of need indicators and political indicators, the more likely it is that Layfield is right. Negative or little impact suggests that Layfield is wrong.

Table 10 summarizes results for two dozen variables in three sets of social services for the urban (county borough) authorities abolished in 1974. The models on which they are based allow for both the direct and indirect effects of need-generating character-istics and national political ideology (indicated by Labour repre-

Table 10. **The influence of area need characteristics and Labour representation**

		Negative or not significantly greater than 0[a]	Less than 0·20	0·20 and less than 0·30	0·30 and less than 0·40	0·40 and more
Personal social services for the aged and deprived children[b]	need	61	9	6	1	1
	Labour representation	9	2	3	5	0
Housing [c]	need	7	1	0	1	0
	Labour representation	1	0	0	1	1
Education[d]	need	0	2	2	1	1
	Labour representation	0	1	1	0	1

[a] At the 5 per cent level.
[b] Nineteen dependent variables. (Source: *Variations in Services for the Aged*, op. cit.)
[c] Three dependent variables. (Source: B. Davies: 'Policy paradigms and local outputs', in R. Fried, ed., *The Quality of Urban Life*.)
[d] Three dependent variables. (Source: 'Policy paradigms and local outputs' op. cit.)

sentation on the Council). The table shows, first, the number of output indicators whose total impact was either not significantly greater than zero or negative; secondly, and subsequently, where the total impact was such that one standard deviation variation in the causal factor ('need' or Labour representation) 'caused' varying positive differences in the standard deviations of output.

The results demonstrate that indicators of need-generating characteristics had little influence on variables in the case of the personal social services. Where there were effects, they were on the patterns of provision rather than on the levels of it. This is similar to the way in which environmental pressures act on constrained resources as indicated by models for seventy variables analysed in one recent study[12] and 150 variables in another.[13] It does not suggest a response to relative need in the amount of resource allocation. For instance, the one variable with a need impact exceeding 0·40 reflects the authorities' response to the ease of recruitment of workers. Again the housing models suggest a modest impact (if their impact on investment is as found by Nicholson and Topham).[14] Demographic need indicators had a strong effect on education models for spending on primary and secondary schools but no need indicators appeared to influence spending on education welfare services.

Labour representation, which indicates the local impact of the main differential between political ideologies at a national level, affects few aspects of personal social service provision, but has a more pervasive effect on education and housing expenditure. However, the effects are indirect only; Labour authorities spend more in total, and the greater spending on education or housing subsidies derives from the greater amount of money available rather than a predilection to direct far more to these sectors. Moreover, the local influences of the national political ideology do not appear to be an alternative to the policy paradigm. A detailed inspection of the results suggests that the impact of Labour representation is greatest on those variables on which need indicators have the most powerful effect.

The overall conclusion is that for this selection of output indicators we have failed to find evidence to suggest that the level of output of these services is in general very sensitive either to area differences in need as implicit in national policy paradigms, or to variations in the local influence of the main forms of national ideological differentiation. These results are not greatly different from those of studies of other outputs. Nevertheless, it remains possible that local outputs are sensitive to variations in citizen preference of a kind reflected neither in policy paradigms nor in national political ideologies. It is not easy to assess this directly from the statistical data now available. We must instead look at the indirect evidence provided by case studies.

3. *The influence of citizen preferences on output-determining decisions*

Fortunately, there is a vast amount of literature on which to base a judgement. It is impossible to review this thoroughly here, but it is feasible to present sufficient evidence to cast doubt on the general assumption that authorities are sensitive to citizen preferences.

First it is argued that the nature of politics in a British local authority is such as to insulate it both from pressures that might stimulate a response to local needs and from the stated preferences of the electorate. L. J. Sharpe, in a seminal paper comparing English and American local government,[15] argued that there were a number of ways in which the British system was less open. In particular, he argued that the British system made less information available, and the press had much less effective access to matters that are potentially of local political interest. Moreover, because it is insufficiently visible, concentrates political power in the party organization, and has an executive that is insufficiently directly accountable, the British system does not identify particular issues with persons subject to election, and hence information is much less readily forthcoming and the issues much more difficult to interpret. That in 1971 many major authorities admitted the press to less than one half of their standing committees is evidence of the reluctance of local authorities to make the system more open.[16]

It is commonly argued that English libel laws can too easily suppress the presentation of evidence and a wider debate about issues of public importance. After his election the councillor tends to be unresponsive to the party because the party has only weak powers of dismissal or control.[17] Local issues can have a major impact on elections, but local voting trends seem to be more influenced by the state of grace of the national political parties. Green's estimate of the relative importance of national in relation to local factors is among the lowest from several studies made; but even he accounts for three quarters of the variation in local voting by national trends.[18] The results of the survey of electors done for the Maud Committee and re-analysed for the Royal Commission showed that local government was not highly commended for its accessibility. The Royal Commission concluded: 'The relationship between local authorities and the public is not satisfactory. The Committee on Management of Local Authorities found that there is both ignorance of and indifference to local government on the part of the public; and indeed, it is not uncommon to hear contempt expressed.'[19] The re-analysis of the data for the Royal Commission showed *inter alia* that 45 per cent of respondents felt that they knew enough about the Council in only two or less of six fields of interest. The same analysis also showed that nearly one third of respondents felt they could have confidence in councillors on less than two of the five issues specified.[20] Again, the development of micro-political activity suggests that the party is frequently insensitive to local opinion.[21] Once elected, the councillor's perceptions are increasingly influenced by the way in which the other councillors look at things. His views become more like those of others in the same stratum of the political élite, party differences being less clear among councillors than among electors.[22] The more influential a councillor becomes, the more restricted his range of contacts; 'the more senior the council member, the more likely his political life will be contained within the four walls of the Council House, the more likely he is to become engrossed by the internal dynamics of council politics, and the less likely he is to consciously bridge the gap between the council and the city as a whole'.[23]

There is little obvious evidence that universal voting behaviour affects the territorial distribution of major resources. For instance, Glassberg's study of capital budgeting in New York and London suggested to the author a local political system that 'appeared to reward and/or punish the electorate on the basis of vote results'. Some have argued not only that the system is insulated from local preferences and conditions, but can also be resistant to them. Dearlove argues that the councillors interpret evidence in the light of their preconceived ideas, and would tend to ignore evidence or representations that were not compatible with these, which is to stress the importance of psychologists' theories about selective perception and cognitive dissonance for the understanding of local politics.[24]

The pressures on authorities to respond to need or demand is weak. Local authorities are area monopolists in many of their services. They enjoy little competition from alternative providers in their areas, and where the alternative providers exist, they are not regarded as rivals for custom, since there is no precise equivalent to profits as an indicator of success. Inter-authority competition is not fundamental to the system. There is little evidence that people are sensitive enough to variations in the structure of outputs as between authorities to locate themselves in the areas of those whose output structure they most like, and since the areas covered by major authorities are large, it is unlikely that they would have a strong incentive to do so. (The incentives to locate themselves in response to variations in the facilities offered within any one authority are much stronger.) Moreover, in many areas, the political structure is such that the dominant party is not subject to political competition over long periods. Some case studies suggest that most initiatives that are not generated by changes in the policy of central government tend to come from councillors and officers rather than from local pressure groups, though there are areas of local government activity where this is changing fast. Indeed, in a system which, by American standards, seems 'obsessively professional', the initiative was taken more often by officers than by councillors. Councillors were more concerned with casework and patronage than with policy. The Maud Committee on Management argued *inter alia* that councillors tended to lose sight of policy issues because they were overwhelmed with casework detail, because the departmental structure was too closely related to professional specialization, and because there was too small a number of councillors of an ability that would allow them to control officers on complex issues taking a long time to work through the system. Some of the case studies of urban renewal and education ascribe influence over policy more to professionals than to councillors.[25] However, others suggest that it is the combined influence of councillors and officers that is important.

It is not necessary for us to prove that authorities are insensitive to citizen preferences. The onus is on the supporters of the Layfield proposal to argue for its adoption. It is enough here to show that a good *prima facie* case can be made out for the view that British local authorities are not as sensitive as they ought to be. It seems clear from this brief review of the evidence that such a case can be constructed.

II The need indicator

The state of play in the development of territorial need indicators cannot be understood without a discussion of the need judgement, policy paradigms, need studies, need indicators and their inter-relation. Need indicators embody the assumption of a relevant policy paradigm, as reflected in need studies. Need indicators can be no better than the need studies and policy paradigm on which they are based. The need studies and need indicators must reflect the conception of the need judgement. Let us discuss each in turn.

1. The need judgement

The need judgement is in essence the outcome of a cost–benefit evaluation: one which should in principle weigh the welfare consequences of an intervention against the opportunity costs of alternatives, however vague, indirect or imprecise the process is in practice. This has not been questioned since Feldstein argued it in 1963,[26] although some (like Majone[27]) see cost–benefit analysis as itself one example of a broader approach. Subsequent writing about need has been compatible with this perspective, though much of it has not made much of the main implications – for instance, that a judgement about one case or service must imply judgements about others; that changes in the costs of producing one dimension of welfare (because of technical progress or the relative prices of inputs) in relation to another makes it preferable to produce more units of the one that has become cheaper and less of the one that has become more expensive, leading to a changed set of need judgements; or that a change in the relative social valuation put on different dimensions of welfare should likewise result in a change in need judgements.

2. Policy paradigms

Policy paradigms are (like Kuhnian scientific paradigms[28]) ideologies or social constructs. They are the entire constellation of beliefs, values, assumptions about cause and effect, and appreciations of the techniques of intervention and the consequences of alternative actions, which are substantially shared by the community of actors, and which therefore influence decisions in the political and bureaucratic process. In short, the policy paradigm is the assumptive world of the actors in that area of policy. The policy paradigm exists because it fulfills an essential function: it provides, maintains, and develops the basis for social action. Sharpe, who has recently used a concept which is similar to but not identical with a policy paradigm, says 'It is impossible for representative bureaucracy to work without a policy paradigm.'[29] It is essential if technical inputs are to be effectively provided for bureaucracies employing professionals with delegated discretion to influence outcomes, or professionals teaching some aspects of the paradigm to general administrators and thus to politicians and other interest groups.

A policy paradigm will only provide a sound basis for need studies and indicators under certain conditions: intellectual, political, and organizational.

(i) INTELLECTUAL CONDITIONS. Certainly one condition for soundness is the degree to which the paradigm is elaborately articulated. It requires articulation in two ways. First, it has to be expressed in a language which will help a sufficiently broad range of interests to accept the structuring of problems and their possible solutions. Secondly, it must be so structured that existing professional and other scientific and bureaucratic skills can be mobilized to serve it. Knowledge and intellectual techniques developed for other purposes can only be successfully mobilized if the intellectual components of the paradigm are made explicit: and the desire of professionals and bureaucrats to exercise power within job contexts can only be legitimately realized if they are thought to possess esoteric understanding and mastery of complex skills. One aspect is the impressiveness both of the conceptual structures used and the degree to which they have been exposed to the 'test' of evidence. It is particularly important that theories should be seen to explain significant outcomes, and that the tools which depend on the intellectual components should be able to achieve the policy objectives implicit in the paradigm. These criteria closely paralleled those which determine the continuing credibility of scientific paradigms. Many intellectual reasons for the collapse of policy paradigms are similar to those for the collapse of scientific paradigms.

(ii) POLITICAL CONDITIONS. To interest groups with political influence the policy paradigm must appear to lead to actions that are at least as satisfactory as any other likely policy. It is important that a policy should attract strong rather than merely nominal support and that it can be easily incorporated into a particular political viewpoint. But it is also important that a paradigm is well articulated and successfully purveyed to a broad public with a general interest in government as well as to parties with a specific interest. Selling the paradigm to the general political market provides the diffuse support which will give it the significance for decision-making that comes from a general perception that action reflecting it contributes to the public interest, and so a role in maintaining a party's position while managing demands.

(iii) ORGANIZATIONAL CONDITIONS. Paradigms can hardly exist in a satisfactory form when organizational structures – bureaucratic or political, such as governments or pressure groups (including professional and client associations) – are unrelated to policy ends.

The policy paradigm is nationally standard. It does not necessarily correspond to the operating ideology of the central government – indeed when the central government holds a version of the paradigm which differs substantially from that of subordinate governments, the policy fails and the central government replaces it. Of course, operating ideologies vary between authorities. But they vary around a nationally standard policy paradigm.

3. Need studies

Perhaps the major weakness of the British studies of need for social services is that they have rarely taken into account the range of factors that it is necessary to consider in sound cost–benefit judgements, and still more rarely has this been done for the variety of circumstances likely to be encountered. This is true for studies in housing, the personal social services, education and other policy areas. Studies of need for the elderly and chronically sick rarely probe the alternative welfare consequences that follow from the application of different services. For instance, apart from some American literature, almost none of the studies have investigated the shortfalls in subjective well-being that are consequent on different packages of service. Indeed, they assume that there is no choice to be made between alternative ways of achieving a desired set of welfare consequences. They have therefore contributed little to an understanding of the 'technology' of the social services as systems of substitutes and complements, the relationship between services having different inputs and outputs. By not doing so, they contribute far less to our knowledge than is required if we are to apply the appropriate logic of resource allocation to the context; since without this understanding, the central government department or the social service manager at the local level cannot select the best combination of services to suit local circumstances.

Circumstances relevant to the selection vary greatly. The surveys implicitly assume that they do not. For instance, they assume that the relative costs of providing additional units of each service vary in the same proportion in all areas. This is not the case. The cost of providing bricks and mortar is quite different relative to that of key professional manpower in an overspill housing estate (Kirkby, for example) and in an outer London suburb or in Brighton. Again the cost of making unanticipated adjustments to the supply of different services differs greatly between areas. Social service departments should not be aiming to provide a uniform pattern of services, even when they are faced with an apparently uniform pattern of need-generating characteristics. The pattern of need-generating characteristics is never exactly uniform from one area to another. There are differences in terms of personal factors that help to decide the contribution to welfare of any given input of services, and also considerable differences in the social settings of areas. The social networks to which the pattern of need relates, and the wide social structure of the locality in which these networks are placed, vary in such a way as to present quite different pay-offs to different forms of intervention.

Cultural differences are also important. For instance, the benefit of receiving a free school meal to a child and his family is affected by many considerations in addition to the family's assessed net income, which in effect is the sole criterion of eligibility or need. The proportion of families earning less than various levels of assessed income will vary considerably between areas when account is taken of the fact that they feel poor in relation to various reference groups; that they have special features (such as lacking a mother or father) that cause them to have a lower level of material well-being than their income suggests; or that they appear to be sensitive to various forms of stigma associated with receiving the service. The benefits to be derived by fixing any one eligibility level of net income differ on this account between areas.

Again, a need study typically fails to consider how the social services system relates to the broader context of priorities in public intervention, and how local authority dispensations relate to private resource allocation. The cost–benefit ratios of social welfare interventions vary between areas in relation to other uses of resources so that the total amount of resources which should be allocated to social welfare also varies. Therefore existing studies fail to take into account yet another essential feature of the need judgement. Most of the need studies can relate only to a Utopia with the odd characteristic that there is no apparent scarcity of resources but there are nevertheless clearly bounded ideas and expectations about what welfares and diswelfares are tolerable. In the context of a cost–benefit judgement, clearly bounded assumptions of this kind can be made only with knowledge of the total quantity of resources available.

Therefore the body of research into need does not incorporate important features of the theory of need judgement. Indeed, this body of literature is not firmly rooted in any body of logical analysis concerning the principles for allocating resources. Politically and administratively valuable as it has been, the absence of a clear intellectual basis has left us with much less of the required evidence than could have been obtained, despite the expenditures of large sums of money on the collection and analysis of data.

4. Need indicators

Much the same applies to the development and use of need indicators. Those who have designed need indicators have neglected the potential cost–benefit nature of need judgements as much as those who have designed need studies. They have failed to recognize that need judgement is almost always about the allocation of resources, even if by indirect means. The designers have therefore failed to recognize that one criterion of a good need indicator is that it should clearly reflect a judgement about the allocation of resources arrived at after considering the evidence. Moreover, the way the need indicator is used often betrays a failure to deal with one essential aspect of the context; that there is substitutability of services has been crucial to the quality of the policy argument. Indeed, the scholarly acumen of many of those who use need indicators has been less than that of those who have developed need studies. The Achilles' heel of the former has been that applied sociology has not been strengthened by applied economics; it has been social policy analysis hopping heroically forward on one leg. In the latter, the work has been supported by neither, and the analysis has lacked any obvious means of forward locomotion.

The definition of the need indicator must be compatible with a concept of the need judgement. The need judgement can either be thought of as the quantity of one form of output that would be sacrificed in order to obtain a unit of another (when the relevant cost and benefit streams have been considered) or as the quantity of resources that would be allocated to produce the pattern of outputs implicit in that judgement. If the need judgement is the estimated amount of resources judged to be appropriately allocated to a potential recipient with certain need-relevant characteristics in the specified circumstances, a need indicator is an estimate of the amount of resources appropriate to some (defined) population of these recipients. It is the sum of the resources judged to be appropriate for each individual in that population. Thus if v_i is the value of the resources judged appropriate for person i, and n_i is the number of client units similar to person i with respect to need-relevant characteristics, the need indicator can be defined as

$$\sum_i (n_i v_i).$$

Need indicators have so far only been used to make comparisons between the needs of populations in different territorial areas for a service or system of services. This is an arbitrary limitation. It merely reflects their origin in the study of territorial justice. It is useful to have need indicators for all those circumstances in which one would be able to compare need judgements. One should be able to use indicators to compare the need for one or a system of services of the populations in different areas. One should also be able to use indicators to compare different client groups within the same area, or different client groups in different areas. Similarly one should be able to use them to compare the needs of populations for different services. The definition of the need indicator that we have just presented is for a total population weighted by the resources judged appropriate to each of its members. One can sum over whatever population is appropriate to the problem in hand. The formula allows summation to be carried out over quite different populations. The conventional type of need indicator is therefore only one case of a general form. The concept of need indicator we are here advocating is as general as the concept of need itself. Most important, it is firmly rooted in the theory of the need judgement.

This concept of the indicator is very different from anything derived from social malaise studies. Indeed its intellectual origin is quite different. It is significant that perhaps the most impressive of the pioneering studies in this country that developed the indicator of social malaise was undertaken by a town planning department.[30] Its intellectual origin lay in the sociology of the city, the social area analysis of Burgess and the Chicago School.[31] The social malaise study is based on theories about the determination of the characteristics of particular areas within the city, and latterly on theories about the determinants of deprivation in 'markets' crucial to life chances.[32] The emphasis of the social malaise study is more on the classification of areas than on the derivation of indicators. It is not based on a normative theory of intervention. It is therefore loosely related to prescriptive theories about the allocation of resource. By contrast, a need indicator of the type described by our formula is based very explicitly on such normative theories, in fact on an entire policy paradigm, such as that which underlies the operation of the personal social services as systems of substitutes and complements in the meeting of needs. The function and level of generality of the two types of indicator make them useful for quite different purposes.

III Data and the development of need indicators

It is clear from the argument of the second section that the development of need indicators has been hampered by the failure to design research in such a way as to take into account the implications of the nature of the need judgement. But we must defer judgement about whether need indicators can be adequate as the basis of territorial allocation until we have considered the availability of data for them.

The more disaggregated the resource allocation decision, the more difficult it is to obtain valid data to develop an appropriate need indicator. Perhaps we should not be too ambitious, and concentrate on the decisions that determine the general availability of finance which sets the framework within which local authority decisions are made. In the personal social services, this requires valid and reliable indicators for perhaps three broad client groups capable of allocating resources to the territories covered by area offices – say territories of the scale of the pre-1974 urban districts with their rural hinterlands, and 'conurban' areas of on average fifty thousand persons. In time it might be feasible to develop reliable indicators for a score or more target groups at that level of geographical aggregation, or indicators for a few client groups for smaller territories, but that seems to be an over-ambitious aim at present.

It is feasible to estimate need indicators directly from the basic formula

$$\sum_i (n_i v_i)$$

only for the broadest of client groups; but for such groups it is the most attractive method. It requires (*a*) the specification of target sub-groups, in each of which the resource needs vary much less than they do among clients as a whole; (*b*) the estimation of the v_i for the range of area contexts found in practice; and (*c*) the estimation and projection of numbers in each of the target sub-groups. Data problems are involved in both (*b*) and (*c*).

ESTIMATING v_i. We have seen that the individual need judgements should be sensitive to variations between clients in the cost and welfare consequences of interventions if resources are to be used most effectively. Some of the factors that affect these are common to interventions in favour of all members of a target group in the geographical area; for instance, the (marginal) costs of recruiting and retaining trained manpower and other inputs, and area characteristics that affect the degree to which inputs can be substituted for one another in the production of outputs. In principle, it is not impossible to estimate the relationships between cost-raising geographical factors and such costs, and to quantify the dependence of technical substitutability and geographical factors; but it requires expensive data to do so. Judgements change through time, so that new data is required periodically; and when (as now) rapid changes in the relationship between demands and resources are occurring, the judgements have to be re-evaluated frequently. To use the relationships to estimate the v_i for each area demands data for a larger number of areas.

Ideally, the pattern of variation in optimal v_i should be directly estimated. This would require the estimation of the sensitivity of need judgements to variation in costs, consequences, and risks. Such estimates are not yet available. What are available are the results of the need surveys mentioned above. These embody a variety of definitions that were intended by those who designed them to reflect ideal need judgements. They can be analysed to predict the association between need and the characteristics for which data could be made universally available at any area level, to test the degree to which different need definitions define similar populations, and to assess the degree to which territorial indicators are in fact sensitive to the choice of need definition.

Unfortunately, how far the best known of the need definitions actually do correlate with the need judgements of others has not been systematically tested – indeed, in most cases it has not been tested at all. Therefore they lack an essential precondition for their validity to be established.

ESTIMATING n_i. The Census is an imperfect data source if for no other reason than that the data on the characteristics of persons and households which would be most relevant to need judgement are not collected. Perhaps social welfare interventions are not important enough for one or two questions of particular relevance to social welfare need to be asked of a small proportion of households in an interpenetrating sample design, allowing the prevalence of combinations of characteristics to be estimated for larger areas. Nevertheless, more use could be made of the Census as the first stage of a multi-stage collection of data. But it would be easier to produce counts of persons and households with combinations of characteristics having particular relevance to social werlfare need. The area counts, particularly the small area statistics, have long been too much influenced by the needs of land use, transport and (to a lesser degree) the education planners. For instance, disability is closely correlated with age (the proportion aged eighty and over who are also disabled being substantial) and because of the correlation between severe physical incapacity and personal morale, age is also correlated with severe depression. The probability of having surviving children is substantially correlated with marital status. Vulnerability to loss of accommodation is associated with housing tenure; inability to cope with increasing frailty is associated with some features of housing amenities and conditions. The absence of continuous monitoring in case of accidents is associated with living alone or with another elderly person. The absence of informal support networks is correlated with indicators for small areas of population mobility and lack of social cohesion. Therefore counts involving combinations of these characteristics could correspond quite well to the specifications of target groups of the number and mix required to use the formula

$$\sum_i (n_i v_i)$$

to produce valid and reliable indicators. Other data can be used to supplement the Census, since client need is sensitive to area characteristics. In this way employment data, data on the geographical incidence of low incomes, and some of the cheaper social malaise data can be used to enrich indicators.

More difficult is the projection of estimates of n_i. The projection of local authority populations in younger age groups is notoriously difficult because of the vagaries of forecasting births and internal migrations. There is substantial internal migration over long distances of persons of about retirement age. But forecasts for up to a decade of those in their eighties and older, by sex, age, and marital status, are likely to add greatly to our ability to plan, despite such migratory flows as that of very old persons to the homes or areas of their children. Again it would be useful to have forecasts of the numbers of persons (by sex and age group) in their late seventies and over who are living alone. Reasonably adequate models are not expensive to construct.

The greatest difficulty in formulating good general need indicators is that no one has tested and validated the survey need definitions which make sense in the context of the normative theory of how need judgement should vary. But if one can take such definitions on trust, there are the data available for two of the three broad target groups of social welfare services to construct territorial need indicators whose sensitivity to variations in need definition can be tested. It is not desirable to depend simply on the crude demographic and social condition variables which have so far been used in the Rate Support Grant formula and the internal allocation decisions of government departments. Although it would be valuable to have large household surveys in each area at a scale appropriate to making estimates of the target groups (n_i), one cannot argue that they are essential for adequate need indicators to be constructed. Moreover, the development of valid and reliable territorial need indicators need neither take much time nor require much research expense.

IV Conclusion

The inadequacy of the data is not a good reason for misallocating resources in the social welfare services through an inability to assess the relative needs of local authority populations. It simply requires research to quantify the impact of cost-raising factors on the expenditure necessary to provide services at a similar standard in different areas. Estimating the resource requirements for producing similar outputs in different areas would be more difficult, but it is perverse to conclude that the technical problems of doing so are such as to make it impossible to develop quickly a knowledge base sufficient to improve the territorial allocation of resources dramatically. If British politics is indeed about to reach a watershed on the other side of which there will be little real growth in public spending, it is vital to deploy public expenditure increasingly effectively. This will require a redistribution not only between services at the local level but also between local authority areas. This has been recognized by the National Health Service, whose Resource Allocation Working Party is committed both to large and explicit redistribution between services and between areas. This commitment has been made even though the redistribution is likely to encounter widespread and fierce resistance. There has been less work on developing need indicators for medical than for personal social services and the problems of doing so are far more complex. Given the spending propensities of local politicians who are virtually unaccountable to the public, it would be quite wrong in a new age of financial stringencies to curtail the improvements in equity and efficiency that a nationally induced redistribution between territories and services could bring.

References

1. Department of Health and Social Security, *Priorities for Health and Personal Social Services in England: a Consultative Document*, London, HMSO, 1976.
2. At constant prices. *Public Expenditure to 1979–80*, Cmnd 6393, London, HMSO, 1976, p. 93, Table 2.11.
3. ibid, p. 96.
4. Department of the Environment, *Circular 45/76: Local Authority Current Expenditure 1976/7*, London, HMSO, 1976.
5. *Report of the Committee of Enquiry on Local Government Finance*, Cmnd 6453, London, HMSO, 1976.
6. See the evidence of the Association of Directors of Social Services to the Layfield Committee.
7. See *First Reports of the General Household Survey*, London, HMSO, 1971.
8. See K. Jones and R. Sidebotham, *Mental Hospitals at Work*, London, Routledge, 1968.
9. Davies, Bleddyn, *Social Needs and Resources in Local Services*, London, Michael Joseph, 1968.
10. Davies, Bleddyn, 'Output and Policy Research in Urban Government', in *Policy and Politics*, vol. 5, no. 3, March 1977, pp. 41–60 (special issue edited by Bleddyn Davies, on 'Urban Policy in Britain – Influences, Processes and Impacts').

11. *Report of the Committee of Enquiry on Local Government Finance*, op. cit.

12. Bleddyn Davies and others, *Variations in Services for the Aged*, London, Bell, 1971.

13. Bleddyn Davies and others, *Variations in Children's Services amongst British Urban Authorities*, London, Bell, 1972.

14. R. J. Nicholson and N. Topham, 'The Determinants of Investment in Housing by Local Authorities', *Journal of the Royal Statistical Society, A*, vol. 134, no. 3, pp. 273–320.

15. L. J. Sharpe, 'American Democracy Reconsidered', *British Journal of Political Science*, vol. 3, no. 1, January 1973, pp. 1–28. However, he also argued that the American system was not as superior in this respect as had previously been suggested.

16. See 'The Public's Right to Know', *Municipal Journal*, vol. 79, no. 39, 24 September 1971, pp. 1305–7. The arguments are summarized in R. Taras: 'Communications and Press Relations in Urban Government', *Policy and Politics*, vol. 1, no. 2, December 1972, pp. 115–30.

17. J. A. Brand, 'Party Organisation and the Recruitment of Councillors', *British Journal of Political Science*, vol. 3, no. 4, October 1973, pp. 473–86.

18. G. Green, 'National, City and Ward Components of Local Voting', *Policy and Politics*, vol. 1, no. 1, September 1972, pp. 45–54. His estimates were compatible with those of Gregory and Steed (loc. cit., p. 54).

19. Cmnd 4040 paragraph 95.

20. Cmnd 4040 – II, 143.

21. See, for instance, Barry Hindness, *The Decline of Working Class Politics*, London, MacGibbon and Kee, 1971. The evidence on this has grown considerably in the last five years.

22. See I. Budge and others, *Political Stratification and Democracy*, London, Macmillan, 1972.

23. K. Newton, 'Links between leaders and citizens in a local political system', *Policy and Politics*, vol. 1, no. 4, June 1973, p. 303

24. J. B. Dearlove, *The Politics of Policy in Local Government*, Oxford, 1972.

25. See for instance, J. G. Davies, *The Evangelistic Bureaucrat*, London, Tavistock, 1972.

26. M. S. Feldstein, 'Economic Analysis, Operations Research, and National Health Service Efficiency', *Oxford Economic Papers*, March 1963, pp. 19–31.

27. G. Majone, 'The Feasibility of Social Policies', *Policy Sciences*, vol. 6, 1975, pp. 49–69.

28. T. Kuhn, *The Structure of Scientific Revolutions*, Chicago University Press, 1962.

29. L. J. Sharpe, 'Instrumental Participation and Urban Government', in J. A. G. Griffith, ed. *From Policy to Aministration*, London, Allen & Unwin, 1975.

30. P. Flynn and others, *Social Malaise in Liverpool*, Liverpool City Planning Department, 1970.

31. See for instance, Brian Robson, *Urban Analysis*, London, Cambridge University Press, 1969.

32. See, for instance, John Edwards, 'Social Indicators, Urban Deprivation, and Positive Discrimination', *Journal of Social Policy*, vol. 4, no. 3, July 1975, pp. 275–88.

Chapter 9
Issues on Representation

Edward Craven

Since the Industrial Revolution our institutions of government have had to cope with the consequences of fairly rapid social and economic change. Industrialization, urbanization and a capitalist mode of production provided challenges to which our system of government had to respond. At a political level, the two-party system eventually came to reflect and pursue the interests of the two main economic classes. Universal suffrage extended basic political rights throughout the community. The range of government powers and functions increased enormously, reflecting the need to control as well as to promote the operation of an increasingly complex and large-scale urban society. Much of this added power was concentrated at national level, as only from there could effective control be undertaken. The formal machinery of government was streamlined and modernized, sweeping away the decrepit, small and inefficient local government units and replacing them with large all-purpose counties and county boroughs.

This process of adaptation is still proceeding and, as always, it produces a good deal of conflict – such changes involve losers and gainers. This is especially so in the 1970s. Probably no comparable period has seen so much upheaval. The list is long and impressive. The National Health Service was reorganized in 1973, and local government in the following year; in England and Wales 1450 local authorities were abolished, and replaced by just 450. The suspension of the Stormont Parliament in 1972 ended, at least for the time being, the distinctive form of government in Northern Ireland. Britain became a member of the European Economic Communities in 1972 by signing the Treaty of Rome. Separate assemblies have been promised to the Welsh and Scots. For the first time since the Irish Nationalists left Westminster, in the early 1920s, we have strong area-based parties in Parliament.

These are important specific changes. At the same time, there is some evidence of a feeling of dissatisfaction and discontent with government in general. The falling turnout at elections, especially in local elections, is perhaps one indication: turnout in county borough elections has fallen steadily from an average of 49 per cent in the period 1948–52, to 37 per cent in 1968–72.[1] A number of surveys, especially the Attitudes Survey done for the Kilbrandon Commission, also show a resentment at the remoteness of government and the unresponsiveness of bureaucracies.[2] Demands for (and the granting of) participation in decision-taking in both the public and private sectors point in the same direction. There is also the growing demand for changes in our voting system. Many believe that proportional representation rather than the present 'winner-takes-all' system would allow a fairer reflection of political preferences, and break the stranglehold of the two main political parties. It is perhaps significant that this demand is now coming not only from minority parties such as the Liberals, but from within the Conservative and Labour parties as well.

It is quite possible, of course, that the dissatisfaction is less with the *processes* of government than with the failure of government to produce the goods, especially in terms of economic growth. Be that as it may, the present arguments about changes in our governmental institutions appear to be fundamentally different from those in earlier times. Usually such debate takes place *within* a set of taken-for-granted assumptions which no one ever seriously questions. The continuing role of our constitutional monarch is one example. Yet, in the 1970s, two of these assumptions are being seriously examined for the first time in many years.

In the past, whatever domestic changes were discussed, no one ever questioned the supremacy of the national Parliament at Westminster. That supremacy rested on the assumption that the basic political loyalty was to the nation, meaning the United Kingdom. There were of course other loyalties, but they were subordinate to this. It was assumed that the political community called Britain was the only one which counted in the end. Now, this assumption is challenged, partly by our membership of the EEC, which for the first time gives supernational loyalties a political form (especially if direct elections to a European Parliament take place), and partly by the resurgence of cultural nationalism in Scotland and Wales.

Secondly, it was assumed that legitimacy was given to government decisions through the ballot box. Because we could choose and reject those who exercised public power on our behalf, we were prepared to accept their decisions, whether we agreed with them or not. The legitimacy of the elected representatives was further supported by our willing acceptance of the value of the advice given to them by their experts, whom we presumed must know more and be wiser than the average citizen. But the legitimacy of the representative democracy is now being seriously questioned. This is shown not only by a demand for proportional representation, but more significantly in the demands for direct participation in decision making. People seem to be less and less prepared to leave decisions to elected representatives who have been chosen largely by a small party caucus, who are unknown to their electorate, and whose ability to control the growing apparatus of government seems to be diminishing.

Many people point to the relationship between the trades unions and central government as one example of this change. The trades unions were not prepared to accept the authority of either a Labour government to impose legal controls over their activities in the late 1960s, or of a Conservative government to restrict collective bargaining and to substitute an administratively defined pay policy in 1973 and 1974. Since then, the close relationship between the TUC and the Labour government throughout various phases of the social contract has been criticized by some as limiting too much the power of a democratically elected government – though others would simply see it as realistic and healthy cooperation in weathering a particularly severe economic storm.

It would be impossible within the confines of this chapter to discuss all the problems associated with these two developments. Two issues however seem particularly appropriate to the theme of this book, as the spatial perspective can illuminate both. How far should we take decentralization of power inside the UK? How far should we adapt our institutions to allow a greater degree of participatory democracy? These two seem to be key issues facing our system of government at the moment.

Decentralization and the spatial perspective

The arguments for taking power away from Whitehall and Westminster and giving it to some form of sub-national authority are complex. The complexity is increased by the various forms of decentralization which are possible. They range from administrative decentralization (the location of central government personnel and some powers of controlled discretion in outposts of the central bureaucracy in various parts of the country) through executive devolution (considerable power to interpret and implement national policy) to legislative devolution (the power to make laws concerning one or more areas of public activity). The strongest form of decentralization would be the creation of a federal state or, ultimately, the conferring of total sovereignty on various regions, i.e. separation. However, there is a basic theme running through the debate which is particularly important for our purposes. This concerns the appropriate spatial scale at which decisions should be taken.

All governments need a spatial area over which to exercise their functions. That spatial area has to be unambiguously defined: it has to have boundaries where responsibility stops and starts. There are two broad inter-related choices to be made. First, how should government powers be distributed between different levels of government, spatially defined – supernational, national, regional, local? Second, at sub-national level, how should we draw the boundaries between different authorities with the same status – for example, if we had regional government in England, how many regions should we have, i.e. how big should they be? The need then for a spatial basis for the exercise of public power presents us with two problems – of level and of size.

There are a number of criteria which help us to make these

choices. One of the most important is to consider how social, economic and political life, with which government has to deal, is organized into spatial patterns. In our everyday life, we live, move and work in a spatial context. Our relationships with others are not random in aggregate terms but exhibit certain regularities. We tend to live close to people with the same socio-economic status. As a result, residential areas become socially segregated. Many travel to work using a few main transportation routes, setting up travel-to-work patterns around centres of employment. We develop political loyalties and use areas as symbols of them – Britain, Scotland, Yorkshire or, on a small scale, the few streets making up Church End, Finchley. Different parts of the country, because of their distinctive economic and social development over the years, differ very significantly from one another. Some areas may have a declining employment base and a legacy of old and outdated physical infrastructure. Others may have booming employment and strong pressure for expansion and growth. Others may be retirement and holiday areas with a peculiar age and employment structure. These spatial variations create problems of quite different sorts for public authorities.

One way of solving problems of spatial level and scale for government is to create some match between the spatial structure of government and the reality of spatial relationships: that is, to draw our government boundaries and distribute government functions so as to reflect as far as possible the spatial patterns of social, economic and political life on the ground. The advantages of trying to do this are many. It is clearly desirable to have units of government which reflect at least some of the loyalties of the citizen. (This is of course something of a chicken and egg situation. The very existence of the units may create loyalties which did not exist before they were formed.) Secondly, a number of problems can be more easily dealt with. It would be difficult to provide a good transport system unless an authority had jurisdiction over the whole area within which the majority of trips were made. Likewise, redeveloping slum areas of cities and providing decent housing requires adequate land for new building fairly close to the main employment centres. This problem would be difficult to solve if the authority with the slums did not also have the land as well. Thirdly, certain services require a fairly large population to make it worthwhile providing them. This applies particularly to important but specialized services in education and health, for instance. The spatial distribution of need for these services often indicates an appropriate size for the authorities providing help.

These points are important for the issue of decentralization because those in favour of it are arguing that, at the moment, there is a *mismatch* between the spatial structure of government and the nature of spatial relationships. This applies firstly to local government in England. The Royal Commission on Local Government in England, chaired by Lord Redcliffe-Maud, made a thorough attempt to build their new local government structure on a knowledge of spatial patterns of social life.[3] They looked at travel-to-work patterns, shopping and entertainment trips, the population size thresholds for the efficient delivery of various services and so on. The final structure of local government which emerges from all this must inevitably involve compromises. For example, an efficient spatial scale for one service will be different from the efficient scale for another service. Also, a spatial scale which is *functionally* efficient may be so large as to make government even more physically remote from the people it serves. Indeed it was these two factors which eventually led the Conservative government in 1972 to introduce a system which was very different from Redcliffe-Maud's. The latter wanted a single set of large unitary authorities which performed all the functions of local government; the 1972 re-organization introduced a two-tier system, with some 'personal' services being the responsibility of the small district authorities which were closer to the people and thus 'more democratic'. Counties had strategic planning functions to perform and responsibility for services, like education, which needed a larger spatial scale.

Some observers, such as Derek Senior, have suggested that the re-organization in 1972 was a disaster.[4] Opportunities to reform local government boundaries in a comprehensive way occur fairly infrequently and Senior suggests that on this occasion the opportunity for a sensible re-organization was missed. Boundaries were re-drawn so that local authorities did not cover areas which were sensible for the provision of health care or water services, both of which needed larger and different areas than those embodied in the new local government structure. Local government powers in these fields were therefore *removed* from local authorities and invested in a re-organized National Health Service and in new Regional Water Boards, both answerable directly to Parliament in Westminster. Thus the choice of a specific spatial scale for local government boundaries led directly to the removal of functions from them and added these powers to an ever-growing central government machine.

Moreover, the new boundaries in the big conurbations such as Manchester, Birmingham and the West Riding were such as to split off these conurbations from the surrounding areas which depended on them, and from which they could draw resources of land and money to help solve their problems. The boundaries were drawn tightly around the built-up area and as the 1971 White Paper admits 'none of these proposed metropolitan counties can practically contain the solutions of all the planning problems of the conurbations'.[5] Inter-authority cooperation might work, but past experience does not hold out much hope for this approach. The differences of interest between the cities and their surrounding counties have been too great.

Local government re-organization failed to take account of the fact that a growing range of problems can only be understood and solved at a regional scale. This fact has of course been recognized in the past. Whenever a regional-scale institution was needed it was set up; but without adequate accountability to the public – water and sewerage, health, police, regional economic planning, etc. People like Senior believe that a regional level of government would not only allow local government to perform its present functions more effectively, but also to take on a range of new functions, now nominally central government's responsibility, making them more democratically accountable in the process. But there is still the problem of exactly what a 'region' looks like. Are we talking about the thirty-five or so city-regions, based on major centres and their hinterlands, which Senior envisaged in his dissenting memorandum to the Redcliffe-Maud Report? Or Senior's later view that, if significant powers are decentralized, fourteen regional authorities made up of combinations of city-regions is the answer? Alternatives are the five provinces outlined in the dissenting memorandum to the Kilbrandon Commission's Report by Lord Crowther-Hunt and Alan Peacock, or the eight standard regions of England now in use for certain planning purposes.

A second and related issue arising from the mismatch of government structure to spatial patterns is the inability of our present system to do justice to the diversity of social and economic conditions in Britain. In theory, *local* government is there to reflect this diversity: policies suitable for one area are not suitable for another. When more and more power becomes concentrated at the centre, these spatial differences are less and less likely to be taken into account. This is especially so when decisions in White-hall are concerned with priorities within, or between, *functional* departments of state – health, housing, education – on a basis of political judgements about the needs of Britain as a whole. These decisions about functional needs at a national level may not make sense in some local areas. Some areas may need schools rather than roads, hospitals rather than housing, yet local authorities have little discretion to switch resources. They are also tied by the tight control over standards of provision exercised by the centre. The argument is then that the centralization of power does not allow local governments enough discretion to pursue policies which accord with their areas' real needs. What is required is that national government should shed some of its powers to sub-national authorities, including the power to fix public spending priorities and to depart, if they think fit, from national standards.

This last argument for decentralization raises a major issue. Historically, the growing centralization of power has brought about some degree of equality in social and economic opportunity between different parts of the United Kingdom. Narrow local oligarchies showed themselves both unwilling and unable to discharge their obligations in this respect: they had neither the resources nor the political desire to do so. Only the central government was able to impose basic and uniform standards throughout the country, to protect deprived minorities and, through its taxing power, to redistribute resources from rich to poor, whether areas or people. Those who wish to see more equality are going to be suspicious of any attempt to undermine the centralization of power.

On the other side, decentralizers bring different values to bear. The concentration of power at the centre is seen as stultifying the individuality of both areas and people, removing control over their own affairs from them, and imposing a uniformity which bears little relation to their real needs. What they favour is diversity rather than uniformity; experimentation rather than conformity; self-reliance and self-government rather than external paternalistic control. The solution, of course, lies in achieving the right *balance* between these sets of values, and it is this that is at issue.[6]

However, no matter how the debate is resolved, there is one important practical implication: significant decentralization to sub-national 'regional' units, whatever the form they take, will inevitably mean another re-organization of local government. It is a very great pity that the Kilbrandon Report on devolution and the Redcliffe-Maud Report on local government were not produced together: they are opposite sides of the same coin. Because local government re-organization took place before any decisions were made on Kilbrandon, the latter's proposals will have to face the inevitable resistance by local government to any more change.

The spatial basis of political community

A third, and potentially more important, mismatch involves political loyalties. The special nature of the Scots, Welsh and Northern Irish has long been recognized in our system of government. Northern Ireland has had a separate legislative assembly since 1920. Scotland has had a Secretary of State since 1926 and separate administrative arrangements in a number of fields of government for some time before that. For Wales, decentralization of some responsibility from Westminster to Cardiff started at the turn of this century, and culminated in a Secretary of State for Wales in 1964.

These arrangements did not imply any disunity among the various segments of the United Kingdom. All these areas were fully represented in Parliament at Westminster, and the discretion of the Secretary of State was always limited by his membership of the British Cabinet. The arrangements sought to recognize, within limits and within a unitary state, the historical and cultural distinctiveness of the Celtic fringe and the attachment of the Celts to their own traditions.

One of the main factors unifying the peoples of the United Kingdom is the existence of two national political parties. Their appeal has never been based on regional loyalties within the UK. Their appeal was broadly ideological, presenting policies and claiming support which had nothing to do with incipent national-ism in the various parts of the Kingdom. Their electoral support was based on the class and occupational characteristics of the population. The Labour party, for example, was able to gain the support of many people in Glasgow, Cardiff and Birmingham because they were all urban working-class people with similar aspirations and similar problems. Broadly speaking, then, the 'spatial' basis of political loyalty was the United Kingdom, and within the UK political loyalty was based on common experience associated with class and occupation.

However, evidence has recently been put forward to suggest that the Scots and Welsh are undergoing a political re-orientation, away from Britain and class-based loyalties and towards loyalties based on 'sub-nationality' and cultural heritage. Attitude surveys and opinion polls are one source of evidence, but far more important is the political support received by the Scottish National party and Plaid Cymru at the polls. The former took 30 per cent of Scottish votes at the October 1974 General Election (see Table 11). A further 5–10 per cent at the next election would see that party taking the majority of Scottish seats. Moreover, evidence from Europe indicates that other unitary nation-states are having similar problems in retaining the loyalties of their

Table 11. **Electoral support for the Scottish National party and Plaid Cymru in General Elections, 1964–74**

	1964	1966	1970	1974 (Feb.)	1974 (Oct.)
Scottish National Party					
candidates	15	23	65	70	71
seats	0	0	1	7	11
votes ('000s)	64	128	307	632	840
Plaid Cymru					
candidates	23	20	36	36	36
seats	0	0	0	2	3
votes ('000s)	69	61	175	171	166

Source: Butler, D. E., and Sloman, A., *British Political Facts 1900–1975*, London, Macmillan, 1975.

various sub-nationalities – the Catalans and the Basques in Spain, and the Bretons and the Corsicans in France, for example.

It is difficult to reach any firm conclusions on why this is happening now. One factor in Britain's case may be a realization that our economic performance over the past twenty years has been very poor; the nation-state has failed as a unit for the creation of wealth. Another may be a resentment, made all the more pointed by the lack of growth, at the regional disparities in economic and social conditions notwithstanding regional policy; the nation-state has failed as a unit for the distribution of wealth. A further possible consideration could be that the internal unity of the UK has depended on a well-developed external role as a great imperial power; once that role disappeared, internal ties weakened. Another, more general, point might be that these new loyalties are a reaction to the complexities of modern industrial urban societies, in which an individual's sense of identity and his control over his own existence is eroded by large-scale change brought about by impersonal and almost unknown sources of power. Being Scottish or Welsh provides a ready-made, easily accessible set of identities on which to cling.

The problem here is how far to recognize these changing loyal-ties in the structure of government. The Kilbrandon Commission was set up to consider this, and its recommendations influenced recent proposals for assemblies in Scotland and Wales.[7] The government plans a Scottish legislative assembly with powers to make laws over a wide range of matters: in Wales, there will be no power to make laws, but there will be executive discretion to interpret and implement law and policy laid down by the UK government. Unlike the previous cases of mismatch, there is little choice but to adjust to these new spatial loyalties: the electoral support for the two nationalist parties are political imperatives which it is exceedingly difficult to deny. But this does not prevent a good deal of worry about the implications of these changes if they result in significant devolution of power from Westminster to Cardiff and Edinburgh.

The first is a straightforward party political point. The Labour and Conservative parties are worried about the effects of national-ism on their electoral support in Scotland and Wales. Both have lost parliamentary seats to the Scottish and Welsh Nationalists during the 1970s. Scotland and Wales are particularly important to the Labour party, which has held a majority of seats there since the war. If the present Labour government does not devolve sufficient power to satisfy the aspirations of Scottish and Welsh nationalists, they may well continue to lose seats to the Scottish National party and Plaid Cymru. On the other hand, if they give too much power away, the whole issue of the over-representation of Scotland and Wales in the Westminster Parliament may come to the fore, and eventually lead to a reduction in the number of Scottish and Welsh seats. In either case, the status of Labour as a national party and its chances of obtaining and maintaining a majority in the House of Commons may be threatened. The present devolution proposals are in part an attempt by Labour to unhook itself from the horns of this dilemma.

Another worry is that these new loyalties may be leading to a narrowing of responsibility. In the past, people's sense of responsi-bility in promoting the welfare of their fellow-countrymen was not limited by internal borders. Few people were prepared to discriminate between individuals on the basis of where they lived, though they were on other criteria. In this sense, the political community within which responsibility was exercised, resources distributed and help given was nationwide. There is now a fear that the limits of responsibility are going to narrow. The Scots will be primarily concerned with the Scots, the Welsh with the Welsh and the English with the English. Neil Kinnock put this very well in the Commons debate on devolution in January 1976:

This proposed devolution creates for the first time in the modern history of Great Britain tangible political and economic borders. They will be in men's minds even if they are not drawn on maps. Where a person comes from could become a deciding factor in his political attitudes. In the past, with the exception of a few paranoiacs in all three countries, most people have been blind to this factor.[8]

Devolution to Scotland and Wales may thus create new barriers. But its divisiveness may be even greater if it results in strengthening the bargaining position of the Scots and Welsh for a share of national resources. The existence of separate Secretaries of State in the British Cabinet has often given Wales and Scotland an advantage in the past. This was acceptable partly because of their cultural distinctiveness and partly because both countries suffered from a number of social and economic problems. Public expenditure per capita in both areas was (and remains) considerably higher than in England. Under the government's devolution scheme, this advantage might well be strengthened, but it might be resented too. The scheme, for example, envisages Scotland negotiating with the UK government each year for a block grant to cover its expenses. The size of the grant is supposed to reflect Scotland's 'needs' objectively defined by specific criteria. It is, however, likely that such criteria will be difficult to find and agree upon. The block grant is much more likely to reflect the unique political status of Scotland with its own legislative assembly. The splitting up of resources will take place with only one or two regions being separately represented around the negotiating table.

Political leaders are sensitive to the effect of this situation on England. England tends to be forgotten in the devolution debate: there are certainly no regional loyalties in the English regions to compare with Wales, let alone Scotland (although the Kilbrandon Commissioners were convinced that they had found some). Yet that regional consciousness may well be fostered by these devolution proposals, and take the form of resentment of and alienation from Scotland and Wales. This was clearly in the mind of Mr Stott, M P for Westhoughton:

England receives £13·1 per head per annum from the Department of Industry, compared with £29·5 in Wales and about £28 in Scotland. I am not complaining. This money has been given to Scotland and Wales to solve their very difficult problems; but while there has been an imbalance in central Government spending over the years, this will be compounded if we go ahead with the Government's devolution proposals. My colleagues and I are not prepared to stand by and see that happen at the expense of our own regions that suffer as much if not worse social deprivation ... I never expected to make this kind of speech to the House, but I have been forced into that situation in order to defend my constituents.[9]

There are two important implications arising from this point of view. First, it is unrealistic to suppose that England can be quickly set aside in the devolution debate. Tinkering with two parts of a system has repercussions on the system as a whole. The second is that giving considerably strengthened regional administration to two parts of Britain may mean that our ways of making national policy may have to change. Simply in terms of public expenditure decisions, the national system may be forced explicitly to start thinking and operating in much more spatial terms. Stott's statements, together with a number of other comments from the English regions, suggest that the idea of territorial justice – to each *area* according to the needs of that area – will become more important in resource allocation. Whether this more territorially based system for distributing resources can be made acceptable without similar bargaining power being held by each of the constituent areas is open to some doubt.

These three cases of mismatch between the structure of government and the spatial patterns of social reality are important for our understanding of the issue of decentralization of political power, and also for making value judgements about its merits.

There are of course many other factors involved which have not been dealt with here. For example, there is the alleged lack of efficiency in central government because it is so overloaded. This is associated with the growing power of the executive – Ministers and civil servants – compared with the House of Commons as a whole. Central government has so much to do that MPs cannot possibly oversee it all. There is the view that the decentralization issue is just a smokescreen which is being used to obscure our real problems. Some argue that our real problem is too much government, so instead of concerning ourselves with juggling the distribution of governmental functions, we ought simply to get rid of some altogether. Others suggest that getting the economy and industrial relations right is the main issue: rearranging government functions is going to make only a marginal contribution to this. Indeed, it is argued that the nationalist support would quickly whither away if the economy could be sorted out.

However, whatever the merits of the last two arguments, it is clear that people's attitudes to our existing governmental system have been changing. Some find it inefficient in providing services and making effective policy. Others find it does not adequately reflect the changing basis of political community. Both wish to change the distribution of governmental functions and the pattern of boundaries. The question is how far we should accede to these wishes.

Participation and the physical environment

Participation can be seen as another facet of the movement towards the decentralization of power. In the past, people's involvement with the political process consisted largely of voting in national and local elections, being members of political parties of one kind or another, and joining with their fellows in pressure groups to influence policy decisions. All these three activities were supposed to enable the grass-roots to influence government at all levels, from national to local. Each involves a hierarchy of organization through which communication can take place. The operation of these channels of communication rests on a number of assumptions: that voting for elected representatives every few years is enough to satisfy most people's aspirations for involvement; that the existing political parties can adequately reflect the range of interests in the population at large; and that our system of government is open enough to allow pressure groups to influence policy.

These assumptions are of course intimately related. They all rely on the acceptance that our system of representative democracy is basically adequate. MPs and local councillors are elected via the two-plus party system: they take decisions advised by their bureaucrats and professionals and after listening to representation by interested parties. Their decisions, taken on this basis, will be accepted if not welcomed. Their authority, then, is derived from and made legitimate by the ballot box and the expertise of their officials.

Two developments over the last few years suggest that things are changing. Both these developments are called participation. The first has been the growth in the number of local pressure groups. Obtaining adequate information here is very difficult. Such groups are often not permanent, but spring up from time to time in response to external threats such as the closing of a school, or the building of a new road. Nor are there very adequate statistics on even the more permanent ones. However, the number of local associations affiliated to the Civic Trust, for example, has risen from about 850 in 1970 to 1250 in 1975. A recent report on voluntary associations states that 'pressure group activities by voluntary associations are nothing new in this country ... however, recent years have seen a dramatic rise in what we call pressure group activities both on the part of established movements and more notably by a large number of brand new movements'.[10] Such pressure groups cover the whole spectrum of social policy from Claimants' Unions on the one hand to amenity and preservation societies on the other. It seems reasonable to assume that more and more people are exercising their democratic freedoms through involvement in the activities of such groups rather than through political parties and the formal democratic system.

A second development has been a growing attempt by people

to become involved with specific institutions of which they are an integral part. These are not pressure groups attempting to influence government from the outside, but clients, customers or employees who are a basic part of the institution itself. Examples would be worker participation in factories and businesses; parent, teacher and pupil participation in the running of schools, and tenants' associations in the management of public housing estates. What seems to be happening here is that the authority of those holding power in an institution to control the activities of others – in our case the manager, the board of governors and the headmaster, and the housing management committee of a local authority – is being questioned. Their right to decide about working conditions in the factory, the curriculum taught in the school, or the repair and re-painting of housing estates is no longer automatically accepted. This kind of participation then raises issues about the exercise of authority within important social institutions.

In so far as these grass-roots pressures have been successful in changing government policy (and there are many instances of this being so), they represent a *de facto* decentralization of power. Indeed, government has had to respond to them by changing decision-making procedures over the last decade. These changes have been aimed at making government more open and responsive. In the physical planning field, there are elaborate consultation procedures in the making of structure and local plans, as there are in transport planning, especially in the siting of major trunk roads. Neighbourhood councils have been set up in many areas to represent the views of local people. In housing, citizens are involved in general improvement schemes and in housing action area projects. The re-organization of the National Health Service led to the creation of community health councils to represent health-users. These are only some of the changes, and are probably, in themselves, the best evidence available that there is local pressure for changing the ways decisions are made.

As with regional loyalties, it is difficult to come to any really firm conclusions about the explanation of these phenomena. But broadly speaking two sets of factors seem to be at work, one of which can be labelled 'remoteness' factors, the other 'awareness' factors. The first have recently been summarized by Harold Wilson. Speaking in Edinburgh he asserted that 'He [the individual] starts from the fact that he is increasingly unable to live his own life, express himself, dream his own dreams, and realize his ideals, because increasingly the decisions which govern his life and the life of his family are taken from him by remote powers or persons he has never perhaps heard of . . . they feel robbed of any real control over how they can live their lives.'[11] In this case, the concentration and centralization of power in large bureaucracies, both public and private, has been necessary to manage an increasingly complex, technological and interdependent society. At the same time it has meant that the individual is constantly baffled by the complexity of institutions and the issues with which they deal, and cowed by the impermeable and inflexible face of bureaucracy. This tendency has been aggravated by the increase in the scale and scope of government activity which extends into more and more spheres of life.

The effect of these factors, it is claimed, is to induce feelings of powerlessness. The Kilbrandon Commission came to the conclusion that the feeling of political powerlessness in the face of government was fairly widespread. However, these social changes, if they do in fact produce feelings of powerlessness, are likely to lead to less participation rather than more. Those who feel powerless in the face of government are not likely to rush out to join community groups and the like. This tendency is probably reinforced by what we know about life-styles in general. Numerous studies have shown the influence of the growth of home-centredness on the use of leisure time: watching television, gardening and doing jobs around the house predominate. The spread of home-ownership and of joint conjugal roles are important here. These factors, which have been at work for a long time, will turn people inward to the family and the home, rather than outward to the community. Thus, while it can be argued that social changes may create a negative potential for participation in that there may be deep-seated frustration and alienation, it is necessary to look to other changes which increase the possibility that this potential may be realized.

This possibility is largely the theme of the second category of changes, 'awareness' factors. The argument here is that the development of advanced industrial societies is leading not only towards the concentration of power, but also towards the de-concentration of power into the hands of the ordinary citizen and consumer. The first factor has been the increase in living standards generally since the war. This has given the individual power as a consumer, and has increased his self-respect in that he has broken out of the deference and acquiescence which goes with low living standards and economic insecurity. Secondly, there has been an expansion of educational opportunity in the school, in further education and in adult education of all kinds. For the increasing numbers of people who grasp these opportunities, horizons are widened, a capacity for independent judgement is created, and a greater confidence in one's own capacity to act successfully is generated. Thirdly, the extension of mass communications, especially television, tends to break down narrow parochialism and to extend awareness of the external world and one's place in it.[12]

The demand for participation seems to be occurring in most fields of public policy, but it is particularly common when attempts are made to change the physical environment. It is important for our purposes to examine specifically the reasons for this. One important factor is the very pace and scale of physical change. Even the low level of economic growth in Britain since the war has brought about a considerable spread of affluence.[13] This has enabled people to acquire more and more material goods and the concomitant of this demand has been pressure on the physical environment. Car ownership has spread, leading to road conges-tion and the building of new motorways inside and outside cities. Owner-occupation has become possible for more and more people, resulting in a further expansion of the urban area. The public sector, financed by increased tax yields and heavy borrowing, has met the demand for roads and pushed ahead with slum clearance and new building. The scale of this change is different from the past. It is no longer a question of widening a road, but building a new one with two or three lanes. Housing estates are not ten-to-twelve-house infill developments, but large developments of a hundred houses or more. New technology has made more large-scale building possible, besides introducing extra pressure on the environment in the form of noise and pollution. Thus, more people are doing more things in a more sophisticated way than ever before.

One reaction to all this has been to try to halt or limit the scale and pace of physical change, and the organizational form of the reaction has been the environmental pressure group. Many of these groups pursue what can be called protective values – that is, they are concerned with protecting the environment in which they live. They see proposed changes having detrimental effects – the splitting up of long-established communities when large-scale demolition is involved; unwanted additions of undesirable people when new housing development occurs; increased noise and pollution when road building takes place; undesirable aesthetic changes when land is built on or buildings changed and so on. On the whole their aim is to maintain the status quo or at least to minimize the scale of change.

The growth of such pressure groups is probably sustained by a number of further factors. The growth of home-centredness has been noted already and this can lead to a narrow concern with family, house and garden. Yet it can also lead to a range of demands on 'public' goods. New wants and aspirations may occur which cannot be satisfied simply by private consumption: as affluence increases, the marginal utility of more private consumption may decline. Moreover, home-centredness cannot be fully realized without certain attributes in the environment surrounding the home – good schools for children, a protection of peace and quiet, defence against falling house prices, etc. To make home-centredness really work, it is necessary to become vigilant about public policy decisions, which can so radically affect the environment. With the spread of home-ownership in particular, more people have a more *material* stake in protecting the environment from unwanted intrusion.

On the other hand, many people may well have an *emotive* stake in protecting the physical environment too. This is not simply a matter of social links with kin and friends which can be disrupted by environmental change. It also involves the sense of identity which close attachment to a particular physical environment can provide. Building and landscapes are functional in a material sense, but contribute to a sense of security and belonging too. With the passage of time, the physical environment can become as familiar and valued as a network of friends and acquaintances: both are anchorages for personal identity in a rapidly changing society.

A further factor which contributes to the growth of such groups and the tactics they employ is the peculiar character of physical development itself – its permanence. A new road, or a new factory, once built, is likely to remain for many years. Unlike a decision to change the curriculum in a school, or to change the ways local discretion in social security payment is exercised, a decision to build or demolish cannot be altered once it is implemented (except at very excessive cost, in financial and political terms). The consequences of such decisions will be relatively enduring. Therefore pressure groups opposed to such physical changes cannot hope to fight again another day to get the decision reversed. Their opposition has to be limited not only in space, to a specific location, but also in time. This tends to lead to the adoption of tactics which are characteristic of dissenting groups, rather than pressure groups.[14] They tend to stand firm on principle and refuse to compromise. Rational technical argument will have less impact than usual. Direct action and confrontation are seen to be as appropriate as discussion and normal political pressure. The disruptive tactics of those opposing the proposed trunk road in the Aire Valley in Yorkshire in early 1976 provided a very good example. In that case, as in many others involving physical change, the government and the local groups were playing a zero-sum game, a game in which the outcome is either total victory or total defeat for one party or the other – the road will either be built there or it will not.

Many people have welcomed these participatory developments. They see them as basically healthy and a necessary antidote to the sickness which has enveloped our political institutions, especially the concentration and centralization of power, and the impotency of elected representatives. Others, however, are worried by this trend. The first worry is that the pressure groups are often basically middle class in their membership and pursue middle-class interests. The outcome, then, will be simply to increase the power of the already powerful to the disadvantage of the less articulate. It is certainly likely that the growth in the size of the middle class has been an important contributory factor in the spread of participatory pressures. In 1951, there were 2·7 million households headed by a chief earner in social classes I and II, comprising 18 per cent of all households. By 1971, these figures had increased to 3·9 million and 21 per cent respectively. There has thus been a sharp increase in that category of the population who normally join voluntary associations, who are most active within them as organizers, who have a high sense of personal efficacy in achieving change, and who know more about public affairs in general. Moreover, a significant proportion of the increase in middle-class occupations is accounted for by professional workers, many of whom are employed by government itself and whose very existence has depended on the expansion of government activity since the war. They have a considerable knowledge and experience of local and central government and seem willing to devote part of their spare time to initiating and sustaining pressure groups of various kinds: 'it is by no means uncommon to find teachers, social workers and the like working in the evening to help organizations to cope with their own professional employer, the local authority, by day'.[15]

Not all of this extra middle-class involvement has been directed at looking after its own material interests: much of the more successful community action in the inner city areas that has attempted to advance the interests of the urban working class has relied heavily on the expertise of sympathetic middle-class radicals of various kinds. But when it has been directed towards self-protection, criticisms have been made that it can result in denying less well-off members of society access to resources they value. This is especially so in the environmental field. New roads allow greater mobility in the search for recreation or work. The expansion of villages through private residential development allows more people access to a pleasant semi-rural life-style which they value. New council houses in the suburbs can provide decent housing for the inner-city slum dweller. Many pressure groups organize to prevent changes such as these. Anthony Crosland warned that these groups attempt to 'kick away the ladder' in order to prevent other people obtaining the benefits which those doing the kicking already enjoy.[16] The reality of social democracy today seems to require the spread of car ownership, better housing and access to pleasant environmental conditions throughout the social structure: certain environmental pressure groups seem to want to prevent this happening.

This kind of criticism relates closely to the idea of the narrowing of the limits of responsibility mentioned earlier. Any major new development will have a wide range of costs and benefits for a number of groups of people. The Aire Valley trunk road, for example, will not only disrupt the peace and quiet of areas through which it passes, lead to the loss of agricultural land and so on; it will also increase the ease of access of people living in the Leeds–Bradford conurbation to the Yorkshire Dales, and reduce pollution, noise and danger on the existing trunk road from Bradford northwards. The problem some people see with many environmental pressure groups is that only those about to suffer the costs will organize politically: those who might benefit will probably not do so. The pressure group may well take a narrow view of the interests involved: only the public authority can take an overall look and attempt to balance the costs and benefits. But this is made more difficult when the political pressure is so lopsided.

There are other worries as well. There is the problem of how the elected representative fits in here. A number of studies have indicated that he sees his job as taking an overall view of people's interests throughout the whole city or region, rather than merely acting as an advocate for the narrow interests of his particular constituents. This makes it difficult for him to become involved in this new form of political action. It is made all the more difficult because pressure groups and the population at large tend to see power residing with appointed officials rather than the elected representative. Thus the tendency of pressure groups to bypass these representatives, or be openly hostile to them, is of some concern. On the other hand, at least one political party, the Liberal Party, has successfully advocated and harnessed such local political pressures. Their brand of community politics was highly effective in increasing the party's representation in both local and national government in the early 1970s.

Concluding remarks

It has not been possible to discuss in detail many other important issues in the political life of Britain in the 1970s – Northern Ireland, the European Economic Community or the move towards worker participation. Moreover, many of the problems discussed in this chapter are not confined to Britain alone. They are, to a greater or lesser degree, characteristic of most advanced industrial societies in the western world.[17] Yet they are perhaps more prominent in Britain because it is both one of the most highly centralized of the western democracies, and one of the least successful in economic terms.

It is, however, a value judgement to see these pressures for change as problems. They may be so for those who wish to retain our present system intact. For those who wish to see it change, the existence of these pressures is a splendid opportunity to bring such change about. The Scottish and Welsh National parties for example were set up in the 1920s, and the demand for regional government covering cities *and* their hinterlands also has a long history. But it is only in the 1970s that it has become politically possible for such demands to be met.

How far they should be met is of course essentially a political decision. It is impossible to conduct any 'scientific' experiments, for example, to evaluate the consequences of a regional form of government. Something can be learnt from looking at decentralized systems of government elsewhere in western Europe, and in North America, but international comparisons can tell us only a limited amount. Nor is Northern Ireland a very useful home-made experiment because of its extreme peculiarity. Moreover, the issue resolves itself not into questions of fact, but into questions of basic value – equality, liberty, national feeling and so on.

The new political loyalties in Scotland and Wales will test the quality of political judgement most. It is not just a question of dealing with the peripheral regions *ad hoc*, as some believe: it inevitably involves the core regions of England as well. Britain has often prided itself (and been esteemed by others) for the maturity of its democracy. Part of that maturity has been an ability to adapt our institutions without violence to meet changing circumstances, pressures and threats. The next big test of that maturity is upon us now: notwithstanding the economic problem, one measure of our success over the next ten years will be whether we make the right choices about the decentralization of power – how much and to whom.

NOTE.

Since this chapter was written the government's devolution plans for Scotland and Wales have been rejected by the House of Commons. One factor in this was opposition from certain English MPs, especially those in the northern regions. A second attempt to introduce legislation will be made in 1978, however.

References

1. Butler, D., and Sloman, A., *British Political Facts, 1900–1975*, 4th ed., London, Macmillan, 1975.
2. Royal Commission on the Constitution, *Devolution and other Aspects of Government: An Attitudes Survey*, Research Paper 7, London, HMSO, 1973.
3. Royal Commission on Local Government in England, *Report*, Cmnd 4040, London, HMSO, 1969.
4. Senior, D., 'Regional Devolution and Local Government', in Craven, E., ed., *Regional Devolution and Social Policy*, London, Macmillan, 1975.
5. Department of the Environment, *Local Government in England: Government Proposals for Re-organization*, Cmnd 4584, London, HMSO, 1971, para. 32.
6. See Craven, E., 'Introduction', in *Regional Devolution and Social Policy*, op. cit.

7. Royal Commission on the Constitution, *Report*, Cmnd 5460, London, HMSO, 1973, and Cabinet Office, *Our Changing Democracy: Devolution to Scotland and Wales*, Cmnd 6348, London, HMSO, 1975.

8. *Weekly Hansard*, no. 1020, 12–15 January 1976, London, HMSO, 1976, col. 294. The whole debate is well worth reading for anyone interested in this topic.

9. ibid., col. 329–30.

10. *50 Million Volunteers*, London, HMSO, 1972.

11. Speech to East Scottish Labour Party Meeting, 20 January 1973.

12. For an interesting discussion see Arblaster, A., 'Participation: Context and Conflict', in Parry, G., *Participation in Politics*, Manchester University Press, 1972.

13. See Ferris, J., *Participation in Urban Planning: The Barnsbury Case*, Occasional Papers in Social Administration no. 84, London, Bell, 1972.

14. See Vallance, E., 'Three Languages of Change: Democracy, Technocracy and Direct Action', in Benewick, R., and Smith, T., eds., *Direct Action and Democratic Politics*, London, Allen & Unwin, 1972.

15. *Issues in Community Work*, London, Calouste Gulbenkian Foundation, 1972.

16. Crosland, A., *A Social Democratic Britain*, Fabian Tract 404, London, Fabian Society, 1971.

17. For an excellent discussion of these issues, see Sharpe, L. J., 'Centralization, Decentralization and Participation', in *Europe 2000*, vol. 1, *Fear and Hopes for European Urbanization*, The Hague, M. Nijhoff, 1972.

Chapter 10
Issues on Financial Allocation

Richard Jackman

Introduction

Since the Second World War there has been a massive expansion of public services such as education, health, housing, welfare services and the like. This development is not unique to Britain but reflects a general trend in relatively affluent societies. As incomes rise, communities typically tend to spend a high proportion of the increase on services of this kind. In the UK such services fall within the public sector and, in particular, within the local government sector. An expansion of local government activity need not, therefore, be regarded as particularly surprising.

In the years since 1950 the current expenditure of local authorities has risen, in real terms, at an annual rate of 5·9 per cent, as against 2·9 per cent for central government and only 1·7 per cent for privately financed consumption. In 1950, local government spending accounted for 9·3 per cent of the Gross National Product, and local government employed 6·2 per cent of the total working population. By 1974 the figures were 17·0 per cent and 10·9 per cent respectively. These figures are set out in Tables 12 and 13, which give a more detailed picture of the growth of local government relative to the economy as a whole.

Table 14 shows the growth of expenditure on the main public services over this period. The increase in expenditure has been accompanied by a marked improvement in the provision of public services. The standard of housing has improved in terms both of amenities and in the number of dwellings in relation to the size of the population. In education, the pupil–teacher ratio (and hence the average class size) has fallen steadily and the proportion of children attending school both before and after the statutory

Table 12. **Growth of local government expenditure 1950–74**

| | 1950 | | 1974 | | |
	£m current prices	% of GNP	£m current prices	% of GNP	Annual real growth %[d]
Local government					
current expenditure	697	6·0	9,289	12·6	5·9
capital expenditure	381	3·3	3,280	4·4	4·0
Central government					
current expenditure[a]	3,397	29·2	22,462	30·4	2·9
Privately financed					
consumption[b]	7,253	62·3	36,690	49·6	1·7
Gross fixed investment	1,702	14·6	16,247	22·0	4·5
Gross national product					
at factor cost[c]	11,637	100·0	73,977	100·0	2·7

[a] Current expenditure of central government and national insurance funds (including subsidies and grants to personal sector) less grants to local authorities.

[b] Consumers' expenditure less national insurance benefits and other grants to the personal sector from public authorities, adjusted to factor cost.

[c] The GNP figure is not the sum of the components of expenditure shown in the table, as some double-counting has not been removed (e.g. gross fixed investment includes local authority capital expenditure).

[d] Annual monetary growth deflated by the price index of GDP at factor cost, which has recorded an average rate of inflation of 5·2 per cent over the period (1974 = 334·6, 1950 = 100).

Source: *Annual Abstract of Statistics.*

schooling age has increased. Welfare services for the elderly and for others in need have expanded very rapidly. In terms of health care, since 1950 the rate of infant mortality has halved and deaths from infectious diseases have fallen by almost 90 per cent, and despite various new hazards of modern living, life expectancy continues to rise.[1]

Despite these achievements, there is strong pressure for further expansion. In part this is due to expectations of higher standards to match the general improvement in the standard of living.

Table 13. **Local government employment, 1952–74 – Great Britain**

	1952 thousands	1952 %	1974 thousands	1974 %	%change over 1952–74
local government	1,448	6·2	2,776	10·9	+91·7
central government	684	2·9	692	2·7	+1·2
manufacturing industry	8,647	37·1	8,238	32·5	−4·7
working population	23,324	100·0	24,365	100·0	+8·8

Source: British labour statistics: historical abstracts 1886–1968, *Department of Employment Gazette.*

Table 14. **Growth of local government expenditure by service, 1950–74 – England and Wales**

	1950/1 £m current prices	1950/1 %	1973/4 £m current prices	1973/4 %	Annual real growth %
Current expenditure					
education	268·7	30·3	3,356·7	34·5	6·4
police	54·4	6·1	534·8	5·5	5·3
social services	27·4	3·1	522·4	5·4	8·4
highways and lighting	75·4	8·5	559·9	5·8	4·1
housing	91·2	10·3	1,491·2	15·3	7·6
Total current	887·4	100·0	9,732·6	100·0	5·8
Capital expenditure					
education	39·8	10·8	457·4	12·2	6·0
highways and lighting	7·5	2·0	296·3	7·9	11·9
housing	233·8	63·4	1,880·5	50·3	4·4
Total capital	368·8	100·0	3,739·3	100·0	5·4

Note: These figures are compiled by a different method from those of Table 12; for example, they do not exclude duplicate reckoning (amounts transferred between accounts of an authority and between authorities). They measure gross expenditure, inclusive of expenditure financed by changes (e.g. council tenants' rents) and hence overstate the cost of certain services (especially housing) to the ratepayer or taxpayer.

Source: *Annual Abstract of Statistics.*

There are also demographic factors, particularly at the present time the increase in the numbers of elderly people. Perhaps more important are social changes as a result of which many traditional family responsibilities (e.g. the care of old people and even, to some extent, children) have been thrown on to the public sector. In addition, the fact that the cost of public services is hidden from the consumer may encourage unrealistic expectations of what can be provided.

The pressure for the expansion of public services has not, however, been accompanied by a correspondingly increased willingness to pay for them in the form of higher taxes. Although the cost of public services may be hidden to the consumer, it is all too apparent to the taxpayer or ratepayer. This combination of pressure for increased expenditure and increasing resistance to higher taxes (and to higher rates) has led to fears of financial 'crisis' in local government.

There are, however, two possible interpretations of the nature of the 'crisis'.[2] One is that public expenditure has become excessive in relation to people's willingness to pay for public services through taxation. The costs of improvements in public services seem often to have been underestimated. At the same time, people may be far less willing to pay increased taxes at a time of economic recession when standards of living are falling than when living standards are rising. On this interpretation, local authorities have to cut back their expenditure programmes to match their financial resources. The second interpretation is based on the financial organization of local government. Local authorities have only one source of taxation, the local property tax known as 'rates', and it is often argued that rates are a particularly regressive and inequitable form of taxation. People might well be willing to pay for improvements in public services through general taxation, but not through an increase in rates. If this is so, what is required is not a reduction of expenditure but a new source of local authority finance, such as a new local tax (a local income tax, for example) or additional grants from central government. The same result can be achieved by transferring services from local to central government so that they can be financed from general taxation rather than from the rates.

While these financial problems are common to all local authorities, their effects will be most severe for those authorities whose financial position is already precarious. It is often suggested that local authorities responsible for old and declining towns and cities are at a financial disadvantage relative to other authorities mainly because of the concentration of social and environmental problems with which they have to cope. This raises a further question of financial allocation: whether the existing system of local government finance deals equitably with different types of authority in different areas and with different characteristics. This chapter is mainly concerned with questions of this type. The first section describes how local government is financed, and how central government grants are allocated between authorities. It concludes that the grant system is, in principle, equitable and should provide finance sufficient to enable all local authorities to provide an approximately equivalent standard of public services. The second section examines whether the general principles of grant allocation deal adequately with the particular financial problems of declining urban areas. While a number of deficiencies are recognized, the conclusion is that, by and large, these areas are not at a serious fiscal disadvantage. The social and environmental problems of declining urban areas are not compounded by a financial system working to their disadvantage.

The third section of the chapter is concerned with a completely different topic: the allocation of finance between services within a local authority. It is often suggested that this process is of necessity largely political and somewhat arbitrary. In consequence, finance is often not allocated to services which might provide the greatest benefit. On these grounds a case is made for the greater use of the approach and methods of cost–benefit analysis, both in allocating finance between services, and in controlling the over-all level of spending.

Financing public services

Some public services are the direct responsibility of central government. These include the health service and the social security system. While such services are administered and operated by regional or local offices (for example, regional hospital boards or local employment exchanges), the offices carry out central government policy rather than formulating their own policies, and are financed directly from central government funds.

Most other public services are the immediate responsibility of local government. These include education, the social services, public housing, planning and land use, parks and recreation, environmental services, etc. Local authorities are empowered both to decide their own policies in these areas and to levy taxes to finance their expenditure. In practice, their freedom to decide their own policies is limited by central government legislation and guidance, and their financial autonomy is somewhat undermined by the fact that two thirds of their income is derived from central government grants.

Indeed it has been suggested that local authorities have become little more than agents of central government.[3] Many of their responsibilities are quite closely controlled by statutory obligations, laid down in central government legislation, and additionally central government departments issue a stream of advisory circulars indicating, often in very considerable detail, how local authorities should carry out the services for which they are responsible. There is little doubt that the legislative and administrative apparatus could allow central government very great control over local authorities, sufficient to reduce them to its agents. But detailed study of the process suggests that this potential control is not in fact exercised.[4]

On the financial side, it might be expected that local authorities' freedom of action might be seriously curtailed because so much of their income is derived directly from central government grants. But if the grants are allocated by formula, as at present, it is hard to see why they should reduce local independence, for the grant a particular local authority receives depends largely on the formula and not on its own behaviour.[5]

Despite the encroachment of central government control local authorities retain significant discretionary powers. This is particularly evident in housing, planning, and land-use policies and, to a lesser extent, in the social services. By contrast, the amount of local discretion in education seems much more limited.[4]

Local government services are mainly provided for the benefit of the local population, and thus it seems appropriate that they should be financed, at least in part, from local taxation. This argument applies particularly where local authorities have some discretion in the quality of services provided, for then it is both equitable and efficient that a local community which elects to provide a higher quality of public services should meet the additional costs from its own resources. Nonetheless, local authorities have received substantial amounts of money from central government grants since the nineteenth century. During the twentieth century the proportion of local authority income derived from grants has increased steadily: from 25 per cent in 1890 to 44 per cent in 1938, and from 52 per cent in 1950 to 66·5 per cent in 1975/6.*[6]

Central government grants serve two quite distinct purposes: to supplement the deficiency of the local tax base and to equalize tax burdens between localities. As noted above, rates are an unpopular tax and while local government expenditure has been rising rapidly, central government has increased grants to reduce the burden on the ratepayer. Local authorities are currently responsible for 32·5 per cent of total (central and local) government expenditure, but rates yield only about 10 per cent of total (central and local) tax revenue.

It should be stressed that financing local government services by grants rather than by rates in no way reduces their cost to the local community. For grants have to be financed by central government taxation, and such taxes fall, ultimately, on households in one form or another. Households pay for local government services either directly through their rates or indirectly through, say, their income taxes, which are collected by central government and passed back to local authorities in the form of grants. The cost is the same in each case; the reason for preferring

* These figures exclude income from charges (e.g. rents from council dwellings).

income tax plus grants to rates is that income is thought to be a more equitable tax base than property values.

The second purpose of central government grants is one of equalization between authorities. Local authorities differ both in their expenditure needs and in their capacity to raise revenue. If all authorities were to provide the same standard of public services their expenditure per head of population (or per household) might differ considerably. For example, a local authority with a high proportion of children of school age in its population will have to incur a greater expenditure on education per head of total population than an area with few children if a given standard of education is to be provided. Such differences in expenditure per head of population required to provide a given standard of services are termed differences in 'needs' between authorities. Clearly, other things being equal, local authorities with greater needs will have to either levy higher taxes or provide a lower standard of services (or both). Households resident in such areas will be at a disadvantage relative to equivalent households elsewhere in that they face either higher taxes or lower standards of services.

Secondly, local authorities differ in their resources. Given that the only local tax is rates, a tax on property values, a rough measure of a local authority's capacity to raise tax revenue is the total value of property located within it. Areas with a high total property value can finance a given expenditure with a lower rate levy (or rate poundage). Households in such areas will pay less in rates than households in property of the same value elsewhere. Likewise households in areas where the total value of property is low will have to be charged in a higher rate poundage to finance a given level of expenditure.

These inequities may be alleviated by a system of differential grants,* which provide additional revenue to local authorities to

---

* In principle equalization could equally well be achieved by an equalization scheme between local authorities – the 'wealthier' contributing to the 'poorer' – at no cost to central government. Such arrangements exist in many countries and in the UK the London boroughs operate an equalization scheme.

compensate for differences in needs, and to supplement deficiencies in resources. These principles are embodied in the general grant from central government to local authorities, now called the Rate Support Grant. The objective of this grant is to equalize rate poundages for a given standard of services across authorities. Local authorities are not all obliged to provide the same standard of services, but if they provide a higher standard they will need to charge higher rates and vice versa.

Having outlined the objective of the Rate Support Grant, it may be helpful to describe how it is administered. The first stage is for local authorities to prepare a forecast of how much, in total, they expect to spend in the coming financial year. While their level of expenditure is a forecast rather than a policy objective, central government will clearly expect them to take account of any guidelines on policy it may have issued. This aggregate level of forecast spending is called total relevant expenditure.* The next stage is for central government to determine what proportion of total relevant expenditure to finance by grants. If this proportion were held constant, the growth of rate payments would have to be equal to the growth of local government spending (on average). By increasing the proportion, the growth of rates can be slower than the growth of local government spending. This has been the normal pattern, as already noted, since the beginning of the century. Similarly, a reduction in the grant proportion means that rates must rise more rapidly than local government expenditure, and this may be used as a means of slowing down the growth of local government spending.†

The next stage is to deduct specific and supplementary grants from the total grant to be provided. These grants relate to specific services: police and law enforcement services, slum clearance and urban improvement programmes, civil defence, transport, and the national parks. Apart from the grants for the police and for

* It excludes housing subsidies and mandatory awards to students, which are subject to separate grant arrangements.

† At the time of writing the grant proportion has been reduced from 66·5 per cent for 1975/76 to 65·5 per cent for 1976/77 to encourage a reduction in local government expenditure.

transport, the amounts of money involved are small, and even in total (including police and transport) amount to little more than 10 per cent of the total grant. The police grant is a 50 per cent matching grant: that is half the cost of each police force is met by the relevant local authority, the remainder being financed directly by central government. The transport grant is allocated to local authorities either according to the extent to which their total estimated and approved expenditure on transport exceeds a 'threshold' level determined by the size of their population, or according to their estimated expenditure on specific purposes (including road building and support of public transport), whichever is the greater. The other specific and supplementary grants are allocated according to a variety of criteria, but the amounts of money involved are very small (about 3 per cent of the total exchequer grant).

After deduction of these specific and supplementary grants, the remainder constitutes the Rate Support Grant. This is divided into three parts, called the needs, resources and domestic elements.

The purpose of the needs element is to compensate for differences in needs between local authorities, differences in needs being defined as the differences in expenditure, per head of population, required to provide some given standard of service. Such differences may arise as a result of variations in the demographic composition of the population (for example, the proportion of children of school age) or for other reasons (housing conditions, for example). The main difficulty with this principle is one of measuring needs. Given all the differences in population and other characteristics between localities, how is the needs element grant to be allocated between them to compensate for differences in needs?

One approach would be to base the grant on actual expenditure. It is clear that such an arrangement would provide every encouragement to unnecessary expenditure and no incentive towards economy or cost-effectiveness in local spending. It would mean that any additional expenditure local authorities were to incur would be financed by additions to the grant, and would impose no additional cost on local ratepayers.

For this reason, the needs element grant is instead a lump sum grant based on the assessed need, rather than the actual expenditure, of each authority. The assessed need is calculated by reference to 'needs indicators' – quantifiable factors outside the control of the local authority itself which are plausibly indicative of differences in expenditure needs. These needs indicators are now identified by multiple regression analysis. (An example to illustrate this method is given in an appendix.) The needs indicators currently in use include the number of schoolchildren, the number of old people living alone, the rate of population decline, overcrowding and other measures of poor housing, the number of children in care, new housing starts and the sparsity of population.* If the needs element is calculated in this way it will, in principle, fully compensate for the differences in expenditure per head across local authorities required to provide a given (average) standard of services.

Thus, after receipt of the needs grant, each authority is in principle left to raise the same amount per head of population if it is to provide the average standard of services. Since the rateable value per head of population varies between authorities, the rate poundage required to raise that revenue will also vary. The second element of the grant, the resources element, is designed to equalize rate poundages. Essentially, it credits 'notional' rateable value to authorities deficient in rateable value, to bring all authorities up to some 'standard' rateable value per head of population. The central government becomes the ratepayer on this notional rateable value, such notional rate payments being the resources element of the grant. Clearly, all authorities that have been brought up to the standard rateable value can raise a given revenue (per head of population) by levying the same rate poundage. The resources element is not symmetrical, however, so that authorities with rateable value per head in excess of the standard level are not brought down to that standard. (At present, the standard rateable value per head is set so high that over 90 per cent of local authorities receive the resources element).

* These factors are not necessarily the same from year to year. Those mentioned in the text apply to the 1976/7 Rate Support Grant.

Thus, taken together, the objective of the needs and resources elements of the Rate Support Grant is to equalize rate poundages for a given standard of services. There remains the third element of the Rate Support Grant, the domestic element. This element of the grant provides for a uniform reduction in the rate poundage levied on domestic properties (dwellings) relative to non-domestic (commercial, industrial, etc.) properties. For example, if the domestic element were 10p in the pound, and a local authority were to levy a rate of 50p in the pound, domestic ratepayers would have to pay at a rate of 40p in the pound with the additional 10p rate being made up by central government grant. Non-domestic ratepayers would pay the full 50p. The domestic element may be justified on balance of taxation grounds: that is, it is thought that commercial and industrial property should be taxed at a higher rate, on average, than domestic property.

These grant arrangements cover all the major services provided by local government except housing. Historically, expenditure on housing has consisted primarily of the cost of construction of council houses and flats. This has been financed neither by grants nor by local taxation but by borrowing. The main form of housing subsidy has been a specific grant to local authorities to meet a proportion (currently $66\frac{3}{4}$ per cent) of the interest charge on the debt. The remainder of the charge had to be met from rents paid by the tenants of the council housing. More recently, however, additional grants have been paid in order to hold down increases in the rents paid by council tenants. (Housing grants are described in more detail in Chapter 7).

Finally, there are grants paid as part of regional policy programmes, rather than in the context of local government finance. Such grants and subsidies (the Regional Employment Premium, for example) are paid to private firms, rather than local authorities, in the hope of influencing their choice of location, and of supporting those already located in areas of high unemployment. The objective of regional policy is to reduce the differences in job opportunities and unemployment rates between regions. While, of course, the availability of employment is one of the most important determinants of the standard of living in different areas, the issues raised by regional employment policy are rather different from those discussed in the rest of this chapter, and are best treated separately (see Chapter 3).

Finance for the inner city

It is often claimed that local authorities responsible for old and declining cities and towns face particularly severe financial difficulties because of the concentration of social and environmental problems with which they have to cope. This section is concerned with the adequacy of the financial arrangements to deal with such problems. But it is helpful first to describe the main characteristics of the process of urban decline and to outline the types of problem that have been created.

The process of urban decline in Britain can largely be attributed to two factors: industrial relocation and 'suburbanization'. New and growing industries have typically been located outside the older urban areas, in new towns and in industrial estates on the outskirts of older towns. This relocation has itself been largely in response to the desire for more space and less congestion both by industry and much of its workforce, and has been encouraged by government policy. This has led to a migration, both of people and of jobs, from the older urban areas either to the suburbs or to completely new towns. At the same time people who continue to work in the central business districts of the older towns and cities tend increasingly to live in the suburbs rather than near to the city centre.

These processes have involved major movements of population, most conspicuously from the inner cities to the suburbs, but also away from the older industrial towns altogether towards the new towns and other areas of economic growth. For the older urban areas, particularly of the inner cities, this has led to problems of 'unbalanced decline'. It is mainly the younger and more skilled of the working population who migrate from the inner cities, leaving behind a preponderance of old people and unskilled workers. Following the movement of population, investment in new social infrastructure (schools, houses, hospitals, etc.) tends to be concentrated in the suburbs and new towns, leaving the inner cities with older, and typically inferior, facilities. A related factor is housing tenure. New properties are built primarily for owner-occupation or for public authorities, so that private rented accommodation is now concentrated in the older parts of cities. Not only is private rented accommodation typically of lower quality in terms of basic housing amenities but its spatial concentration encourages the formation of immigrant ghettos and the segregation of others who are economically insecure and largely dependent on this type of accommodation.

It is often alleged that a further factor contributing to the decline of inner cities is the high level of rents and of property values. But this is to confuse cause and effect. If no one wanted to live or work in the inner city, rents and property values would fall. If rents are higher in the inner cities than in the suburbs, it can only be because people are prepared to pay more to live or to run businesses in the inner city. While many industries have moved out, other economic activities such as commerce and government administration have developed rapidly. Cities continue to offer, for many people, the greatest variety of job opportunities and higher levels of pay. At the same time the high population density means that cities can offer a greater variety of services, shops and entertainments than other areas. These are indeed the traditional economic advantages of the city – that it allows a large number of economic activities to operate more efficiently by being located close together. The growth of professional and managerial employment in cities has provided a counterweight to the decline of industry and helps explain the apparent paradox of high land values in areas of urban decay.

The purpose of this section is not to analyse this process of urban change in any detail, but rather to examine its effects on the finance of public services in the inner cities. It is clear, however, that there are likely to be particularly heavy demands on local government services in areas of urban decay. Higher expenditure may be expected on services such as housing (where the existing housing stock is poor), education (where, for example, there are immigrant communities with language problems), social services (where there are many old people separated from their families) and so on. Local authorities responsible for areas of urban decay, then, have higher expenditure needs. The first question to be asked is whether they receive correspondingly higher grants from central government.

To answer this question it is first necessary to identify the local authorities responsible for areas of urban decay, and then to compare their expenditure, and receipts of grants, with those of other local authorities. But in Britain urban local authorities (outside London) are quite large so that a single authority is responsible for a whole city or town. By contrast, areas of urban decay are rather smaller and normally confined to the inner cities. Thus most urban local authorities are likely to be responsible not only for inner city areas (which may be in decline) but also for more prosperous residential suburbs and new industrial estates.

Thus it is not possible to identify specific authorities responsible for areas of urban decay. Nonetheless, the administrative structure of local government in England and Wales* does provide some useful information in this context. Outside London, there are two types of local government structure. There are the metropolitan counties which consist of the large conurbations of the north, the north-west and the west Midlands, and the non-metropolitan counties which cover the rest of the country. Most of the older industrial cities and towns are now parts of the metropolitan counties (Newcastle, Sunderland, Leeds, Sheffield, Manchester, Liverpool and Birmingham, for example). While there are a few large towns isolated from any metropolitan conurbation that form part of non-metropolitan counties (Bristol or Leicester, for example), by and large it might be expected that areas of urban decay would be concentrated in the metropolitan counties. Table 15 presents figures on expenditure and on grants for London, the metropolitan counties, the non-metropolitan counties in England, and the Welsh non-metropolitan counties.

These figures indicate, as expected, that in England metropolitan

* Separate arrangements apply in Scotland and in Northern Ireland. To avoid additional complication, discussion in the text is confined to England and Wales.

Table 15. **Expenditure per head of population, 1974–5**

	London	Metropolitan counties and districts	Non-metropolitan counties and districts	Wales
Expenditure	£	£	£	£
education	72.89	66.68	64.35	70.85
housing	35.41	17.20	9.11	13.37
social services	17.61	10.93	8.35	10.07
police	20.71	10.24	9.01	9.90
highways	10.47	9.49	11.50	12.09
other	52.23	38.79	30.87	38.78
total	209.32	153.33	133.19	155.06
Specific grants				
housing	26.93	13.64	6.82	9.96
police	10.35	5.12	4.51	4.45
other	4.87	4.34	4.56	5.57
other credits	4.97	0.74	1.75	1.23
total	47.12	23.84	17.64	12.21
total net expenditure	162.20	129.49	115.55	133.85
needs element	43.45	41.13	36.12	40.36
net expenditure less needs element	118.75	88.36	79.43	93.49

Source: CIPFA, *Return of Rates 1974–5*, Table 5.

counties and districts typically spend more than their non-metropolitan counterparts, and London spends more than the metropolitan counties. Only the Welsh authorities seem an exception to the association of urbanization with higher spending. The major service where there are substantial differences, again as might be expected, is housing. Otherwise, the higher expenditure of urban authorities is spread across a wide range of services, and particularly heavy demands on the social services, or the police, which might be associated with various types of urban problems, are evident only in London.

In so far as expenditure variations are largely attributable to housing, which is itself largely financed by specific grants, it might be expected that specific grants would go a long way towards reducing these expenditure differentials. Payments of specific grants are shown in the second part of Table 15. As the table shows, housing grants finance, on average, around 80 per cent of the differences in housing expenditure between different types of local authority. Nonetheless, there remain significant differences in expenditure net of specific grants. In so far as differences in expenditure reflect differences in needs, such differences should, in principle, be compensated by the needs element of the Rate Support Grant.

It is clear from Table 15 that the needs element does not compensate the different types of local authority for differences in their net expenditures. As compared to (English) non-metropolitan counties and districts, metropolitan counties and districts spend, on average, £20.14 per head more, which is reduced to £13.94 by specific grants and to £8.93 by the needs element. Similarly, the Welsh authorities spend £21·87 per head more than the English non-metropolitan counties and districts, and this differential is reduced to £18.30 by specific grants and to £14.06 by the needs element. The failure to achieve a full equalization is particularly evident for London. London authorities spend £76.13 more per head than the non-metropolitan counties and districts, which is reduced to £46.65 by specific grants, and to £39.32 by the needs element.

It is possible to interpret these figures in one of two ways. One is to accept that differences in expenditure are attributable to differences in needs, from which it follows that the needs element grant is failing in its purpose of compensating for such differences. The other is to argue that differences in expenditure reflect differences in standards of service, which should be a charge on the local ratepayer and not matched by payments of a needs element grant.

The first interpretation, that the needs element grant systematically undercompensates for the needs of the cities, may seem implausible, given that the formula for the distribution of the grant is calculated by regression analysis (see Appendix). In searching for a formula which best explains observed expenditures, a regression analysis will assign coefficients to variables associated with urban areas which, on average, fully account for their observed higher expenditures. By basing the needs grants formula on these coefficients it follows that the higher expenditure of urban authorities, on average, will be fully compensated by a higher grant.

The force of this argument is rather weakened, however, by the fact that the figures for the expenditure of the London boroughs were excluded from the needs element calculation. Since the London boroughs have urban characteristics and abnormally high expenditure, their exclusion has the effect of reducing the co-efficients on those variables associated with urban areas. Thus the needs grant payments associated with such characteristics are reduced. But whilst this may well have led to an inadequate needs grant for London, it is not clear that the metropolitan counties' needs have suffered as a result.

The second interpretation is based on the idea that different expenditure levels reflect differences in the standards of services. The question that must then be asked is why certain types of authorities might wish to provide better or worse services than others. One suggestion is that there is a 'tax effort' effect. It will be recalled that the objective of the resources element in the Rate Support Grant is to equalize rate poundages. But rate bills depend not only on rate poundages, but also on rateable values. Rateable values vary quite considerably between areas so that a given rate poundage will correspond to a much higher rate bill in some areas than in others. Authorities where the general level of rateable values, particularly of residential property, is high may thus levy below average rate poundages since their rate bills would otherwise be abnormally high. And authorities where rateable values are low may feel able to levy above average rate poundages without imposing excessive rate bills.

Table 16 compares expenditure per head net of specific grants and of the needs grant (the last line of Table 15) with average household rate bills. It shows that, outside London, those types of authority with relatively high net expenditure have relatively low rate bills, and vice versa. Thus it suggests that, at least to some extent, the availability of financial resources has an effect on spending. The discrepancy between average rate bills in England and in Wales is particularly striking in this context.

Table 16. **Expenditure and rates**

Authority	Net expenditure less needs grant per head £	Rate payments per household £
London	118.75	95.30
Metropolitan counties and districts	88.36	71·81
Non-metropolitan counties and districts	79.43	75.12
Wales	93.49	36.52

Source: CIPFA, *Return of Rates 1974–5*, Tables 1 and 5.

It seems reasonable to conclude from all this that outside London the grant system operates reasonably effectively, and that the cities are at no significant financial disadvantage. Only London seems an exception. Its expenditure is much higher than anywhere else, and this is by no means compensated for by higher payments of grant, so that rate burdens in London are higher than elsewhere. Further, the exceptional position of London seems to some extent to be the result of official policy, in that London's expenditure is deliberately excluded from the needs element calculation. How then is grant policy towards London to be explained?

The main point seems to be that London is exceptionally well endowed with rateable value. As the resources element of the Rate Support Grant is asymmetric, London boroughs are not pulled down to the standard level of rateable value per head but are left, in many cases, with rateable value far in excess of that level. If their net expenditure after receipt of the needs grant were the same as authorities elsewhere, it could be financed at a below average rate poundage. In this way, the London boroughs might be said to gain unfairly from the asymmetry of the resources element. This gain is, in a sense, balanced by the deliberately inadequate treatment of London in the needs grant calculation.

Indeed, on this logic, London may be said to be at a financial advantage, for, despite its inadequate needs grant, rate poundages in London tend to be lower than elsewhere in the country, reflecting its excess of rateable value. If the Rate Support Grant were to achieve its objective of equalizing rate poundages, rate payments in London would be even higher relative to those in the rest of the country than they are under the present arrangements. It might indeed be claimed that the objective of equalizing rate poundages works to the disadvantage of the cities, and of London in particular, since property values are typically higher in the cities and this implies higher rate payments for a given rate poundage.

But high property values are not purely arbitrary: they reflect the balance of economic advantages of different areas. Households resident in areas of high property values may expect to enjoy such economic advantages, and in that sense, are better off than households elsewhere. It should be recognized, however, that while this argument is true on average it is not necessarily true for every household. There is a great deal of immobility, particularly amongst older people and as a result many people may find themselves occupying property of high value in the cities while not enjoying any of the economic benefits. Although there is a Rate Rebate scheme which is specifically designed to assist people in this position, its operation is far from satisfactory. In consequence, local authorities in areas where rateable values are particularly high may feel obliged to levy lower than average rate poundages in order to alleviate the burden on poorer households.

Finally, there is the question whether the movement of population, and of business, out of the inner cities has itself been induced, or at least encouraged, by the system of local government finance. In the United States it has become generally accepted that the decline of the inner cities has been exacerbated by the fiscal system. It is claimed that the inner cities have higher expenditure needs, and in consequence have to levy higher taxes. The higher taxes drive out some businesses and some of the wealthier residents of the inner city. This leads to an erosion of the local tax base in the inner city, but not to a comparab'e reduction in its expenditure needs. Expenditure cannot be reduced in proportion to the outmigration of population, in part because those of the population in greatest need tend to remain in the inner city and in part because those who do migrate may well commute back to the inner city to work, and hence still require some local government services. The combination of a falling tax base with unchanged expenditure commitments can be resolved only by a further increase in tax rates, leading to a vicious circle of further outmigration, further tax increases, and so on. Eventually, the inner city is unable to meet its expenditure commitments, and even basic services like education or police can no longer be provided.

While such a process leading to complete financial breakdown might appear alarmist in the British context it is clear that these fears are real enough in the United States. The financial crisis of New York City provides a sufficiently serious example. There are those, in the United States, who dispute the importance of fiscal factors in the process of inner city decay,* but the relevant question here is whether the same process might be at work in British cities and towns.

There are three major factors in the British arrangements that should prevent any fiscal encouragement of migration out of the inner cities. First, as has just been argued, the needs element of the grant compensates local authorities for the higher expenditure needs of the inner city areas, so they have no need to levy higher taxes. Second, any outmigration from the inner cities which had the effect of eroding the local tax base would be compensated by payment of an additional resources element grant. Third, urban local authorities outside London are quite large so that a migra-

---

* A careful study[7] of the distribution of taxation and benefits between inner city and suburban residents of Washington D C suggests that the fiscal system probably benefits the inner city residents at the expense of the suburban, rather than the other way, as commonly supposed.

tion to the suburbs will not, in any case, erode the local tax base, for both inner city and suburbs are under the jurisdiction of the same local authority.

As a result of these arrangements, local authorities responsible for inner city areas should be safeguarded against the erosion of their tax base. But there remains the problem of the provision of services in the inner cities to non-resident commuters. This problem is unlikely to be serious outside London, for London is the only city with separate authorities for the central districts and for the suburbs.

The main point to make about this argument is that the services accounting for by far the largest share of local authority expenditure are provided almost exclusively for the resident population (for example, education, housing and social services). The main services which may benefit non-residents are road maintenance and lighting, the support of public transport, libraries and parks. Not only do these services account for only a small proportion of the expenditure, but they typically possess 'public good' or shared cost characteristics, in that if the service is to be provided for the resident population the additional cost of making it available to non-residents also is small. Public transport subsidies may be an exception in that their main benefits often go to commuters.

Table 17 sets out the expenditure of the inner London boroughs, the outer boroughs and the Greater London Council on various services. It is clear that the higher expenditure of the inner boroughs is concentrated on services such as education and housing where the benefit accrues to residents. By contrast, the additional expenditure on other services, which might in part benefit non-residents, is small. Nonetheless it remains appropriate that such additional expenditure should be compensated by means of an additional grant. This is being done, for the first time, in the 1976/7 Rate Support Grant, where the needs element for London boroughs includes an allowance for the excess of 'daytime' over resident population.

The purpose of this section has been to ask whether the cities are at a fiscal disadvantage relative to other parts of the country as a consequence of the system of local government finance. The conclusion must be that, by and large, the cities are at no serious disadvantage. This is not to say that cities may not face continuing decline and many other social or economic problems, but that it would be wrong to attribute such problems to the present procedure of financial allocation between local authorities.

Table 17. **Expenditure in London per head of population, 1974/5**

	Inner boroughs	Outer boroughs	GLC
Service	£	£	£
education	85.12	66.69	—
housing	40.64	16.61	9.33
social services	26.37	12.36	—
police	—	—	20.71
highways	6.37	6.40	3.73
other	38.96	24.74	17.52
total	197.46	126.80	51.29

Source: CIPFA, *Return of Rates*, 1974–5.

Resource allocation within local government

Should a local authority build more houses or more schools? Should it provide special facilities for problem children or more home helps for the elderly? Should social services be expanded or public transport subsidized? To a local authority facing a limited budget* these choices appear as financial constraints on their spending that have to be resolved by procedures for financial allocation between the different services.

To describe these choices as problems of financial allocation is in a sense misleading, for it suggests that some re-organization of financial arrangements might remove the need to make them. It is necessary to choose between, say, better schools and better housing because productive resources of labour, capital and land are

* The local authority's budget is not fixed, of course, but limited by the level of rates its ratepayers are prepared to pay.

scarce and if they are employed in providing new schools they will not be simultaneously available for producing other goods (better housing, for example). It is the scarcity of productive resources rather than a shortage of money that necessitates such choices.

How, then, are the decisions to be made, and on what basis is finance to be allocated to the different services? It is often argued that such issues are essentially political, and that any type of objective analysis is impossible. While political factors are clearly important, studies of political decision-making in local authorities (for example, G. W. Jones's *Borough Politics*)[8] have stressed the arbitrariness of the political process. Individual personalities play a major part, as do the traditions of a local authority (themselves reflecting dominant personalities of the past). An observer of local government politics would be likely to argue that money would be allocated to the housing programme or to schools according to whether the Chairman of the Housing Committee or the Chairman of the Education Committee happened to have a more forceful personality. Since this is largely a matter of chance the procedure is clearly not a very rational one, and is unlikely to lead to an efficient use of resources.

The question must then be asked: is there in fact a more rational procedure for the allocation of finance between different services? To date, the most logical and systematic approach appears to be one based on techniques of cost–benefit analysis. The idea is that all the social benefits and social costs of a public expenditure project can in principle be evaluated, in monetary terms, and that resources should be allocated to projects which offer the greatest excess of benefits over costs. Cost–benefit techniques are already used extensively in transport planning, but they could be applied to all decisions involving the use of resources. The raising of the school leaving age, the treatment of juvenile offenders, the care of the elderly, the choice between slum clearance and rehabilitation, all have implications for the use of resources, and all are issues to which cost–benefit techniques can be applied.

There are two main advantages of cost–benefit analysis. First is the requirement that the benefits of a project are evaluated, which

291

in turn requires that the types of benefit expected from some project are made explicit and also that an attempt is made to assign monetary values to them. An example might be the benefits to be expected from a housing project. The main one here is the better quality of accommodation provided for tenants. The value of these benefits might, in principle, be discovered from evidence of rents charged and prices paid for accommodation in the private sector. Such information will also indicate the types of accommodation people prefer (as shown by a willingness to pay higher rents), which may be useful in guiding a local authority's housing policy. There is, for example, evidence from private sector rents that people prefer low-rise buildings to tower blocks even at quite high population densities.

It might be suggested that local authority housing not only benefits the tenants, but also provides more general social and environmental benefits. Since it is often claimed that poor housing conditions are a major cause of crime and delinquency, a second benefit of a housing project would be its effect on the crime rate. Here the cost–benefit analysis would have to estimate the type of crime that is reduced by better housing, and by how much. Over the last twenty years housing conditions have been improving steadily while the crime rate has been increasing rapidly. This evidence must at least cast doubt on the effectiveness of housing policies in reducing crime. Cost–benefit analysis is useful in this context because its emphasis on quantification necessitates an investigation of the evidence rather than a reliance on what are sometimes unsupported articles of faith among social reformers.

Plainly there are other, less contentious, social benefits of better housing, for example, the benefits to public health of improvements in sanitation and heating should be included. A precise assessment of these may, however, prove extremely difficult, a point taken up in more detail later.

The second major advantage of cost–benefit analysis is that it emphasizes the cost-effectiveness of public expenditure. It gives preference to projects which achieve given objectives at relatively low cost. This might seem so obvious as to need no mention, but local authorities might, for example, well have taken from an early stage much more interest in the rehabilitation of properties, rather than in large-scale redevelopment, had their housing policies been geared to consider the relative costs involved.[9]

The introduction of cost–benefit analysis implies a radical change from existing modes of thought about the provision of public services. It is normal practice to discuss public services in terms of 'needs', 'entitlements' or 'rights' – 'every family has a right to a home' or 'children are entitled to an education that enables them to develop their talents fully' or 'no child should be allowed to die as a result of a shortage of social work staff'. Such principles, though too vague for direct application, tend to become established as 'absolutes' which override financial considerations. Again a good example is housing, where the principle of the right to a home has been translated to mean that the existing housing stock is inadequate and has to be replaced by good, new accommodation with all modern facilities. This then means that large areas of cities and towns have been laid waste during the course of redevelopment, which often extends over many years, results in the break up of local communities and causes considerable disruption to those involved. More modest improvement of existing properties, to remove their worst defects and install modern facilities, might have overcome the worst housing problems much more rapidly, have been just as acceptable to those involved, avoided social and environmental upheaval, and have saved a great deal of money.

Nonetheless, the idea that the benefits of public expenditure can be measured in financial terms, rather than in terms of providing people with services to which they have a right, is perhaps the major obstacle to the introduction of the use of cost–benefit techniques. All that need be said is that if it is felt that people have a right to more services than the local authority can in fact afford to provide, a choice has to be made. Such a choice must, at least implicitly, depend on a comparison between the importance of these different services and the costs involved. Cost–benefit analysis simply makes the basis of choosing more explicit. As long as there is scarcity of resources, the logic of cost–benefit techniques can hardly be disputed.

A second reason that may explain why cost–benefit analysis has not been adopted more widely is that it is a complex and difficult procedure, and much too cumbersome for use in day-to-day decisions. As we have seen, it may run into quite involved and subtle problems concerned with the evaluation of benefits or costs. The techniques available for dealing with such problems have been developed considerably over recent years, and there has also been a great increase in its application to specific projects. These issues will not be pursued further here (for an excellent survey of recent developments, see R. Layard, ed., *Cost–Benefit Analysis*),[10] except to point out that despite increased familiarity with the technique it remains a costly way of making decisions.

None of this should suggest that cost–benefit techniques will, or should, remove the political element from decisions on financial allocation. Some aspects of such decisions, for example, the distribution of benefits and of costs between different groups in society, are essentially political matters. On occasions it may be as important to 'reflect the public mood' in decisions as to seek the greatest social benefit. But cost–benefit analysis provides a rational procedure for financial allocation which can make a useful contribution, and sometimes a major contribution, to decisions on public expenditure.

Finally, cost–benefit analysis may be relevant in deciding the size of a local authority's budget as well as its allocation between services. If projects being considered by a local authority show a consistent excess of costs over benefits, it suggests that the local authority is not making sound use of public money, so it would be better not to go ahead with the projects but to reduce the level of rates instead. If, by contrast, a large number of projects show an excess of benefits there is a case for increasing the rates rather than having to choose between the projects.

Conclusion

Over the post-war period there has been a very rapid expansion of public services and, as mentioned in the introduction, substantial improvements have been achieved. Nonetheless many urban problems such as homelessness, crime and delinquency, illiteracy and various types of urban squalor seem, if anything, to get worse. This must at least raise questions about the effectiveness of huge increases in public spending in dealing with such problems.

In any event, the economic difficulties of the past few years have forced a halt in the growth of public expenditure. As a result more attention is being given to assessing the effectiveness of existing public expenditure programmes than in seeking areas of further expansion. It may be hoped that this reassessment will encourage the introduction of more logical and systematic techniques of expenditure appraisal (as discussed in the previous section).

The Report of the Layfield Committee on Local Government Finance,[11] published in May 1976, has suggested another possible reason for the lack of effective expenditure control in local government. This is the problem of accountability. The committee suggests that existing arrangements are confused in that local authorities are nominally responsible to their electorates but in practice subject to extensive central government interference. Thus people have come to regard central government as responsible for local authorities, and consequently local government responsibilities, such as the level of rates or education policy, have become major issues in central government elections. The Committee suggest that either this centralist trend be formalized, and local authorities become the agents (or regional offices) of central government (rather like the French system) or that local democracy and local accountability be restored. They argue that local democracy can only be a reality if local authorities have to raise the major share of their revenue from their own electorate. Clearly people are likely to take a much greater interest in local government if every decision is reflected in their local tax bills.

Thus an essential condition for the restoration of local democracy is a substantial reduction in central government grants. Central government grants (as argued on page 274) have two purposes in the existing system: to supplement the deficiency of the local tax base and to equalize tax burdens between localities. If rates at present constitute an inadequate revenue source, new local taxes can be introduced, for example local income tax. Also the rating system can be improved, for example by improved rating assessment procedures, which could increase the yield of rates. On equalization, the Committee accept that grants should remain in order to equalize tax burdens between localities, and also accept, as has been argued in this chapter, that the existing arrangements for such grant allocation are broadly satisfactory.

References

1. Central Statistical Office, *Social Trends* no. 6, 1975.
2. Foster, C. D., *Local Government Resources and Finance*, Association of Metropolitan Authorities, 1976.
3. Robson, W. A., *The Development of Local Government*, 2nd edition, London, Allen & Unwin, 1948.
4. Griffith, J. A. G., *Central Departments and Local Authorities*, London, Allen & Unwin, 1966.
5. Institute of Fiscal Studies, *Proceedings of a Conference on Local Government Finance*, 1973, pp. 51–9.
6. Peacock, A. T., and Wiseman, J., *The Growth of Public Expenditure in the U.K.*, Princeton, 1961; Central Statistical Office, *Annual Abstract of Statistics*, various years.
7. Greene, K. V., Neenan, W. B., and Scott, C. D., *Fiscal Interactions in a Metropolitan Area*, Lexington, 1974.
8. Jones, G. W., *Borough Politics*, London, Macmillan, 1969.
9. Needleman, L., *The Economics of Housing*, London, Staples Press, 1965.
10. Layard, R., ed., *Cost-Benefit Analysis*, Penguin Books, 1974.
11. *Report of the Committee of Inquiry into Local Government Finance* (Chairman: Mr F. Layfield), London, HMSO, 1976.

Appendix

Calculation of the needs element

It is helpful to start with a very simple example, in which local authorities provide only one service, say education and in which expenditure depends on only one variable factor, say the number of school children. The information relevant for the needs element calculation is set out in Table 18:

Table 18. **Example of data inputs for the needs element**

Local authority	Population	Number of schoolchildren	Schoolchildren per head	Total expenditure	Expenditure per head
				£	£
A	400,000	60,000	0·15	2,600,000	65.00
B	100,000	18,000	0·18	740,000	74.00
C	200,000	34,000	0·17	1,420,000	71.00
D	100,000	16,000	0·16	680,000	68.00

The first stage is to carry out a regression analysis, with expenditure per head (X) as the dependent variable and the number of schoolchildren per head as the independent variable. In this example the result of such an analysis would be a regression equation of the form:

$$X = 20 + 300N$$

As can be seen from the table it is possible to predict from this equation the expenditure of an authority from the number of its schoolchildren.

The purpose of the needs element is to compensate for differences in expenditure per head of population that result from differences in needs, as in this example. Thus the expenditure net of needs grant in each authority should be equalized. If the needs grant per head is written G, this objective takes the form that, in each authority, $X - G = K$, some given amount equal for all authorities.

Appendix

It follows that $$G = X - K$$

i.e. in this example, $$G = (20 - K) + 300N$$

Assume for example that the given amount each authority was to provide net of needs grant was £50 per head of population. Then the needs grant formula would be:

$$G = -30 + 300N$$

The expenditure and grants received by the authority are set out in Table 19.

Table 19. **Relationship between local authority expenditure and grants**

Local authority	Schoolchildren per head (N)	Expenditure per head (X)	Needs grant per head (G)	Expenditure net of needs grant per head
		£	£	£
A	0·15	65.00	15.00	50.00
B	0·18	74.00	24.00	50.00
C	0·17	71.00	21.00	50.00
D	0·16	68.00	18.00	50.00

Thus the needs grant compensates in full for differences in expenditure per head of population.

In this simple example, the regression equation fitted the data exactly. In general this will not be the case, and although the regression technique will compute the equation which comes closest to fitting the data, it will not fit exactly for every local authority. Some local authorities will turn out to be spending more than might be expected on the basis of the regression equation (given the number of their schoolchildren) and others less. The needs grant, however, is based on the regression equation (as in the example). Thus local authorities will receive in needs grant a sum related to the amount they would be expected to spend on the basis of the regression equation, given the number of their schoolchildren, rather than the amount they actually spend. The advantage of this procedure is that it means a local authority's receipt of grant is independent of its own expenditure decisions.

Clearly this example is highly simplified in assuming that local authorities provide only one service and that there is only one needs indicator. Local authorities provide many services and there are many needs indicators but this does not affect the basic principle. Multiple regression analysis can be used to derive an equation which best explains differences in expenditure, and the needs element grant can then be based on this equation.

Notes on Contributors

Peter Hall. Professor of Geography, University of Reading.

A. G. Champion. Lecturer in Geography at the University of Newcastle upon Tyne.

Kenneth Warren. Lecturer in the School of Geography at the University of Oxford.

Morgan Sant. Lecturer in Geography at the University of New South Wales. He was previously director of a research unit at the University of East Anglia and Associate Professor of Geography at the University of Toronto.

Patrick O'Sullivan. Associate Professor in the Geography Department at Florida State University. He was formerly Director of the Transportation Center at Northwestern University.

Ross L. Davies. Lecturer in Geography at the University of Newcastle upon Tyne.

Reg Hookway. Director of the Countryside Commission.

A. A. Nevitt. Professor in Social Administration at the London School of Economics.

Bleddyn Davies. Currently Director of the Personal Social Services Research Unit at the University of Kent at Canterbury.

Edward Craven. Lecturer in Social Policy at the Civil Service College. Formerly Fellow at the Centre for Studies in Social Policy

Richard Jackman. Lecturer in economics at the London School of Economics.

MORE ABOUT PENGUINS
AND PELICANS

Penguinews, which appears every month, contains details of all the new books issued by Penguins as they are published. From time to time it is supplemented by *Penguins in Print*, which is our complete list of almost 5,000 titles.

A specimen copy of *Penguinews* will be sent to you free on request. Please write to Dept EP, Penguin Books Ltd, Harmondsworth, Middlesex, for your copy.

In the U.S.A.: For a complete list of books available from Penguins in the United States write to Dept CS, Penguin Books, 625 Madison Avenue, New York, New York 10022.

In Canada: For a complete list of books available from Penguins in Canada write to Penguin Books Canada Ltd, 2801 John Street, Markham, Ontario L3R 1B4.